HOSPITALITY SALES AND PROMOTION
Strategies for Success

Dedication

This book is dedicated to Evie, Jacob, Ellie, Theo, Jonah, Joshie, Angus, Benjie and Connie.

HOSPITALITY SALES AND PROMOTION
Strategies for Success

Derek Taylor

Series Editor: John O'Connor

OXFORD AMSTERDAM BOSTON LONDON NEW YORK PARIS
SAN DIEGO SAN FRANCISCO SINGAPORE SYDNEY TOKYO

Butterworth-Heinemann
An imprint of Elsevier Science
Linacre House, Jordan Hill, Oxford OX2 8DP
200 Wheeler Road, Burlington, MA 01803

First published 2001
Reprinted 2003

British Library Cataloguing in Publication Data
Taylor, Derek, 1932 Aug. 5–
    Hospitality sales and promotion: strategies for success
    1. Hositality industry – Management   2. Hospitality industry
    – Marketing

Library of Congress Cataloguing in Publication Data
A catalogue record for this book is available from the Library of
Congress

ISBN 0 7506 4986 0

For information on all Butterworth-Heinemann publications
visit our website at www.bh.com

Typeset by Avocet Typeset, Brill, Aylesbury, Bucks
Printed and bound in Great Britain by Biddles Ltd,
www.biddles.co.uk

Contents

Contents

About the author

Derek Taylor was the first salesman in the British hotel industry, back in 1954. Most of the systems and procedures we use today were first developed by him.

He served on the main board of Grand Metropolitan – the parent company is now part of Diageo – as Sales Director for the hotel division for 13 years. He eventually controlled a sales force of nearly 200 around the world.

As a lecturer he has run courses in 30 countries and, as a consultant for the past 20 years, he has worked for almost every major international hotel company.

He is a Cambridge graduate, a Past President of the Hotel & Catering International Management Association and a much-loved journalist. This is his ninth book and in it he brings together all the new developments in modern hospitality marketing, to ally to the classic methods which have stood the test of time.

He lives in North London and is still very much in harness as a consultant. He is married, with four children and nine grandchildren.

Foreword

When you talk to anybody in the British Hotel Industry about sales and marketing, the first name that comes up is Derek Taylor, a man who has dominated the field for more years than most of us can remember. I worked for him as a salesman in the late nineteen sixties and seventies and Derek has continued to be a consultant for me through Ladbroke, Stakis and now Hilton.

An astonishing number of sales and marketing systems which are now standard in the UK hotel industry were actually first created by him. As Sales and Marketing Director of the old Grand Metropolitan Hotels and for 20 years subsequently as a consultant, he has invented everything from marketing Short Break Holidays and the 4 o'clock Automatic Cancellation to Special Events Departments. Thousands of hotel and hospitality executives have attended his courses and he has been a prolific writer on the subject. He brings to this field, his passion and his hobby, a formidable intellect and a total willingness to go on learning and experimenting.

This book gives you this state-of-the-art as it is now. That doesn't mean it will fail to change in the future. You would, however, be very sensible to adopt the processes detailed in the book and start to improve on them from there. A very large number of us, his friends, hope that this is exactly what Derek Taylor will be doing for many years yet.

David M.C. Michels
Chief Executive
Hilton Group PLC

Introduction

When you came into the industry, did you think you would need to know a lot about sales and marketing? A great many of our best management didn't and, indeed, still regret that it is necessary. When I wrote my first book on the subject back in 1964, the second chapter was entitled 'Is selling respectable?' and a lot of people still think the answer is 'No'. Selling, in their minds, is linked to double glazing, people knocking on doors or ringing you in the evening to sell you anything from a fitted kitchen to a new credit card.

Most hotel schools have been in the vanguard of teaching the industry that marketing needs studying. In the nineteen sixties the subject didn't feature. Then there were optional modules and now there are mandatory ones. The problem is that the average hotel school curriculum must inevitably cover an enormous amount of ground. Furthermore, the operational side of the industry must get the highest priority. Therefore, the amount of time which can be devoted to marketing is very limited.

The fact is, however, as you know – or will soon find out – if you don't handle your marketing well, your revenue will suffer substantially. There is only so much you can do to control costs. When you have done your best in that area, you are forced back onto marketing to increase your profits.

So we find that large numbers of executives who have to sell and market their products as part of their jobs, get only the most rudimentary training in how to go about it. And the whole topic may not be one that appeals to them and, in its exercise, even scares them; picking up the telephone to try to persuade a complete stranger to give you business is emotionally stressful until you have done it on a large number of occasions. It is one of the reasons why you find that a lot of marketing people smoke.

Often, of course, you find that people come into the industry because they like dealing with people, enjoy cooking, the atmosphere of hotels and restaurants, and the opportunity to travel all over the country and, indeed, all over the world. If, however, you had told them at the outset that they had to sell, as part of their job specification, many would have seriously considered another profession.

Let me reassure you right at the start. Selling is eminently respectable. We have bad apples in our barrel, like anybody else, but the vast majority of selling is – and must be – ethical, moral, professional and honest. Good salesmen don't cheat their customers in our industry; we are too anxious to have them come back again and again, and people who feel cheated, don't do that. We don't lie to them about the product because it is impossible to remember who you lied to and you would get caught out quickly enough. We also recognize that persuading the client to buy a good product is doing them a favour; they are going to get good value for money and an enjoyable experience.

To the sales executives who are proud of their products, the alternatives available to the customer are inferior to the quality and service they intend to provide. The vital thing is to put your best foot forward and to market your products in the most professional way possible.

Producing a good product is, unfortunately, not enough. The public don't beat a path to your door automatically. There is a lot of competition out there and you absolutely have to promote your product as effectively as you possibly can.

This book is about how to promote hotels, restaurants, pubs, cafes and everything else in the hospitality industry. Obviously you will have to decide what applies to you. What you can be certain about is that there is a right way to go about it. I have been selling in this industry for nearly 50 years – did I mention I was very old? – and I could write a book twice as long as this about how not to do it. Been there, done that.

Of course, a lot has changed in those 50 years in Britain, where I have always been based, although I have advised hotels all over the world. The British industry has expanded beyond anybody's wildest dreams. Because of the quality of the UK's heritage attractions, the enormous growth in the number and quality of hotels and restaurants and the hard work of the nearly 2 million people who work in the industry, the sector has flourished. The best of British hospitality marketing is recognized as among the very best in the world.

Naturally, much has changed in the world of selling over the years. It is not just the introduction of higher technology; the impact of computers, of international booking systems, of the Internet, the fax and emails. It is also that we've learned a great many extra skills in the selling field itself. For example, we have learned the value of closing techniques, body language and buying signals, we've mastered the skills of advertising and we're much better at direct mail.

It remains true, however, that many of the methods we used in those early days are just as applicable now as they ever were. Indeed the old-timers would insist that we were more efficient in some ways before computers, than we are currently!

What is beyond argument is that the same sales methods work all over the world. We are very much an international industry. I have lectured on sales promotion in 30 countries now and, while there are minor adjustments you have to make – don't use the Royal colour, purple, in Thailand; don't cross your legs or blow your nose in front of the Japanese; always shake hands with the French – the core skills of selling remain exactly the same.

The name of the game is to take the best of both worlds. To conserve what was good in the past and to welcome any innovations that help us.

So, what will you find in the book? It starts with how to plan your sales promotion. Chapter 1 helps you see the trees for the wood. There are so many things you could do. You have to identify how you should go about the task of organizing your marketing plan: what to work on, what to spend and who is going to do what. At the end of this and subsequent chapters, there is a case study to illustrate how the processes work out in practice.

When that is clear, you have to decide how to organize your sales office. Chapter 2 covers that. It tells you what paperwork you will need and how you keep it to a minimum. How to get the best out of sales people and how departments, like Reception, Banqueting, Restaurants and Bars, should approach the marketing task.

In Chapter 3 we deal with the markets. There are over 20 of them and they have their own characteristics. You can't approach them all in the same way.

Chapter 4 deals with face-to-face selling: what to say and how to say it. Office interviews, body language, closing the sale, overcoming objections, entertaining and showrounds, dealing with different personalities and overcoming price resistance. All vital and all with the right way of doing it and many, many wrong ways to avoid.

In Chapter 5 we review telephone selling. You spend a lot of your time selling on the telephone and it is very easy to aggravate the customer. (That's why you yourself have so often got the sales executive off the phone as they've tried to get your attention when *Coronation Street* was on in the evening.) Well, you don't want the same thing to happen when it is you who wants their attention. So how do you avoid it?

In Chapter 6, we look at the new technology – in simple language. It is not surprising that we have a saying in Britain 'if all else fails, read the instructions'. The more complicated the subject, the easier it is to blind us with science. Yet, if you examine the technology carefully, it isn't all that difficult to grasp the methodology. What are GDS systems, designing a website, the principles of yield management, etc. I would like to thank David Bearman, Tony Dessauer, Gareth Gaston, Mike Hope and Hugh Taylor for their valuable advice here.

Chapter 7 sees us examining banqueting sales: maximizing the turnover, improving the ratio of success with enquiries, using the many secret weapons which are available to make sure you are the final choice for the client.

Chapter 8 looks at a marvellous sales weapon – direct mail: its construction, its databases, the thinking behind it and the proven methods of achieving success. Of course, direct mail is about writing a form of sales letter. With sales letters, the techniques haven't changed over the years, but there has been a terrible decline in the standard of literacy throughout the country. As people have become more computer literate, they have become less literate – and less numerate for that matter. Letters remain, however, a most powerful selling tool, if they are constructed correctly and that is what we must look into.

Which brings us to Chapter 9, which attempts to tell you all about the principles of advertising in one fell swoop. While this is a long chapter it may be the first time you have had the opportunity to examine those precious rules.

We then move on to that form of advertising which is most often used in the hospitality industry – promotional material. All those brochures, posters, menus, wine lists, flyers and tent cards which you hope will encourage the guests to buy your products. The problem that has to be resolved in Chapter 10 is that most of the material you see – all over the world – breaks many of the classic rules of the advertising industry. This is not because the hospitality industry is different from other forms of economic endeavour. It is because most of the material hasn't altered in form for over 100 years. I could show you Victorian hotel brochures which – apart from the use of colour photography – are indistinguishable from the modern variety. Well, the world has moved on. The rules of successful advertising have been developed through trial and error – and the loss of kings' ransoms when expensive mistakes have been made. It is high time we absorbed the lessons the advertising world can teach us.

In Chapter 11 we take a look at public relations, a very important facet of sales and marketing. Not only because it covers our relations with the press and media, but also because it's the first line of defence when something goes drastically wrong.

Chapter 12 studies the business you could invent. There are three kinds of business we can go after; the business we have, the business our competitors have and the business we invent. The London to Brighton 'Old Crocks' Race is an Edwardian invention to fill a hotel in Brighton. Trivial Pursuit evenings in today's pubs are an invention. Short Break Holidays I invented myself back in 1964; they did alright. Even Mother's Day is an invention. The question is how can you best go about inventing business?

Finally, there is a bibliography and an index. The index is very important to you. It quickly refers you to the area which is giving you problems. When you have read the book, you will need it all the time as a reference when you run into difficulties.

Right: if you're ready, we could get started.

1 The marketing plan

The background

Whoever is keen to protect trees should complain about the production of marketing plans. They are usually vast documents. There are statistics of the performance of other hotels, SWOT analyses (Strengths, Weaknesses, Opportunities, Threats), computer print-outs, spreadsheets, Old Uncle Tom Cobley and all. All too often they then go on the shelf and lie there till the same exercise takes place again next year.

Marketing plans have to be working documents, cut to the bone, so that it is simple to identify what needs to be done at any given moment. Then they need to be reviewed on a regular basis. The format of the plan would be 12 monthly lists of things that will need doing. So if you are making out the plan in June, you will remember to put into it the mailing you want for Burns Night the following January, under the December list of things to be done.

There is another major reason why this is vitally important. No matter how busy you are, the tables have still got to be laid, the food cooked, the beds made. When it's all hands to the pump, the only area which can safely be neglected without immediate chaos is sales and marketing. Fail to make the chase call, don't send out the direct mail, don't put out the tent cards for the special offer and absolutely no crisis will ensue. You will get through today unscathed. You may go broke in six months time, but today you'll survive. So prepare for that problem. If you have got a marketing plan, keep to it at all costs.

Of course, you could fail to make a profit with some of the initiatives. In fact, it can be absolutely guaranteed that even if it is a good, comprehensive marketing plan, you definitely will. You can't get it right all the time. And if you do nothing and finish up in the same profit position as all your neighbours, that's the perfect excuse for not making more money. What is more, if your organization punishes marketing failure, the safe option is not to do anything remotely revolutionary – and to look for a better company!

When deciding which markets to tackle, the trouble with the hospitality industry is that there are too many clients. The majority of the population could eat in your restaurant. Large proportions of your incoming tourists could stay with you. Then there is every travel agent, association, tens of thousands of commercial companies, million of potential Short Break holidaymakers ... the list goes on and on. In developing your marketing plan, where do you start? What are your priorities? Who is available to do the work? Let's take it one step at a time.

Bringing back the old business

Protect the business you have got. You don't want the additional business you get to just replace the old business you have lost. So, how are you going to get the old business back?

It is difficult if you don't know when the decision makers for the group bookings are going to start planning the next event. And you need more information than that. Whether you put the details on a sheet of paper or in a computer, the minimum you want to know about everything you want back is:

- The name of the organization.
- The decision maker.
- The type of business it was.
- The date they are going to start thinking about it again.
- The value of the business – if time is limited, go after the big ones.
- The telephone number.

Then put the correspondence in alphabetical order in a file. When the time arrives to talk to the client again, you need to be reminded by the system. So either the sheets of paper are in trace date order or the computer program can give you the list of organizations you should be tracing this month.

That takes care of the group business you had. But what if the old correspondence hasn't been touched for years? What if there are no trace dates to try again? Then get in temporary help to put it all together for you. You have to validate the old records. You contact the organization who gave you the group business and you ask them three questions:

- Does the business still exist?
- Who is the decision maker now?
- When do they make up their minds?

Eliminate what isn't happening again. Keep a record of what does exist. Your hard working and overqualified staff don't need to be involved, except to supervise the student. Then see the records are kept in the future, so you don't have to go through the exercise again.

You can move on from there. Does the organization have any other business you could quote for? It is an easier market to approach than people who have never used you before. 'We look after Tom, Dick and Harry. Could we look after you?'

Of course, it would be nice if you knew something about those old decision makers. Are they teetotal, fusspots, lazy when it comes to administration, divorced (don't cheer then for the joys of marriage), old timers, New Turks, etc. etc. If they are strangers to you, the right personal approach is more difficult to guarantee. Can you visualize the National Accounts Manager for Unilever not knowing the colour of the Tesco Purchasing Director's bed socks? Yes, I know nobody kept that information for you. They should have.

Getting more business from existing customers

After protecting the old group business, you then need to apply the most important four words in improving your business; 'Why? And Who Else?' If you are looking after one branch dinner, why not the other branches? If one cricket club has their annual party with you, who else plays in their league? If you have stockrooms for one shoe manufacturer, who else is selling shoes in your town? Again, it is then a matter of research. Go through the list and identify who could need you.

Whatever business is available to you, there is a crucial question before you go after it; do you want it? What is the point of going after 25 organizations who have parties on Friday nights in December? Just open the doors in Banqueting and they will pour in without doing any selling at all. You want to concentrate on the rare kinds of business.

Filling the gaps

When you have taken care of the bread and butter business, marketing is about filling gaps that won't fill themselves. It obviously isn't about getting business for any time at any tariff. Yet many hotels offer companies corporate rates lower than their published tariff, without having any idea whether the bednights they get as a consequence will improve their occupancy. The corporate rates are based on promises to provide bednights; not on promises to provide valuable bednights.

Who has the valuable bednights? Well, take one example. Suppose you have a serious weekend occupancy problem and your hotel is in a dull, uninteresting town. You are not in London, Sydney, Las Vegas or Rome. One source of weekend business then is conferences by charities. Who could tackle that market? And supposing I recommend that you hire a member of staff just for that. How do you justify the expense?

Say you have 50 unoccupied bedrooms on an average of 30 weekends a year and you would like £50 a bedroom for the two weekend nights. If you achieved that, you would get £50 × 50 bedrooms × 2 nights × 30 weekends = £150,000. And say that you can make 50 per cent profit = £75,000. And say the member of staff costs you £15,000. If you fill 20 per cent of the gap, you will get your money back. Fill six weekends – and the staff member has the whole year to do that – and the expense has been self-liquidating. Anything over six and you are in profit.

Your marketing budget should never be an expense. It should be a question of feeding geese who lay golden eggs. That's why it is so stupid to cut the marketing budgets when business goes sour. If the sales effort is professional, you can hardly avoid making a profit. A cut in the marketing budget should mean increasing your loss.

Certainly, you can hope the business will come without the sales effort – what is called Milking the Product – but often it won't. The gaps were there before; they will be worse when times are hard.

Correspondence research

How do you find the business that will fill the gaps? Well, why aren't you full on Sunday evening? People have gone home to work on Monday morning, there aren't many holidaymakers in the winter, nobody has got any money, etc. etc. Then the next question is 'why aren't you totally empty?' Because all those things don't apply to the people who are eating or sleeping with you. Who are they and why don't they apply? In a hotel there should be a Reception staff member who specializes in finding the answers.

Often they tell you in their letters, for example, they are coming for an event, which is specified – 'I'm attending a conference at the hospital' from someone who signs himself Dr Smith. A twin bedded room on company notepaper probably indicates a company function where the partners are invited. If their title is Sales Manager, there may well be a sales conference somewhere. Examine, investigate, research. Where you find that one person is coming for a dog show, where are the others who are coming? Part of your marketing plan must always be to learn more about the market.

You have to concentrate on those bad days, those empty sessions. In your district, within a few miles, there will be ample customers to fill your restaurant or hotel every day of the year. The problem is who are they and how can you appeal to them?

The soft option is to say that everybody is quiet, so you are quiet too. The professional approach is that you have no objections to everybody else being totally empty – as long as you are 100 per cent full!

Yield management

Yield management is a contemporary term for getting as much revenue from selling the product as you possibly can. It involves you in deciding what percentage of the product will be sold at full rate, what needs to be sold at a reduction, and what is the lowest price you can accept that still makes a contribution towards your fixed costs – rent, rates, management salaries, etc. – after you have taken out the marginal costs – food, soap, etc.

Look at every night, every meal occasion, from that point of view. Then decide what you want to charge and that is part of your marketing plan too. Yield management is studied more closely in Chapter 6.

Forecasting the future

The famous American evangelist Billy Graham once said that faith is not reducing speed when driving over the brow of a hill, satisfied that the road you are on will continue. In hospitality industry terms, the road you are on is the business pattern over the past years. If you have been full on Mother's Day for 10 years, the likelihood is that you will be full this year again, if you make the same marketing effort. If you have been empty between December 26th and December 30th for the past 10 years, that will reoccur too – unless you do something about it.

Therefore, you need the records as far back as you can go. It is worth the staff cost, going to work to drag them out. Hotels complain about the lack of commercial business in the weeks before and after Easter. Well, there will be an Easter next year again. So the marketing plan sets out to do something about it. For example, company pension clubs don't mind when they have a social outing, so long as the price is right. They are a good market for before and after Easter.

When you know where you have come from, you still have to ask yourself if the future will replicate the past. To some extent, this is out of your hands. If the Japanese Stock Market crashes, you will get fewer Japanese tourists; the Japanese won't have as much spare money – what is technically called discretionary income. If there are riots and civil unrest in a country, it is likely a lot of tourists will stay away until the situation has returned to normal. If the lira crashes, you will get fewer Italians. The important thing is to recognize that these stories in the City or Foreign News pages of the newspapers really can affect your future business. When I was discussing prices with an American travel agent and we weren't far apart, I would always settle for his price if it was going to be paid in dollars; it was always a fair bet that sterling would weaken against the dollar and I would finish up with my price at least.

The timetable

Far too many marketing plans are pious hopes of what may happen on a good day in a fair wind, unless there are unforeseen circumstances. What they need to be is detailed plans of how it is going to happen. Who is going to do what, and by when, and at what cost? Then you need to monitor regularly that this is what actually takes place.

It is seldom possible to correct a revenue disaster if it comes upon you without warning. It is normally a question of too little, too late. With planning, the disaster doesn't have to happen in the first place. Suppose you are quiet in January. You look at the forecasts at the end of December, when the Christmas and New Year rush are over and you say 'We must do something about this.' It's too late. You should have planned for it months ago. And you say 'But we didn't have time months ago. We were busy.' Well, say you want to start sending out direct mail in October to get January business, and

October is a desperately heavy month. You had no time to write the direct mail, run it off, address the envelopes and frank them in October. So do it all the previous January! Just put the material in cardboard boxes and get it out and post it when October comes around. Are you really surprised when business is bad? Sometimes, yes, usually, no.

Looking for improvements

There are certain marketing areas which benefit from particularly careful monitoring:

- What percentage of the banqueting enquiries are converted into definite bookings?
- What percentage of the enquiries to Reception for bedrooms are converted into definite bookings?
- What percentage of Brochure and Tariff enquiries result in definite bookings?
- What percentage of the old group business comes back?
- Is the level of the sleeper/diner ratio improving? (i.e. More people staying in the hotel are eating in the hotel.)
- How do the restaurant covers change when you advertise locally?

Those are the ways in which you know that the marketing is working. Plus, of course, your accommodation revenue and your restaurant and banqueting turnover. Notice that it is accommodation revenue that counts and not average room rate or average occupancy. You can easily improve your average room rate by refusing to accept any booking below rack rate. You can put your average occupancy up by cutting your tariff in half. It is revenue that matters.

How much should you spend a year on marketing?

The answer won't be a percentage of your annual turnover. Say you and every hotel for miles around are packed out with the visitors pouring in for the Agricultural Show or for major sporting or cultural events. On the days those events are happening you don't need to spend 0.0001 per cent of your revenue on filling the hotel or restaurant. It will fill by simply opening the doors. On the other hand, you may have been dead in the water on Sunday nights for years. If you can build a profitable market, it may be necessary, originally, to spend 30–40 per cent of the additional turnover that results on the marketing. Not for ever, but originally. It is still a good investment if you eventually come out with a peak period instead of a disaster area.

What's included in a marketing budget?

The most profitable marketing item in your list is, undoubtedly, entertaining clients. First, because it isn't very expensive; everything except the food and wine is among your fixed costs. Second, the value appears much greater to the clients because they don't buy at cost like you do. Third, because the expense buys you at least an hour of the client's time, which you can spend on selling your product and on research. The fact that most Assistant, Reception and Banqueting Managers seem to have little time to entertain, illustrates the mistaken way in which administration so often gets a higher priority than selling.

A list of items you need to consider when you create your marketing budget are:

- Entertaining.
- Staff costs.
- Print production.
- Photography.
- Origination costs – lay-outs, graphics, cartoons, etc.
- Advertising media.
- Public relations – including press relations.
- Mailing costs.
- Stationery.

- Postage.
- Travel.
- Entertaining.
- Buying research.
- Contingency.

All of these will be obvious to you except, perhaps, the item for contingency. If you get a good marketing idea after the budget has been approved, you don't want it delayed for up to a year until the new financial year starts because no money has been allocated for it. So put some contingency money into the budget in case you think of something new.

How do you decide what to spend the money on?

Obviously, that depends on many factors. One point is vital: never let any part of the marketing budget be sacrosanct. 'We've always had a big brochure, so we must go on having a big brochure.' No, every element of your marketing expenditure has got to be in competition with the other ways of spending the money. If it can be more profitably spent on something else, then that's where the money ought to go.

There are companies who will agree a sizeable advertising budget but take on no more sales staff; their idol is head count. Head count does, of course, matter when the staff are used to service customers. Agreed, if very few customers ever eat in the restaurant on Monday nights, there is little point of having a full brigade on duty. Marketing cannot be judged by a yardstick of head counts. The money is spent to make more profit than the marketing costs; that is the marketing yardstick.

Of course, that also implies that the hospitality industry expects a one-year payback. So it does. If the money is spent in this financial year, then the view is that the profit has at least to balance the expenditure during this financial year. Well, it's nice work if you can get it, but there are few other industries who look at marketing in the same way. Almost everywhere you will find that markets need building over a long period of time. When Grand Metropolitan Hotels started their Stardust Short Break Holidays we lost money for the first 4 years; we made a fortune, though, in year 5 and from then on.

Certain parts of the marketing budget are spent simply because you are in business in the first place; you have to have a tariff, a menu, a wine list, etc. You have to spend money on telephones, on travelling and on desks. Anything like that is an inevitable expense. There is a difference, though, between telephone costs and a telesales campaign. With the latter, you could identify the cost and the profitable results. Wherever it is possible to do a Profit and Loss account, you should attempt it.

This is not, however, in order to decide whether your expenditure on sales personnel was wise in the first place. The effort to do that leads many companies into serious planning errors. They are so anxious to know whether the sales people are worth having, that they put that cart before every more logical marketing horse. For example, they insist that sales people are, primarily, there to get new business. The theory is that, if they get new business, then you can set the value of the new business against their cost and know whether they are valuable to the company. Well, what is new business? If you had a group using your product in 1985 and they haven't been back since, a sales executive who brings them back in 2001 is surely producing new business. And if they were with you in 1990? In 1995? When does a failure to return become new business if the sales executive persuades them to do so?

The logical answer is another question. Does it matter? So long as they come back, that's money in the bank. Who brings them back is totally irrelevant. Yet, for example, we find sales people beating the boondocks to find brand new business while Banqueting has no time to try to bring the old business back. Worry about the turnover, not about who brought it in.

Are there other exceptions? Yes, if the local vicar tells you in advance of all the wedding parties booking his church, the least you can do is to take space in the church magazine. If you want to support a tourist board or advertise in the brochure of your major travel agent supplier, then that is realistic too. That is a quid pro quo, however, and you want to keep that expenditure as low as you possibly can.

Where's the time going to come from?

Where indeed? If the kind of marketing plan I am outlining is far more than you have tried to implement before, then extra time has got to be found from somewhere. As hospitality industry staff are not underworked – far from it – you have to look at what is occupying their time, with the intention of cutting out anything that is really not absolutely necessary. For example, when you are writing letters, do you write '£100.00' or '£100'? Agreed, '.00' doesn't take much time to write. Do it thousands of times a year unnecessarily and it's worth writing '£100' instead. Now, there are a lot more time consuming examples than that. Identify them and cut them out.

Are the team qualified to carry out the marketing plan?

In most cases, it is not very likely they are. The management haven't usually worked as sales executives or in advertising agencies and they haven't studied the subjects as much as they deserve. Therefore, your marketing plan should give a lot of thought to what training needs you have. Management who can write letters to their grandparents are not, thereby, experts on direct mail. Get at least one book for the executive who is given the direct mail portfolio. See that the F&B Manager learns more about advertising. This book is a start, but it isn't the whole story. There are libraries where you will find the whole picture.

If there are areas of the marketing plan that don't work, the reason could be that overseas economies are under pressure, new competition has to be overcome or government economic policy has temporarily lessened discretionary income. It should never be because you have carried out the marketing plan inefficiently. That last criterion is under your control.

Case study

This case study illustrates:

- Small companies can work on small areas of promotion that larger company marketing departments often ignore because success wouldn't make enough difference to their profits.
- Whatever size of company, you always need to be able to monitor the results of your work.
- No matter how remote your location, there will always be Unique Selling Propositions if you look for them hard enough.

Milton Hotels, a small hotel group in the Scottish Highlands, who engaged me as a consultant, obviously had only a limited amount of money available to spend on marketing. It was even more essential than usual therefore that we could monitor the results of the expenditure.

There were many ways to do this. The company built a new Leisure Club. The marketing budget was for a brochure describing its attractions and direct mail to send the material to people who could afford the membership fees. This included the postage costs and the cost of selecting the right people to mail. As a result of the mailing we had a large number of enquiries and converted a considerable proportion into members. The revenue from membership from that exercise could be set against the costs of the promotion to identify the success of the operation.

A lot of bus groups stayed at the hotels but they spent very little extra. So we produced a Liqueur Coffee card. The extra revenue generated by something like this can be easily calculated by identifying how many liqueur coffees were sold before the card and how many afterwards. The difference represents the result of the advertising. From the additional revenue you have to subtract the cost of the ingredients. The question of VAT is best dealt with by deducting VAT from both your expenditure and your income.

When it snows in the Highlands you get good skiing – if the winds aren't too high. So when conditions were good, we would take space on television (teletext) and advertise the skiing. Bookings would come as a result. It could, however, be coincidence that skiers book at the last minute without seeing the teletext. They could learn of the good conditions from other sources. So in order to estimate the value of teletext, you have to subtract a part of the revenue as not applying to the investment. From the revenue of the rest you must deduct the marginal costs (room cleaning, breakfast food, etc.) and then you finish up with a profit – or a loss. We finished up with a profit.

The marketing budget included the cost of sales people. Here the important factor was how much business they produced when the hotels needed it. The Highlands is a difficult area to sell in the winter, so any business they could find during that period was very helpful indeed. On the other hand, if the sales people came in with August business it could be said that others would have stayed if the new business hadn't done so. You had to examine the dates on which the business came in to judge their effectiveness. One advertising promotion which worked well in the winter was directed at Senior Citizens and had a headline 'Over 60 and bored witless?' In cooperation with the Scottish railway company, this produced a lot of business.

In an area as remote as the Highlands you don't get a lot of local commercial traffic. Your marketing budget inevitably includes a lot of travelling for your sales people. You may take a stand at events like the World Travel Market in London. The results then might seem to be in the lap of the gods. Either potential customers will come by or they won't. You can help the gods by contacting the people you want to talk to in advance and making appointments for them to drop in at the stand at specific times. It is the difference between reactive and proactive selling.

Perhaps the most crucial marketing expenditure was on Central Reservations staff. It isn't the highest paid job in the world so the staff weren't originally world beaters, but converting enquiries for groups was vital to the success of the company. A great deal of sales training went into maximizing the staff's effectiveness. I asked one of them which Closing Technique they found most productive. They said the Silence Close. You could find any number of London luxury hotel advance reservations staff who wouldn't know what a Closing Technique was. The conversion rate of the central bookings department became impressive.

Some elements of the marketing plan demand intelligent work, rather than large expenditure. Correspondence research is one of these. Why are people coming and who else could come for the same reason? Among the markets that emerged from a careful examination of the correspondence were painters coming to Oban because of the excellent quality of the light in the area. There was also a lot of business associated with the building of a new shopping centre – shop fitters, staff training, architects, etc. A scouting party looking for suitable locations for a film led to the housing of the cast of *Braveheart* when they started shooting.

A lot of promotional material may seem necessary but unproductive – hotel brochures, menus and wine lists, for example. They are, however, all selling documents and the ones we produced in the Highlands were highly unusual. For example, they used a lot of headlines. For one hotel, the headline on the page read 'You'll be just as well looked after as were Robbie Burns, Henry Campbell Bannerman and Grand Duke Nicholas of Russia' – all distinguished guests from the past. There were captions to the photographs – one for a conference room reading 'So peaceful, you could hear your brain ticking over'. Just using marketing money to go through the motions and provide information is not enough.

THE MARKETING PLAN

Marketing is about identifying Unique Selling Propositions: the training of divers in a loch with sheer sides in Fort William, the international standard of a lake for trout fisherman outside Stirling and the council business in Inverness (councillors come from a long way away to reach Inverness and often have to stay overnight).

Successful marketing is about monitored expenditure, aimed at need periods, making every penny count, identifying every USP and always looking for better selling methods. It is also about recognizing that if you finish up with an incremental profit you wouldn't have had otherwise, then there is no reason to stint on your marketing expenditure.

2 Organizing a sales office

OK, you've got a marketing plan. Now how do you organize a sales office?

Sell selling

Your first problem is that many of the staff who have to sell, didn't come into the industry with that in mind. They haven't been taught to sell, they may consider it beneath their dignity, because there are unfair stereotypes of sales people, associating them with high pressure tactics and sharp practice. It hardly needs saying that professional sales people are highly ethical but the profession has not always had a good press. The staff may be terrified at the prospect of persuading a managing director to do anything. They may feel humiliated when the client says 'no', and not want to go through that experience again. They may consider they have been conned into being sales people and resent it. Your first task is to sell selling as a respectable, professional activity which benefits both the client and the hotel. They must believe that the client would be wise to spend their money on your product. If they have little confidence in the product, they won't sell it with any enthusiasm.

They must also recognize that selling is not a difficult skill to master. It is a commonplace to say that everybody in the hospitality industry is a sales person. It is true that waiters, hotel receptionists, bar tenders and banqueting staff have a selling responsibility as part of their job specification. To say that they are all sales people, though, is the same as suggesting that if you can make a cup of tea, you are a chef. There is a great deal to learn and you have to make plans to train them properly in a skill that is not covered well in hotel schools and is seldom an important part of an induction process. Conference coordinators might read in the job advertisement that the successful candidates will be able to handle a Fidelio system, but it will seldom say that they will be able to sell.

Train it in

Who is going to do the training? Well, the General Manager or the Sales Manager. They know most about the subject. Yet sales managers are usually employed to go out and visit clients. They are not usually involved in improving the standard of selling in the Banqueting and Reception departments, or teaching the waiters how to sell more liqueur coffees. They should be. There is little point in going out to get new business while you are losing a lot more unnecessarily back at the ranch.

You can have one-to-one training and group training. If it is group training, then the audience should get the impression of a discussion more than a lecture. You are not only trying to teach; you are also trying to win them over to your way of thinking. If they feel that everything is cut and dried and that they can have no effect on the final outcome, then they may reject this take-it-or-leave-it approach. A discussion where you win them to your way of thinking is far more likely to get them to carry out a policy, which they can see makes sense, where they have had their say, and where, therefore, it's a team effort.

It isn't sufficient to train, though. Remember that the audience is often not that keen on the subject. You also have to set up a monitoring system. Are the sales policies actually being carried out – and carried out effectively?

Take a simple example. Everybody wants to keep regular guests. When they read the papers, they are inundated with special offers from your competitors to leave you. In a hotel this is less likely to happen if you get their next booking before they check out. For that to happen, the receptionist who checks them out, needs to say 'We have a number of busy periods coming up, Mr Jones. If you know when you're coming back, why not make your next booking now. We hate to disappoint our regular guests.' And, as the client waits for the bill, they have nothing better to do than get out their diary and make their next booking.

That's all there is to it. It is easy to teach and easy to understand. But will it happen? And happen every time?

What would you need?

1 A list of the clients who are to be approached in this way.
2 The Sales Manager to do the first batch of sales, so that the receptionists can see that it isn't all that difficult.
3 The Sales Manager to then observe the Receptionists trying it, and to correct and help them when they go wrong.
4 A Next Booking Card for the client to fill up.

You then have to handle the objections from Reception. They haven't got the time, do you realize how long the queue is at 8.30 in the morning, etc.? Right, so you handle the objections. You produce a notice for the Reception desk which reads 'Booking out tomorrow? It's the end of the queue. Ask your breakfast server for your bill.' And on the breakfast tables, a tent card which reads 'Booking out today? It's the end of the queue. Ask your breakfast server for your bill.' Use the notices when Reception can't cope in the morning.

Every sales policy you want carried out needs the same process. Decide what you want to do, train it in and then monitor it.

Suppose you can't afford a sales manager?

The hospitality industry is full of small companies. So a great many of them would find it impossible to employ a sales manager. It would just be too expensive. That applies, however, to fewer companies than it actually should. When you look at the profit you are losing from unsold space, you need to ask yourself just how great an improvement a sales manager would have to produce to pay back their salary and still leave you with a profit.

It is a mistake to regard a Sales Manager as an expense. It is often a good investment. Having said that, it remains the case that sales managers are not feasible in many situations. Then everybody who sells has to decide to learn more about the subject. Any additional knowledge and experience they obtain will stand them in good stead in the future course of their career. Yet, so often, it is expected that they learn instead about health and safety at work, industrial legislation, fire precautions and the like; very important – but so is how to sell.

What sort of people make the best sales executives?

You may be recruiting sales people or trying to decide who to give the selling responsibility to in a department. If people want the job, they will tell you that they are keen as mustard and will be enthusiastic, hard working and loyal. All of which is very desirable, but will they make good sales people?

The key is to look at the CV. Have they ever shown any inclination to sell when they didn't have to? Did they take a vacation job in a shop? Did they ever try to sell Avon cosmetics? Anything to do with selling in their past is good. Next, are they stubborn, obstinate and difficult? Very good qualifications if they are going to make a living in sales. Do they play team games or enjoy one against one sports: golf, tennis, squash? Those who choose one-to-one are better prospects for selling, because they are more likely to enjoy the battlefield with the client. Even if they are totally non-sports minded, what about their hobbies? It takes plenty of patience to be a bird watcher, it takes persistence and intellect to do *The Times* crossword. Large jigsaw puzzles demand enormous concentration over long periods. If they do those kinds of things for enjoyment, the persistence you need in selling won't worry them. Never was it more truly said than in sales, if at first you don't succeed, try, try and try again.

From the point of view of personality, almost everybody can be a good sales executive. If they are shy, they can overcome it with time. If they are scruffy in their appearance, they can become smarter. If they are sloppy in their paper work, they can become more organized with practice.

The one thing that a good sales executive must have is a good working brain. Selling is an intellectual exercise. The sales executive has to out-think the client. He or she has to come up with convincing counter arguments, to persuade logically and clearly. A sales executive has no other weapon. You can't hold the client up with a gun and demand the business. Without the ability to think, it is very unlikely that you can become a good sales executive.

Now, of course, everybody has some capacity to think. We are not talking here about brains that win Nobel prizes. But the ability to think also involves not being distracted by other considerations. That the client is being unreasonable, that you don't like them, that nobody treats you like that. Yes, many clients are unreasonable, dislikeable and they can go on treating you like that. Because the object of the exercise is to get the business. When you do that, the client has lost game, set and match.

How do you judge a sales manager?

The answer to this is, exactly the same as you judge any other executive from an operational point of view: skill at handling staff, timekeeping, etc. But the important point is how do you judge them from a sales point of view?

Most sales people are judged by the number of client calls they make a day and the amount of business they bring in. This is wildly simplistic. What is the point of going out to make calls if the Banqueting Department haven't got the time or the ability to write good selling letters to clients who have enquired about group business? Surely you are more likely to get more additional revenue if you lend Banqueting a hand. What is the point of bringing in business which the hotel didn't want, or could have replaced at as good or better a rate?

ORGANIZING A SALES OFFICE

Sales managers should be judged by criteria such as:

1 The amount of useful business they bring in.
2 The improvement in the conversion of enquiries for group business.
3 The improvement in the volume of old business that comes back.
4 The improvement in the conversion of enquiries for reservations.
5 The improvement in the conversion of Brochure and Tariff enquiries into definite business.
6 The volume of bookings that come from prepaid reply cards.

The counter argument is that the business would have come anyway. No, all of it wouldn't. If you know your success rate at the moment, you know how far it can be improved. Selling is a team exercise. Where the business comes from doesn't matter – so long as it comes.

What weaknesses should you watch out for with sales people?

Obviously, the answer is going to be a generalization, but there are three weaknesses which are very prevalent in sales personnel in hospitality industries.

1 They don't have enough product knowledge. Why is a 1986 Burgundy cheaper than a 1989? Few could tell you. What are sight lines and point loading? Now, *you* know that sight lines are those which divide areas from which you can see the whole of the stage from those where a part of the stage is obscured. Do the sales people? And you know that point loading is the weight a part of the floor can take without collapsing. Sight lines are important when you are selling major conferences and point loading if you are selling exhibitions. A 1986 Burgundy is, of course, less expensive than a 1989 because 1986 was 5 but 1989 was 6. If the sales people are still

none the wiser, the quality of French wine is measured on a scale of 1–7. If you are selling wine, you need to know why one is better than another.

The excuse you hear is that sales people can always refer the client to the Chef or the Wine Waiter or the Banqueting Manager. In the client's office? No, they can't.

Consider; you are being told about a car by the sales executive in the showroom. You ask what a knob is for on the dashboard? 'I've no idea. I'll go and get a mechanic' is the answer. Do you buy the car from that individual? I suggest you don't. And any sales person with good product knowledge is in a far stronger position than the one who has to go off to get the information.

2   They are inexperienced in managing staff. Just because they can sell well, doesn't mean they are good managers. And particularly in those situations where they need to persuade their colleagues in other departments to accept advice, they haven't been trained how to do it effectively.

3   They have often not been taught how to train. A great many hospitality industry staff get On the Job Training qualifications, which are excellent. To how many sales people does this apply? The ability to train effectively is vital, but not easy.

So if you want to finish up a first class sales person, capable of going on to run major companies and sit on a board of directors, these skills have to be acquired. If your ambitions are pitched lower, you still need to become as expert as you can in these areas.

Where do you locate the sales office?

You locate your sales office right by the people who were order-taking and who are now going to sell as well. What is more, the staff need to be told that the Sales Manager is there to improve their selling standards; and that you are holding the Sales Manager responsible for that.

There may be circumstances in which you may have to help the Sales Manager do their job. For example, it is possible that the Banqueting Manager is a middle-aged man and the Sales Manager a young woman. The Banqueting Manager might be resentful at being taught things by a younger executive of the opposite sex. You have to make it clear that this is your policy, and make those being taught happy that this is going to happen.

What's the right ambiance?

The best example is that of the relationship between a student and supervisor at university. The student can treat the supervisor as a friend, as an equal, and the supervisor will do the same with the student. The yardstick is always the correctness of the facts. The facts can be argued over, but they are paramount. And as the supervisor usually knows the facts better than the student, he or she retains their senior position on those grounds.

Why is that the right ambiance for a sales office? Because the young sales people have got to get used to talking on the same level as senior management. To feel comfortable with that, they have to practise on somebody. Their boss is the best practice available.

Furthermore, the state-of-the-art in selling improves all the time. There has to be a desire for that to happen in your sales areas. If the boss, effectively, says 'Don't argue with me. I'm in charge' this will be a far slower process than is necessary.

If you can get all the people involved in selling in the same room, so much the better; Advance Reservations, Group Sales, Banqueting Sales and Sales can support each other. It is easier to build a camaraderie. That does not mean that, if the banqueting staff are busy, the advance reservations staff can answer the enquiry equally well. That would only be the case if the staff were multi-skilled in the product knowledge of the different departments. You can set out to achieve that result, though.

Part of the ambiance is the setting of standards. Like Manchester United or the SAS, the standard which brings the best results is one of perfection. If you make mistakes in your selling, the clients or the competition may punish you for them. So perfect punctuation and spelling matters in your letters, an impeccable appearance, spot-on time keeping and never missing a chase date to try to bring in business, are all essential. If you set high standards, the staff will be proud to work for such a quality company.

The ambiance has got to include a belief in the minds of every member of the staff that you can be successful. As you struggle to get business, the temptation to quit is considerable. 'We've tried to get hold of him six times. Let's just file the correspondence in the cancellation file.' No, you haven't lost till the final whistle blows and the client books somewhere else.

What about the competition? Part of believing you can win is believing that the competition won't. When the staff think of the competition, it should be with healthy and amused contempt. You have to believe you can do better and then there's a far better chance that you will. How can you have contempt for the Rolls-Royce of the competition? They'll have weaknesses. Every product does. Concentrate on the weaknesses.

How do you organize the paper work?

You want the sales staff to spend as much time as possible selling and helping others to sell. You have employed sales staff because they know how to do it. Not because they can type. So, unless you are satisfied that they can type fast – and unless you want to pay a sales manager's salary for a typist – have a typist do the typing for them. The same principle applies for reports, statistics, contracts and similar. When they are doing those, they are not selling. Now, they may not complain. It is a lot less wearying doing the paperwork than trying to persuade reluctant clients to buy things. You have to keep their shoulder to the wheel, however.

In trying to make sure that your sales people spend their time selling, you need to recognize the difference between selling and research. In the marketing plan it was a student who validated the information on business you have done in the past. Apply the same idea to research on increasing your share of markets; if you look after one dinner for a team in a hockey league, do the other teams have dinners too? That's the researcher's job, not that of your small, skilled, selling resource.

A word about contracts. Everybody sends out contracts nowadays. When they are signed, they ensure that, if there is any dispute, you will win in court. The only thing is that you practically never would finish up in court anyway. And if you did, whatever is in the correspondence is just as much a contract. Indeed, if you agree to buy a biro from me for 10p in front of a third party, that is a contract too; without any correspondence. Yet the time spent on writing contracts is immense – and costly.

Some paper work is vital. Particularly the records of the old business and the Call Reports. They are discussed in the chapter on banqueting. But, frankly, the Call Reports can be handwritten just as well as computerized. And it is much quicker.

You need your correspondence about future group bookings filed in date order for when they are coming. You need the old correspondence filed in alphabetical order for easy reference. File the old files, so that you haven't got a mass of unnecessary paper. Of course, we are only talking about the paperwork you need for selling purposes. Operational paperwork is not part of this book. There is, in both areas, however, likely to be a lot of unneeded duplication. The rule is, if you don't need it, don't bother to produce it.

One of the most important pieces of paperwork for any sales office is the record of the company's performance in years past. Say you have a large banqueting room which takes 250 guests. You are offered a party for 150 on a date in the future. Do you take it or not? Well, that depends on how heavy was the demand for that room on the same day in years gone by. The same applies for hotel accommodation, party bookings in the restaurant, etc.

The sales people need to be able to refer to those records at all times. Just producing business, irrespective of the demand pattern, is often useless. For example, you give a corporate rate to a company which books a lot of bedroom accommodation. The agreed price is lower than rack rate. You then find that the company only books Tuesday night during peak periods. Every booking you take at a corporate rate costs you money. So check which nights a company with a corporate rate is booking.

There is also a concept called the 80/20 rule. This holds that you need to concentrate on the 20 per cent of your customers who give you 80 per cent of your business. Well, you certainly need to prioritize, but this is the wrong way to do it. It's fine for selling baked beans. Which tins you sell don't matter. But in a normal banqueting situation, one of those 20 per cent of clients may give you a group banqueting booking on a Friday night in December. Another, too small to be in the 20 per cent, gives you a booking for a Monday night in January. Which client is the most important? The one who gives you January. Your priority is the client who fills gaps for you.

In hotels you also need to keep records of the performance of travel agents booking groups. To get a lower price, many travel agents offer a series of bookings which include off season and shoulder season groups. Then they cancel the off season and shoulder periods because – as they knew – few people buy them. When, next year, they try it again, you need to know what their performance was on each date. Then you can negotiate more intelligently.

Then you need a record of what happened to the requests you got for Brochures and Tariffs. Did you get the bookings or not? If you are checking, it is more likely that Reception will do the necessary work.

Entertaining reports

Entertaining is one of the best ways of getting business. The more skilled the staff in this complex area, the better. So it's necessary to have a review after every occasion while what happened is fresh in their mind. There is no need to push the problems under the carpet. If the research wasn't done properly, if they failed to identify the other group business available, then, with luck, they will do so next time.

What kind of meetings would be helpful?

Again you need to decide your priorities. For example, meetings to reflect on how much business you have booked are enjoyable, but they don't take you forward.

Weekly Provisional Review Meeting

What you need is a Weekly Provisional Review Meeting (WPRM). The day before you hold it, you get out a list of all the provisional group bookings you have in the diary. During the meeting you review all of those which you are really keen to see converted from provisional to definite. The others round the table can put in their ideas for solving problems. For example, you are going to lose the business because you haven't got exercise equipment as good as your competitor? Then somebody round the table will correctly suggest hiring it in. You can't leave all the thinking to the single individual who is handling the group; they can't think of everything. Selling should be a team effort.

The WPRM also gives you the opportunity to check that the correct work has been carried out to get the business. Has the client been invited to come to lunch, have you visited them? Have you written a good selling letter or just sent a brochure with a compliments slip?

Forecasting meetings

You need to keep the future position under review at all times. If business looks better than last year, you may decide to take fewer cut price groups, or put the rates up. If business is looking worse, then you have to find ways of dealing with the problem. Special events need long gestation periods but you often know a long way in advance that you are going to need them. Bank Holiday Mondays in hotels, Monday nights in restaurants, the weeks before and after Easter: the marketing plan sets out the policies to be adopted but the regular meetings give the specific parts of the plan extra relevance.

Appraisals

It is important to agree with a sales executive how they can improve their performance. It is also important not to undermine their confidence. The appraiser needs training too. It is confidence that keeps sales people going when the going gets rough. A formal annual appraisal is, therefore, a dangerous exercise. Much better to chat with them about other matters on a fairly regular basis – the performance of an important company, the development of a market – and turn the conversation into the need for them to improve their personal performance. You agree you are not getting enough repeat business. Would it be a good idea if they studied the techniques of direct mail a little more thoroughly. What do they need to do that? How can you help? By when might it be done?

Morning Prayers, F&B meetings, etc.

In Victorian times the day in a hotel started with the staff – and often the guests – attending Morning Prayers. To this day, the morning meeting to discuss the happenings of the day retains the title. When such meetings are concerned, primarily, with discussions and timetabling, they involve little emotional strain. The sales people will be happy to attend, particularly as little which is said affects them. So don't have them there, except when topics that involve them will come up. You need them to be selling to customers. Don't take them away from that for a minute more than necessary.

Marketing plan review meetings

As I have said, all too often a marketing plan takes weeks to produce and then sits on the shelf till the time comes to write

ORGANIZING A SALES OFFICE

a new one. Yours should be reviewed every two months at least. At the meeting you need to know what is happening.

At that point don't accept the excuse that the work hasn't been carried out because of a lack of time. If that is the case, then you wanted to know weeks before, so that you could give the executive additional resources, or change the executive responsible to somebody who did have the time.

How do you get the best out of sales people?

Sales people need a lot of encouragement. They spend a lot of their lives trying to get business from clients who often give them a hard time: clients who won't speak to them or who turn down their proposals, who keep them waiting, don't ring back or are even rude. Professional sales people take all this in their stride, but they are not looking for more of the same when they get back to the office. If they come up against resentment when they are trying to help a colleague sell better, they will just switch off.

The General Manager needs to praise them, encourage them, support them and coax them into the best possible performance. You have to be on guard against the sales people going through a bad patch and losing confidence. If they haven't sold a thing for a couple of weeks, reassure them that business will get better soon. When they are successful, there should be general rejoicing. A combination of criticism when they are pointing up errors, and indifference when they are bringing in the business, is not best calculated to keep their enthusiasm up to fever pitch.

You also need to set out an equivalent of the Marquess of Queensberry rules on differences of opinion in how to approach sales problems. The important point is that discussion, even heated discussion, is essential to try to come up with the right solution. Discussion needs to be encouraged. But, if there is disagreement, it must be couched in intellectual terms and it must not become personal.

It is also important for sales people to recognize that improving sales techniques does not mean condemnation of their existing efforts. It is the difference between a trial and an inquest. A trial is held to identify the guilty party and punish them. An inquest is designed to find out why the sale died and try to make sure the next sale doesn't. Everybody needs to be reminded that you don't hold trials; you hold inquests.

On that basis, it is more likely that errors will be brought to light and discussed in a positive way. If the sales person sees everybody's objective as to make fun of them or criticize them, then they will put the sales skeleton in the cupboard and lock and bolt the door. Nobody will know the truth and the same mistake may be made in future.

The sales people should only know one enemy; the competition. If they are at war with the other departments, they cannot devote their maximum energy to burying the opposition.

In most companies there is friction between the sales side and the operational side. Why can't the sales side sell what we operational people want to produce? Why can't operations deliver what the clients want to buy? Someone has to keep the peace. The cause of friction is often that neither side understands sufficiently the problems of the other. Don't they realize how stupid it is to block us up on Tuesday night? Don't they realize that if I don't give them Tuesday night, I can't get the big party in January? Both sides need educating.

A great deal of a sales person's time should be devoted to selling on the telephone. The bosses who say that they want the sales people on the road all the time are mistaken. They forget that they are selling a product that the public will probably want to see before they buy it. The objective is to get the client to visit the property, but this can be done on the phone. If most of the time is spent on the phone and on showrounds and entertaining, the time that has to be devoted to travelling is reduced to a minimum. Time really is money.

One of the important factors in successful selling is to be relaxed when you are doing it. If the sales person is nervous, the nervousness comes out in their voice. Selling requires total concentration, so when a sales person is selling, never interrupt them. For the relaxation to be as complete as possible, you may find the sales person slouching back in a chair or even putting their feet on the desk. This is good. It relaxes the stomach muscles. It may not look professional but it is.

While their posture may be sloppy, their appearance must be immaculate. They represent the product and, in the hospitality industries, part of the attraction of the product is its elegance. On the other hand, their appearance should fit the client they are approaching. Morning dress scares the daylights out of young secretaries in companies. People who book jazz bands don't take kindly to dark suits. It is also true, though, that if you are selling to someone with a military background, your shoes had better be well polished. So many clients believe they can sum up an individual as soon as they see them. You can't, but if the first impression is poor, it is that much more difficult to get the sale.

Answer the phone

A sales office exists to get clients to contact you if they need your product. When they do so, you have to answer the phone. Does that happen within three rings? Because that's the standard you should aim for. It is unforgivable to work for a couple of years to get a client to offer you business, and then when they are finally ready to do so, fail to pick up the phone before they ring off.

It isn't always easy. You may be on the phone already, showing potential customers around the place, out on a call, or in the loo. You can't be in two places at the same time. So then you have to have a fall-back position. Who is going to answer the phone if the sales people can't? Draw up a list of extensions to which the call should be referred. And tell whoever is on those extensions that they are on duty for the calls if the sales people are otherwise engaged.

What happens at the moment? I will lay 10–1 the telephonist will say 'There's no answer. Can I take a message?' To stop this pernicious practice, you need to put up notices in every office which read 'We don't take messages. We help!' After all, it is ridiculous that, in a hotel for instance, you can book a bedroom for, say, £50 from 7 in the morning till 11 at night, but you can't spend £10,000 on a major dinner at 11 in the morning because there is no one to answer the phone.

The reason given for this disastrous situation is usually that only the relevant department can make decisions and provide all the information. The answer to that is to train others to do so nearly as well. Because, if you don't, a lot of people are not going to bother to wait for you to ring back.

Differentiate between sales promotion and sales activity

The difference between success and failure in selling is often a small one. It's like making a shot on the golf course or the tennis court: get it slightly off line and you lose the hole or the point. You equally deviate from the straight and narrow when you undertake sales activity rather than sales promotion.

Let's take as an example the Christmas parties that so many organizations arrange. Perhaps you produce a brochure to advertise what you can offer. You send it out to clients who have been with you in the past or who may be arranging something of the kind. When do you send them the information? Well, perhaps September? October? That's sales activity.

Sales promotion is to send them the material when they are ready to make up their minds – that is when it will get the most favourable attention. Not long before, when it will go into the basket. Not after they have made their arrangements, when it will also go in the basket. You recognize, of course, that this means far more detailed organization. You need a file for posting for each month. If a particular client decides on the Christmas party in May, then write to them in April. And if you don't know when they make up their mind, ring them and ask. Tedious, boring, routine, time consuming – professional, far more successful and sales promotion.

You find that business is quiet in January. Right, then there is time to contact clients, to do a sales blitz, to send out direct mail. That's sales activity. Who is to say potential clients are ready to make up their minds in January? Only research and contacting clients with a regular flow of business throughout the year can be done effectively in this way. That is sales promotion. The rest is sales activity.

ORGANIZING A SALES OFFICE

If you are going to have a sales blitz, it is extremely unwise to tell anybody who isn't a professional sales person to take part in it. Professionals don't mind contacting complete strangers and selling them things. They don't mind calling at the offices of potential clients, without an appointment, to try to see them. For the inexperienced, this kind of sales activity is torture. When they can't get an appointment they feel rejected and humiliated. When they can, they are terrified of being asked questions to which they don't know the answers. They are afraid of fluffing their lines and making fools of themselves. If you really want to turn youngsters off selling for ever, put them on a sales blitz. Don't fool yourself that they are just being thrown in at the deep end. It's normally a disaster.

Taking ownership

Each part of the marketing plan needs someone to take the responsibility for seeing that it is properly carried out. Those responsibilities need to be handed out and the executive given the authority to ensure they get any support they need.

The Disaster Squad

One member of the department needs to be constantly on the lookout for news that will involve the use of hotels. To take a simple example, on those rare occasions when there is a rail strike, a lot of the regular passengers who commute to their offices every day are unable to do so as easily, so the most senior stay in hotels until the emergency is over. That kind of problem – and a great many more – leads to windfall business, so long as you react quickly when the opportunity presents itself.

Here are just 20 types of events that will fill somebody's hotel:

- Transportation strikes.
- Aircraft delays.
- Tourists flown out of areas that have suddenly become war zones.

- Snow closing down airports to which flights from your country are going.
- Bad weather closing down your own airport.
- Passengers of broken down ferries.
- Survivors of shipwrecks.
- Floods preventing journeys to and from the affected area.
- Juries who can't make up their minds and have to stay in hotels overnight.
- When two countries fall out, they repatriate their own nationals.
- When countries announce a moratorium on their overseas debts, there is an influx of overseas bankers to try to resolve the situation.
- State funerals.
- Sports match replays.
- Government enquiries into major accidents.
- Groups lobbying government.
- Government conferences with disaffected groups.
- Government initiatives to implement their policies.
- Protest group demonstrations.
- Journalists covering newsworthy stories.
- A fire at another hotel.

Of course, if not taking some of this business made it 0.1% more likely that the tragic events could be prevented, I know you would happily sacrifice the business. It won't, so you might as well go after it. (See the case study at the end of Chapter 3.)

Summary

In organizing a sales office, you have 12 objectives.

1 To persuade everybody in a sales role that selling is a worth-while activity.
2 To train in the sales techniques.
3 To train in the product knowledge.
4 To make everybody understand and agree with the sales policy.
5 To set up effective control systems.

6 To create the most effective ambiance.
7 To keep the paperwork to a minimum.
8 To keep meetings to a minimum.
9 To stick to priorities.
10 To build a winning sales team.
11 To tolerate failure in a good cause.
12 To carry out sales promotion and not sales activity.

Case study

This case study illustrates:

- The thinking behind the creation of a culture for a sales office.
- Staff development.
- How to grow a sales department.

When I started in 1954 there was just me in the Grand Metropolitan sales office. By 1980 there were 190 of us and they were spread all over the world. Over those 25 years decisions had to be made on how to expand, responsibilities, authority, selection of personnel, etc.; how to organize a sales office. The thinking behind those decisions needs explaining because you have the same challenges today.

First, who was to be in charge of sales: Operations or Sales? Since Operations knew very little about sales and marketing techniques, it was decided that I would be in charge, subject to final approval by the CEO. Not a General Manager, but the CEO. The correct sales and marketing decisions were unlikely to be reached at that time by a committee of amateurs, no matter how enthusiastic and hard working. The same may well apply to you today. So, if you have a dog, don't bark yourself.

After several years I was given an assistant. The question then arose of how to recruit good people and what would the office culture be. Selling is like chess; to be successful in negotiation, you have to counter every move your opponent makes – and, in this case, your opponent is the customer. So almost everybody I recruited had a degree. There were exceptions – not everybody likes hitting the books – but the vast majority of the staff who passed through my office had a certificate that said they weren't idiots.

Now the culture. I had no previous experience of running an office. So I asked myself who had got the best out of me. The answer was undoubtedly my college tutor. I did my best work for him, so I decided to run the department like a university. Everybody was on first name terms. People who might be coming into their first job after college would immediately have to call their boss by his first name. As a side benefit, this gave youngsters the opportunity to practise being equal with senior management. When you are selling to a managing director, it doesn't help to be terrified of the individual just because of his or her title. The other advantage is that nobody in the department could be right simply by virtue of seniority; they could only be right because they came up with the correct answers. Any other system simply switches off the brains of the junior staff. They ask themselves why they should bother thinking, when their arguments are refuted by someone who pulls rank on them.

The department developed to somebody handling commercial business and someone else the travel trade. Eventually there were departments for Advertising, Short Breaks, Special Events, Public Relations, offices in America, France, Japan, South Africa, etc. The problem was to decide which markets to tackle. The key was to aim to fill empty space. From the beginning I had been told I was there to fill the winter. Anybody could fill the summer, so I had to concentrate on the period between November and April. The Special Events department only worked on the deadest periods. It started with winter weekends and Short Break Holidays. As Short Breaks grew in numbers, there was a need to hive it off into a separate department. When you develop a market to a size where it needs to go off on its own, you have produced a great deal of extra business. The employment of sales executives to solicit business from Third Party Agents is just the latest in this kind of development.

As the Sales Department spread, the question of morale became ever more important. When you are surrounded by your staff, you can spot problems as they come up. If you have a Sales Manager in San Francisco it isn't that easy. Staff have personal problems from time to time. There is a view that personal problems are nothing to do with the boss. They are outside office hours and no business of ours. I rejected this. I believed that anybody with problems would be less likely to give the client their best shot. So if I could help with the problems, that would get the staff member back on track soonest.

If staff were scattered around the world, there had to be a newsletter. It was a message from home; always cheerful, personal, upbeat. It told of successes and it talked of the 'family' of the department. At a company conference there was once a teamwork exercise. The Sales team finished streets ahead of the General Managers; the family unit worked better.

Appraisals were important. You have got to help staff improve. I never told the staff when these appraisals were going to happen. If you make a date for an appraisal the defences go up and confrontation is far more likely. So I did it when the opportunity occurred – when I handed out salary rises, when we were travelling together on a plane after a sales trip, in the pub. Relaxed, friendly and starting 'How are you getting on?'

If you have good staff, they are going to be poached. How do you stop them going? They are going to be offered more money and higher positions but you have still got to try to keep them. I tried to make my staff believe they were playing for Manchester United. To leave was to go to a team at the bottom of the Third Division.

They developed a contempt for our main competitors because they believed they (we) were better.

To keep up their spirits there was another cardinal rule. If anything went wrong it was the fault of the head of the department. If there was a success, it was down to the junior who had made the sale.

Most of the personnel came from hotel schools. They knew the product. If the hotels tried to tell them something couldn't be done, they knew whether it was an attempt to blind them with science. They knew their wine lists and their menus. They were professional hoteliers as well as sales people.

Many things change over the years: websites, yield management systems, GDS and email. People don't change to the same extent. A lot of the senior sales management in the British hotel industry are ex-Grand Metropolitan. A number of the industry's CEOs also spent time in my department during the course of their careers. We must have been doing something right.

3 Buyers and customers

How are you going to fill all the bedrooms in your hotel all the time? No yield management system will fill your hotel, *if there isn't sufficient demand.* The demand comes from many different markets, but how do you approach them and what do you specifically want from them?

Association conferences

When we talk of association conferences, they can be national conferences or international conferences. The procedure is the same; the difference is just that selling international conferences takes you further afield.

As nobody can force an association delegate to stay anywhere, if you are going after association conferences, getting the conference to your town or city is just the beginning of the work.

How do you get an association to decide on your city for its next conference?

1 There will be a decision-making process. You need to identify what that process is.
2 Normally, the decision and booking will be made two years or more in advance. Few association conference venues will remain undecided for the present year.

3 An association normally has branches or chapters. Each can invite the association to come to its city or country for the next year where a decision has not yet been made (known as the Next Open Year).

4 In many countries there is considerable pressure by government on association chapters to issue invitations. For a chapter officer in your country, the alternatives are to work very hard arranging the gathering in their own country for a couple of years, or to go off for a few days to Hawaii or Rio de Janeiro as a delegate! It is not surprising that many choose the latter route. Prestige and patriotism are your best friends in trying to get them to take the former.

5 There will be a committee to consider the offers. This committee may come to a conclusion:
 – on which venue to recommend to their members;
 – on which venues not to recommend;
 – to get all the members to vote on their preference.

6 The final decision on where to go next is usually made, or rubber stamped, at the Conference itself. It, therefore, follows that if you want the meeting in your city, you probably have to get the local chapter to agree to issue an invitation.

Assume your local chapter has agreed to invite their association to meet in your city. You should try now to arrange a FAM (familiarization) trip for the decision makers.

You should identify the decision-making process. Suppose the committee will meet to decide on their recommendation to the Plenary Session beforehand. Can your local chapter make a presentation? Can you be part of the local chapter presentation committee?

The essential point is that, as far as the local chapter is concerned, you are not just one of the hotels they are going to use if they are successful. You are a full partner with them in their endeavours. You are on their team.

Chance and last minute bookings

When a client wants a room at the last minute, the pressure is on getting the room, rather than on getting the best price. The latecomer has to sleep somewhere. This poses you two problems:

1 How to tell the potential clients that you have the space more efficiently than the competition.
2 How to persuade the clients who come on the day to stay with you, preferably at, or as near to, rack rate as possible.

Those last minute bookings are either:

(a) Enquiries on the phone, or
(b) Enquiries at the reception desk.

So how do you solve the problems?

Informing the clients

1 Make a list of the contacts who could give you last minute business. Make sure the list includes their fax numbers.
2 During any period which is remotely busy, let these clients know you do have space by fax during the night. The Night Porter will have the time to send these faxes.
3 Help the Night Porter by programming your fax machine, so that it can send the faxes out more quickly and simply.
4 Help yourself by having sets of letters available – with fax numbers filled in – so that you just have to overprint a set with the date and give them to the Hall Porter.
5 Remember, the business can come from travel agents, corporate companies, in-house plants, transportation companies, booking agents, other hotels, tourist offices, etc. The more people who know you have the space, the more likely you are to fill it.

How do you deal with last minute enquiries?

1 With phone or fax enquiries at the last minute, you can probably get the business because you have the space. 'We do have one room available at £X' would be the message.

The enquirer would be pleased to have solved the problem where they anticipated difficulties.

2 With potential clients who come up to the desk, the first question will be whether you have room tonight, and the second will be how much is it?

3 The answer on price is normally to quote rack rate and then be prepared to drop to the 'lose it' rate if the client finds the rack rate too high. There is a better way though. The response would be something like:

'We have a number of different types of rooms, sir, and they are at different prices. I'm sure you have a figure in mind. What type of room would you like? There is a Suite for £X, an Executive Room for £Y, a Superior room for £Z or we have one or two rather smaller rooms at £N.'

You will notice that the objective is to move the client from his or her initial position of the Principle of Maximum Choice – you or somewhere else – to the Principle of Minimum Choice – Club Room or Suite, but both with you. (This is called a Closing Technique; they are discussed fully in the next chapter.)

The more your reception staff know about the bedrooms, the better. Where the rooms are located on the floors, what the view is from the windows, what size the beds are, how big are the TV screens, etc. etc.: 'The more facts you tell, the more you sell.'

You can, of course, use the same day selling strategy on the reservation systems as well.

The charity market

There are two aspects of the charity market which can bring business to the hotel:

(a) Fund raising events.
(b) Organizational meetings.

Fund raising events are little different from any other form of function handled by Banqueting. Organizational meetings, on the other hand, need careful analysis. They can be very useful in filling quiet weekends. People who work for charities often do so on a part-time basis without payment. They do their normal jobs during the week and, therefore, can only get together with the charity at weekends. It follows that many charity organization meetings are held then.

Obviously, charities do not have a lot of money to spend on hotels. Nevertheless, they have to meet and, if your accommodation is going to be empty otherwise, there is no harm in reducing prices to accommodate them. The advantage is that prices cannot be reduced for most markets without a knock-on effect. If you're going to lower a corporate rate for one company, the others will want the same reduction. So corporate rates have to be standardized. Nobody is going to object, however, to your reducing prices for a charity.

The important thing is to find out which charities meet at times of the year when you are definitely going to have the space empty if they don't use you. That means research. There are many hundreds of charities in the UK, so it is a long business finding the right ones. But when you find the right charities, you'll probably be one of the first hotel companies who have ever contacted them direct.

Coach companies joint promotions

Coach companies are natural partners for hotel promotions. Hotels may normally be seen in the travel industry only as suppliers – the coach company decides what trips to run and hotels just provide the bedrooms. But this does not have to be the whole story.

Let's look at it from the coach company's point of view. A coach in the garage earns them nothing. Worse, they have to keep the drivers, because good drivers – like good anything else – are hard to find. Every coach company wants to keep the coaches rolling. What can you do to help? You can provide a reason for the coaches to be occupied. If you buy tickets for a big sports event, the coach company can package that up locally and sell it to the sports enthusiasts. You've helped them fill a bus. The same could be true for an important pop concert.

BUYERS AND CUSTOMERS

Coach companies can be your sales force in that town or area. They know where to advertise, which are the local clubs, they have the contacts and the public trusts them.

The coach company marketing budget is designed to be as low as possible, allowing that all the seats on the coach need to be filled. Now see what happens if you offer to put money into that marketing budget to help fill more of the coaches in which you're interested. Say the coach company is promoting a visit to the tulip fields and you have a hotel in the vicinity. You would like 100 guests but they're only running one coach. So you're going to have 50 empty beds. The coach company spends, say, £500 on promoting the coach – £10 a seat. If they have other coaches in the garage, why don't they spend £1,000 and fill another coach? Because they don't think they'd get another 50 people. So you offer them £500 of your own money. Now, they have no risk. The only condition is that however many people book the second coach, they will agree to run it.

Now look at the kind of costings that are involved, and we will keep this simple.

Package cost £300. Made up of:

Hotel × 3 nights	£150
Advertising	£10
Coach costs	£50
Event tickets	£30
Coach company profit	£60

Of the £150 that comes to us – and remember this is an off-season exercise – let us say we make £100 profit. You now put in £500 to fill the second coach. Obviously, if you do fill it, you make a lot of extra profit. But what is your break-even point?

If your marketing cost was £500 and your profit for every extra passenger is £100, you only need another 5 passengers on the extra coach to break even. Indeed 4½ – because you get back the £10 per seat which is allowed for in the original marketing budget. Usually, of course, the break-even point is higher than in this example, but if you can break even if the coach is 25 per cent full, it is worth trying.

Remember, these promotions are for specific events during the low season. They are agreed with coach companies you trust, who have a good track record and are good marketing people.

There will be occasions when the offer doesn't work and you lose money. If the promotion works, you are going to have found a way to avoid losing so much in quiet periods. That is how Short Break Holidays started in the UK – from that premise.

There is one last advantage. Let us say a competitor finds out about these packages and asks the coach company what you are charging. The competitor is told £150 and offers £125. The coach company says 'Will you put in £500, up front, win, lose, or draw?' Your competitor only offers low rates. 'Then' says the coach company 'we'll stay with our existing hotel.' You're a partner, not a supplier.

The corporate market

The corporate market may well be your most valuable. It splits down into a number of different types of organization. These are:

1 Local companies who book direct.
2 National companies.
3 Multinational companies.
4 Travel agent in-plant operations.
5 Major consortia.
6 Hotel booking agents.

In attempting to maximize turnover from all these sources, we also need to keep in mind:

- Overrides and retroactive discounts.
- New accounts.
- Keeping existing accounts.
- Loyalty programmes.

Companies

The amount of business you get from a company may be quite small. The important point, though, is when does it come? If it comes when you need it – a regular visitor on Thursdays, a sales conference in January – then that's an important client. Set up a proper chase system, just as if it was a major multinational. Don't just leave the records in the old correspondence in the basement or the attic.

Travel agent in-plant and out-plant operations

Many companies have enough travel and hotel needs to justify a travel agent asking for a contract to book it for them. This is cheaper for the company than employing their own staff. Basically, the cost of the company Travel Department is then paid for by the commission earned by the in-plant or out-plant agent from hotels, airlines, etc.

If the travel agency has a branch office within the client company complex, it is an *in-plant* operation. If it works from its own headquarters, it is an *out-plant* operation.

The agency may charge for doing the work, but the company get the benefits of nett rates. These dedicated offices can be paid a management fee (fixed annually, or flexible). Or the fee could be based on turnover or on projected savings. Or the agency could be paid for each booking it makes and each amendment.

What does the in-house agent want from a hotel?

1 Commission or the best nett rate available. (Depending on the type of agreement they have with the company they're servicing.)
2 Availability.
3 Speed and efficiency.

These in-plant agents carry out the instructions of the company. Their recommendations on the best bargains available are obviously valuable. At the end of the day, though, the decisions come from the company. This is a most important point.

If you deal with the in-plant agent, you will be asked to quote for individual and group business and then the quotations will be passed to the company executive who wants to make the booking.

Dealing with the in-plant agent, you will not be dealing with the decision maker. Obviously, the in-plant agent doesn't want the executive to make the booking direct. If that happens, the need for an in-plant agent is undermined. On the other hand, if a company executive wants to talk to a hotel, that's their privilege. So long as the final booking is done by the agent, there should be no problem.

You, therefore, need to identify who are the executives who need hotel accommodation in bulk – though, probably, individual bookings for the most part. If you bring them to the hotel for lunch or a showround, they may be more inclined to choose the hotel. It isn't enough to know, and be on good terms with, the in-plant agent.

Often you may find some executives in the company who don't use the in-plant agent. They have been instructed to, but they may be important enough to ignore the instruction. They may be antagonistic towards company instructions – it does happen. They may only have one group booking a year and prefer to deal with it off their own bat.

Major consortia

These are individual agents or companies who join together as consortia to get lower prices from suppliers. Again, the agreement of the price with the consortium is only the first step in getting their business. After that, you have to identify the decision makers among the individual members.

Hotel booking services

You could describe them as travel agents who only book hotel accommodation. They are not only clients to hotels but also serious competitors, as they endeavour to get companies to use their services instead of coming to your hotel direct.

Some hotel booking agents like to suggest that, as they brought a client to you in the first place, you should not try to get that client back, except through them. They suggest, furthermore, that if the client does come back, the hotel booking service is still entitled to commission because they introduced the business.

Such contentions are illegal under EC and British law. If they were accepted, they would restrict competition.

Hotel booking services, like travel agent in-house operations, want commission, availability, speed and efficiency. The temptation to get more of their business by increasing their commission levels during quiet periods is considerable. If you do that, however, your competitors will do so as well and the situation will deteriorate year on year.

As with any other type of competitor agent, the best way to get the business is to reach the client before the client reaches the agent. Offer a better service, more attention for the client's VIPs, value plus, if he or she comes direct. Value Plus is giving more for the money, rather than reducing your basic price.

It always needs to be remembered, with corporate accounts like any other, that the value of the business depends on:

● The business on offer coming when you need it.
● Overall, the business on offer coming at a price you can't improve on from other sources.

Overrides and retroactive discounts

A word about overrides and retroactive discounts. If you want to buy a product for your hotel, most manufacturers or retailers will offer you a price. If you want to buy a lot of the product, they will offer you a wholesale price, lower than the full price. *But only if you do buy the larger quantity.*

The hotel industry has become too accustomed to offering a lower corporate rate before the client has provided the business to justify it. If the business doesn't materialize, you may not renew the offer, but you have still sold the bedrooms thus far at a lower price than you wanted – or may have been able to get. It is, therefore, fair – and very much to your advantage – to endeavour always to agree instead that when they have spent a certain amount with the hotel, they will get a retroactive discount, i.e.: the agreed tariff is £50 a room night but there is a 10 per cent retroactive discount when the company has spent

£10,000 on bedrooms during the year. So, when they've spent £10,000 at £50, they get a retroactive discount cheque for £1,000. If you have to agree a corporate rate for the first time, this can be another incentive.

Such an agreement can work to your advantage in another way – and, again, it doesn't affect the client at all; start the contract *at the end of your dead season*. See the effect of that; assume you are quiet in January and February and the contract starts on 1st March. On 1st January you ring the client and point out that they have already spent £X in the hotel and if they only spend another £Y in the next two months, they'll get their retroactive discount, worth £Z. This means that you pay the retroactive discount from extra income when you would normally be quiet.

Who is the decision maker?

The answer is unlikely always to be the executive with whom you have been negotiating. You may have a contract with the client, but there can be a number of instances where their organization still doesn't use you.

- You are not the only hotel with which most companies have a deal. There may be several hotels within your price bracket. The booker can still, therefore, choose other hotels. It is up to them whether to use you or a competitor.
- You haven't got the space at the last minute.
- The client company objectives are more important than which hotel they are using; if the Vice President, Sales wants to use Hotel A for a new product launch, his responsibility for the success of the launch outweighs whether the company has a deal with Hotel A or not.
- If the client company executive is important enough, he may simply override the company policy on which hotels to use.
- Even less senior executives may decide not to follow the company policy, because they have a favourite hotel. You are unlikely to be fired for using the wrong hotel.
- The business is social and the client company is merely subsidizing the cost for its staff.

How do you identify the decision makers? Well, when the company executive did the deal with you, he or she then had to tell a lot of people who make bookings what the result was. So ask for the list of the people whom the executive will inform of the terms of the deal. Now you have a lot of decision makers. The list needs splitting down into two:

1 The executives organizing group bookings, who should be handled by your Sales Department or somebody senior.
2 The secretaries or reservations clerks making individual bookings, who should be looked after by the Reception Department.

If you have an important booker of individual reservations, you need to arrange for him/her to have a one-to-one with your Reception Manager over lunch. This helps you to identify new sources of business within their organization, to deal with any grumbles and to identify quickly if there has been a serious problem which hasn't come to your attention. (The company executive may complain to the booker without complaining to the hotel.)

Depending on the number of important bookers, you need to make out a list of those you want entertained and how often you want it done; twice a year is ideal.

Of course, you want to build up a picture of the organization's hotel needs and keep that record where you can refer to it. *Don't let the information be found only in the head of the executive handling the account.*

Why are you better than the competition?

The answer to this does not only lie in the quality of the hotels. You may be planning major refurbishment next year, in which case the hotel may be tired, compared to the new hotel which has just opened across the road. You still have to be better than the competition.

What does the individual booker want?

1   To get through easily.

How easy is it to get through to the hotel during peak periods?

Do you need a restricted telephone number for VIP bookers?

Do you need a VIP fax line? The danger is that if a booker is busy and they can't get through easily, they'll book a competitor where they can.

2   To be recognized.

They need to be reassured that their instructions will be carefully followed. If they are recognized by the person they talk to, they are going to be reassured.

3   To get accommodation.

Obviously, you try never to turn down a good client. Nevertheless, there may be occasions when the hotel is packed solid. In those cases, don't say 'No'. Just promise to find the accommodation for them at another hotel. They then know that, when they want space, you will always come up with a room.

4   They may not want to waste time confirming bookings.

They are busy people. If they are satisfied with a confirmation from you, and they're good clients, you don't need confirmations from them. If their clients don't turn up, the fact that you have a confirmation from them won't help, if they say they cancelled the booking over the phone. You are not going to take them to court.

Education

I have dealt with universities in their appropriate section later in the chapter. Promotions that involve education come in a number of additional forms, however.

Schools

There are a number of markets you can consider:

1   Teachers' parties at the end of the school year.

Teachers tend to have a party at the end of the school year. Where that happens in July, the resulting banqueting comes at a time of the year when most hotels are very quiet. You would, therefore, be able to offer reduced prices which, at least, cover your marginal costs and make a contribution to fixed costs.

It is the fact that the parties are held when you are quiet which makes the functions attractive. The approach should be to the Head Teacher during the beginning of May.

2   Where there are boarding schools near the hotel, the parents of the boarders will visit their children during term time.
The market is for both accommodation and entertaining the child, and it is, of course, normally at weekends. Parents Days and Speech Day bring the largest demand. You'd advertise in the school magazine. Most school magazines will take advertising and the rates are very low.

3   Most boarding schools will have reunions of former pupils. The former pupils may come from all over the country. This is an accommodation market too.
The way to reach the former pupils is by a prepaid reply card (PPRC) which goes out with notification of the reunion taking place. There will probably be an Old Pupils' Association and the person who can agree to the PPRC is probably the Secretary of the Association. It shouldn't be a difficult sell, particularly if you offer a rate. The rate, of course, depends on how quiet you are likely to be on the night.

Educational seminars

A lot of people want to learn about a lot of things. There are, of course, many companies who put on seminars for this purpose. There is no reason why you can't do the same thing. Examples in the past have included buying tickets for a popular exhibition on Monday morning, and selling the tickets – including overnight accommodation – for the Sunday night. Or attracting hairdressing salon owners by putting on a teach-in with a famous hairdresser. Or a teach-in for architecture students by a panel of first class architects.

Association meetings

There are a number of teachers' associations (head teachers, assistant teachers, etc.) They may well hold their events during periods when you are very quiet.

Government, embassies, the law and the armed services

There is a great deal of business to be obtained from government sources, in all their many guises. In many instances, the price that may be paid for hotel accommodation is set by government ministers or the Civil Service. In such cases, nobody has any room for manoeuvre and you must either take the business at the price offered or let it go to another hotel which will. Only in emergencies, or if the top officials waive the rules, can higher prices be paid. Obviously, the more senior the official who needs accommodation, the higher the price will be. Also, if you're negotiating for a delegation, the price agreed will be the price for the most senior member of it. It is unlikely that junior members will be put in different hotels, though they would be accommodated in less prestigious rooms than their superiors.

National government

There are a number of markets to consider:

Departmental conferences

Within a Department of State – Agriculture, Industry, Defence, etc. – there will be a need for conferences on various subjects. There may well be a Conference Officer within the Department. That is a very valuable contact. Remember, though, that the Conference Officer is the implementer, not necessarily the decision maker. The Officer may make the decision on where to hold the conference or may take instructions, from someone higher up, to book it at a specific hotel. You, therefore, need to identify which sections of the Department hold regular conferences, who is involved within the section and where the decision maker is located.

While a Conference Officer may come to lunch to see the hotel and test its quality, that may well be the extent of the hospitality you can provide. In Britain, bribing an official is a criminal offence and a bottle of champagne at Christmas would probably be returned.

Meetings are also held to discuss how to carry out the manifesto pledges of political parties. One government was elected on a manifesto that included maintaining village shops in the face of competition from area supermarkets. The Department concerned was persuaded by a hotel sales department to hold marketing training courses for village shop owners in their hotels. Study party manifestos. Then decide how carrying out these objectives may result in additional hotel business for you.

Lobbying

Before the government takes decisions, it may listen to the views of national experts, association delegations, etc. These delegations will need accommodation because they will be drawn from all over the country and will need to meet in advance to agree their approach to the Minister. Here, the decision makers will be within the lobbying groups – probably the Director General – but the government departments would know who is coming to lobby.

Political conferences

There are political conferences of all kinds, arranged by the political party Conference Officers. Don't neglect the smaller political parties; they often fit more comfortably into hotels than into vast conference centres.

Emergencies and inquiries

There are many kinds of emergency in which government is involved: natural disasters – floods, cyclones, tornadoes, etc.; wars abroad may involve getting a country's citizens repatriated. (Who looked after the expats flown out of Sierra Leone by the RAF in 2000 when the civil war broke out?) If there is a major accident, there will be an inquiry. That produces business. Planning inquiries have to be held somewhere and can bring expert witnesses who need accommodation.

Overseas aid

Many governments offer overseas aid to underdeveloped countries, in terms of advice on how to develop their economies. This involves groups visiting the developed nation to learn of the techniques involved. These delegations need accommodation.

Trade delegations

To improve the level of exports overseas, many trade delegations are organized to visit the UK. The list of groups coming will probably be known to the commercial attaché at the Embassy.

Local government

Within local government there are any number of activities; everything from sewage disposal to schools and fire brigades to policing. For everybody working in these sectors, there is a need to understand best practice and to communicate. These factors lead to the holding of conferences. How is it decided where to hold them? There is no one answer. One possible scenario is that it goes in turn; in which case, when is the turn of your region coming? Or it may be decided by who invites the group to meet in their area next time. In which case, you'll have to persuade your local area to issue an invitation.

Even ordinary council meetings can provide accommodation business. Local councillors may come to meetings from homes a considerable distance away. In which case, they may well need overnight accommodation. Then there are training budgets for fire officers and Income Tax inspectors. There are social clubs, like those for prison officers, who go away for a Short Break.

Town twinning

There are official visits from the towns with which yours is twinned.

Court cases

Court cases involve the attendance of lawyers, experts witnesses, witnesses, plaintiffs, defendants and members of the police. Whenever these people come from a long way away to court, there is a need for accommodation.

Much of the information you need can be obtained from the Courts as it is not private. There may also be a department within the Courts which helps to arrange hotel accommodation or, at least, deals with enquiries by recommending local hotels.

Armed services

Again, there are a number of potential markets:

1 Armed services personnel are often on the move. There may be some accommodation on American air bases, some embassies own houses locally, but normally the personnel have to put up in hotels. The military attachés at the embassies will often know of these movements and may well make the hotel bookings.
2 Where there are meetings of alliances – NATO, etc. – the bookings may be done by the organizations holding the conferences. Then there are exhibitions of military equipment – the Farnborough Air Show, for example.
3 As the armed services need new recruits, there are often teams of army, navy or air force personnel visiting different parts of the country. They need hotels too.
4 Friendly countries send over marching bands or teams to take part in various shows. That involves hotel accommodation as well.
5 If your hotel is in a naval city, visiting ships may send officers on shore leave to hotels.

Ground Handlers

Let's imagine you are a travel agent. You are arranging to send a lot of tourists to a foreign country where you have no branch of your organization. Who is going to look after those clients? Well, there may be a guide or a coach driver when they are actually on their way. But who is going to arrange the coach, the driver, the meal stops, etc.?

The answer is a Ground Handler – a company that exists to provide the local help a foreign company needs. These Ground Handlers may deal with the same client year after year. Or they may look after a single event – an international conference, an overseas fact finding mission, an incentive, a one-off group. They have to be very reliable; the originating company's reputation depends on their doing a good job. Their recommendations are taken very seriously.

Their loyalty is only to the originating company. Their interest is only in keeping the originating company's business in the future. They will switch from one hotel to another without a single thought, if they think the business is at risk. There are two main ways in which you can help them more than your competition.

1   You can help in their selling to their prospective clients. These clients may not have seen Britain. They may want to come on a FAM trip. The Ground Handler wants to look after them, but some of the cost may have to come out of his or her own pocket – and they don't want to skimp.

If you decide that the prospective client could be good for you, there is no reason why you shouldn't go into partnership with the Ground Handler to get the business. The handler sells their services and you sell yours. You would pick up the tab for the hotel expenses and – if the prospects were good enough – for the flights as well, if necessary.

As the Ground Handler is a good customer of car hire companies, coach companies, etc., the Ground Handler can pick up the tab for those areas of expense. If there is any chance of building loyalty from the Ground Handler to you, it could be because you are a good person to rely on to defray the Ground Handler's promotional expenses.

2   There are occasions when you know of a foreign client using the hotel who needs a Ground Handler to look after the business. You know it before the Ground Handlers. If you introduce the client to a specific Ground Handler who then gets the business, they now owe you. You have moved from being a supplier to being a client. Maybe, if the Ground Handler looks after you, you can find some more customers for them.

If such an opportunity arises, make sure to have the Ground Handler and the client meet each other with you as host. You don't want there to be any doubt in the Ground Handler's mind that you were the original contact with the client.

Ground Handlers can't normally make decisions on whether to use the hotel or not. Remember, though, that they know the client's objectives, peculiarities, decision-making process, etc. Unlike most markets, you have a very good chance of getting properly briefed on the client before you meet them.

Health services

The amount of money spent on health in any developed country is very large indeed. Part of that money is already spent on hotel services and a lot more could be.

The health service market divides into several sections:

1 Patient services.
2 Training.
3 Conferences.
4 Visitors.

Patient services

The cost of keeping a patient in hospital is about £350 a day, without medical services. There is track record in the UK for patients to convalesce in hotels when the hospitals are under pressure. There are several emergencies when this solution is attractive to the hospital authorities.

1 Where waiting lists for particular operations are so long as to be unacceptable and the problem is a lack of beds in hospitals. Patients recovering from varicose vein and cataract operations, for example, fall into this category.

2 Where the patients are sufficiently recovered to be sent home, but there is nobody at home to care for them. This applies to a lot of elderly people. If they were to convalesce in hotels until they were fit to go home, it would release beds during, say, a flu epidemic.

3 There are a large number of patients in hospitals recovering from mental illnesses. With mental illness, many hospitals don't want the patients to go from recovery to running their lives again in one step. They prefer them to stay a few weeks in a hotel, to get used to normal life again.

There are peak periods in hospitals. One tends to occur in the depths of the winter, when there are flu epidemics, etc. That would mean pressure on hospital beds in January and February, where a lot of hotels need more clients. Sometimes governments provide additional funds to reduce waiting lists. These occasions cannot be forecast in advance, but when the money is available, the hospitals want to take advantage of it. These are known as waiting list initiatives.

How do you get a hospital to use a hotel for convalescing patients?

In the UK each hospital has a Chief Executive. He or she would discuss any initiative like this with a Consultants Committee and reach a conclusion. The benefit to the chief executive is a saving in costs, a reduction in charges to patients and a more profitable hospital. The benefit to the consultants is that they can carry out more operations – therefore, more income.

Is all this really feasible?

There are precedents in the UK already, and there are many purpose-built American hospitals with adjoining hotels. If it works in one country, it can work in any country. It helps the hospitals, the patients and the hotels.

BUYERS AND CUSTOMERS

Training

Health services expand every year and more trained personnel are constantly needed. Furthermore, as the health state-of-the-art improves all the time, additional training is needed to keep up to date.

The sort of training business which is available for hotels, is:

1 Where the hospital's own training rooms are inadequate for the demand and they have to obtain additional ones in hotels.
2 Where a hospital has a particularly expert unit. For example, a hospital in Wigan developed the hip replacement operation. Doctors have come from all over the world to watch this operation being carried out. They need to stay somewhere.

Conferences

The world's health improves because doctors come up with better cures for more diseases. They research independently, though, and like to get together to compare notes and listen to their colleagues. As a consequence, there are a massive number of conferences for that purpose – both national and international.

Most hospitals have visiting lecturers and a programme of meetings to which doctors come out of interest, many from a long way away. You need to find out how your local hospitals organize all this.

Visitors

If the patient has been sent to a distant hospital which has a specialist unit, then their visitors may well need to stay overnight. In such cases, you need to have a mention in the documentation sent to patients before they enter hospital that, if their visitors need overnight accommodation, there is a special price arranged with you by the hospital.

'Momma & Poppa' agents

You will, very naturally, spend a great deal of time working on the major travel agents and tour operators. There is a lot of sense, though, in also giving thought to the small agents – the 'Momma & Poppa' agents.

There are three important things about these organizations:

1 You usually deal with the owners – and, therefore, whatever decisions they make, are likely to be carried out. A major chain of travel agents are only as good as their branch managers and instructions from Head Office don't always get carried out.
2 The owner is interested in paying the bills and making profits. The branch manager is interested in making his bonus and keeping Head Office quiet, but is less committed to the profits than the Momma & Poppa agent. They go bankrupt if the business fails to make a profit; the branch manager just looks for another job.
3 When you are quiet, the Momma & Poppa agent may be quiet too. If the depths of winter are off-season for you, they are probably off-season for the Momma & Poppa agent as well. So, anything you suggest to help produce hotel revenue during the off-season also produces much needed commission for the Momma & Poppa agent.

To an extent, working with Momma & Poppa agents is similar to working with Coach Operators. You aim to be a partner more than a supplier. Take, as an example, a town we'll call Superville. You want to encourage the local Superville Women's organizations, garden lovers, sports clubs or golf club members to stay with you, As it is a small town, the chain travel agent companies may not think it worth their while to have a branch there. The market has been left to the Momma & Poppas. It is the best of those that you want to work with. They know who to talk to, where to advertise, how to do the direct mail, where to put up the posters, how to get the local newspaper on their side and what are the timetables of the clubs when it comes to deciding their social programmes.

BUYERS AND CUSTOMERS

When you work with them, it is the same system as the coach operators.

NTOs – non-tour operators

A group approaches a Travel Agent and asks them to get quotations for a visit the group wants to make; for example, a Townswomen's Guild Group going to an art exhibition or a supporters' club going to a big game. The agent rings a hotel and the hotel's Group Reservations Department offer space and a price. They agree an option date with the agent. They follow-up at the option date to see if they got the business. If they didn't, was there anything more they could have done?

Well, imagine now you are the Secretary of the Townswomen's Guild and you have gone back to the travel agent to see what they have done. And they tell you 'The Splendide will charge you £50, The Intergalactic will charge you £40 and the Travalanche will charge you £30.' And they choose on the basis of price. Suppose, however, that the conversation went like this. 'The Splendide will charge you £50, The Intergalactic will charge you £40 and the Travalanche will charge you £30. But if you go to the Splendide, they'll arrange for the curator at the museum to come to your dinner the night before and tell you all about the exhibition. They'll provide you with packed lunches because the food at the museum is pretty terrible, and they'll serve you breakfast at 7 o'clock, so that you can get to the museum early before the queues build up.' Now who gets the business?

That's typical 'Value Plus' selling too. Your ability to use this technique obviously depends on identifying what kind of business you're being offered. The member of staff who takes the original booking must always do this. Then it's up to you to provide the Value Plus items which seem appropriate.

Off-peak markets

The problem is not usually the lack of business in the quiet seasons but which ones to go for. In addition to the ones discussed in detail in the chapter, you need to consider the following.

1 It has to start with the researching of last year's correspondence to identify the markets you have.

2 Research all the correspondence for the quiet periods this year, as it comes in, to identify new markets.

3 Go through the old banqueting books to identify off-season business.

4 Check the tourist board database for conferences held in the off-season.

5 Create Special Events for the off-season.

6 Research the pensioners' clubs in major companies. These people are often prepared to travel when the offer is right.

7 Sell prepaid reply cards (PPRCs) for all the functions held in your towns in the off-season; not just at your hotel but anywhere else – other hotels, banqueting houses, the Town Hall, etc.

8 Sell PPRCs for weddings held anywhere in your town in the off-season.

9 Identify minor events like dog and cat shows, flower shows, antique fairs, etc. and telesell exhibitors, judges, the press, etc.

10 Everybody staying should get a letter inviting them to stay on at a reduced rate.

11 Where you have horse racing in the off-season, owners, jockeys, course officials, bookmakers, race readers, journalists, etc. need rooms.

12 Estate agents will be visited by out-of-towners thinking of moving to your city. Those visitors have to stay somewhere. A simple hotel flyer could be sent when confirming appointments. Give the estate agents commission. Try also to sell them the idea that, if the client buys the house, the agent will pay the hotel bill.

13 Newspaper readers trips.

14 Radio DJs to run listeners' trips.

15 A special package designed for children. Get the parents to bring the children for an educational, fun-filled few days, marketed through newspaper trips and comics.

16 Prize offers of a stay in the hotel if the public buy a large

BUYERS AND CUSTOMERS

item; a car for instance. Do a deal with a major car area dis-
tributor just for the off-season. The dealer pays for the
hotel.

17 One-parent families can be reached through their
Associations. The offer should include some service for
keeping an eye on the children, to give the single parent a
rest. Day nursery, baby listening at night, etc. Although a
lot of one-parent families are not well off, that doesn't
apply to them all. You only need a small percentage of the
market to buy.

18 The disabled. There is a need for special programmes for
them.

19 Offers through department store mailing lists. These could
be tied in with sales periods for credit account customers.

20 Special trains in conjunction with the railways. Advertised
on stations, joint advertising in newspapers. The local
railway marketing people should know their market, just
like the agents and bus operators.

21 For some neighbouring tourist towns, your off-season is
their high season; their prices are steep. Offer your hotel
where the prices are lower and let the guests bus, or go by
train, to the tourist towns.

No, the problem is not the lack of opportunity. The problem
is the labour resource and the budget you will need to trans-
form the situation.

Senior citizens

Senior citizens are flexible on dates. If you are retired, one
day is the same as another. If the children have grown
up, you don't have to go on holiday during the school breaks.
The downside is that senior citizens expect reduced rates.
Often they won't be able to afford you unless you provide
them. Not that senior citizens are, necessarily, poor – far from
it – but you do need to identify the better off within the senior
citizen market. These can either be found as individuals or
groups.

As individuals:

1 There are companies who have researched all the houses in your area, identifying who lives there and what their likely financial position is. In the UK these organizations have names like Acorn and Mosaic. An advertising agency can point you in the right direction.

2 If you tell these companies what kind of people you want to reach – wealthy, children have left home, American Express Platinum Card, BMW or better, etc. they can give you the addresses.

3 There may well be periodicals read by senior citizens or media with an older reader age profile. An advertising agency can help you identify these too.

4 There may be companies specializing in looking after the senior citizen market; in the UK the most notable is Saga Travel.

As groups:

1 By membership of clubs designed for the senior citizen, or clubs where the age profile is high. Bowls, for example, attracts a lot of elderly people. So bowls clubs would be a way of reaching sections of the market. They very often move in August.

2 By membership of pensioners clubs run by major companies for their past employees.

Clubs have social programmes and you can produce programmes for them, advertise packages in the appropriate magazines, etc.

What do senior citizens want?

They want no hassle. They want arrangements to be simple, easy to understand and carried out at a relaxed pace. They have plenty of time and do not take kindly to anything stressful. They are happy if there aren't a lot of stairs to climb, long distances to walk, lots of forms to fill in and lots of noise. They dislike being ordered about but enjoy set programmes, once they have agreed to them.

What do you want?

You want the committees of pension clubs/senior citizen clubs to include a visit to your hotel on their social programme each year. You want this to be advertised in their newsletter. You would like the decision maker(s) to come on a FAM trip to see the hotel and what the city can offer.

Agents specializing in the senior citizen market drive hard bargains, but they have the capacity to deliver large numbers at times of the year when it is difficult otherwise to fill the space.

Do you want anything else?

Yes, there can be annual lunches for members of pension clubs. These are paid for by the company for whom they used to work.

Show business

The bookings for show business are normally made by the agents of the performers, or the impresarios who are putting on the performances. Show business people are no different from any other strata of customers; they are mostly very nice, but there are the occasional megalomaniacs and oddballs. One famous artiste walked out on a major hotel in Paris because he couldn't get an omelette at 3.30 in the morning! So handle them with tact and give them that little bit more attention to avoid problems.

The business can be very important. Shows can go on for weeks and even months. Groups coming to see the show can be sold packages which include the tickets and the hotel accommodation.

How do you get the business?

1 Get the upcoming programmes for the theatres and concert halls in your area. Try to make arrangements with the auditoria that you will be given advance notice of the shows

which are coming. Nobody can book hotel accommodation until the contract for the hire of the auditorium has been signed. Therefore, the theatre knows before anybody else. There is no harm in offering commission to the theatre on any bookings which come about because they've given you advance warning. Be careful if the theatre is run by the local authority. Again, bribing a public employee is a criminal offence. But there would be no problem if the commission was paid, say, to the Mayor as a contribution to his or her favourite charity.

2 Identify the agents and the impresarios. This is another market to research. There may well be a yearbook available.
3 Identify whether there are forthcoming shows for which they will need accommodation. Now you're attacking the market from both ends: the auditoria and the agents and impresarios.
4 Pay particular attention to the unusual needs of this market. They may need the ability to rehearse – a piano, etc. They may need food and drink at the theatre during rehearsals; picnic baskets. They may need meals before or after the show.
5 There may be press conference parties and opening night parties.
6 Show business people tend to be informal. The morning dress approach can be a big mistake.
7 Make absolutely sure what the impresario or agent wants to be billed for, and what extras should be paid by the guest before leaving the hotel.
8 With overseas artistes, you are unlikely to sue for unpaid bills if you are not paid by their agent within the country. So be sure that the money is available.

Sport

The hotel business associated with sport breaks down into three parts:

1 Clubs and teams.
2 Supporters and spectators.
3 The press.

Clubs and teams

The decisions on where to stay for away games can be taken by many officials. The most likely decision maker is the team manager.

For major international events, the organizers may offer accommodation, may even build it specially, but most deal with hotel accommodation only in an advisory capacity. For an overseas tour, involving many stays in different towns, the appointed travel agent may make the hotel bookings.

Team managers, when booking hotels, have many concerns. Among them are some which emerge from superstitions. The managers will be considering:

- The hotel's ability to provide individual menus at odd times.
- Before a match, each player may prefer to eat particular dishes and the team players know what suits their individual stomachs.
- A team room for discussions before and after the games.
- A Leisure Club with a gym would be attractive.
- Security for the players, to stop them being pestered by fans.
- Parking for the team bus.
- Some team members want particular rooms, perhaps facing in a particular direction; superstitions have to be understood and tolerated.
- The manager may need a room for press conferences.
- Travelling team owners and directors are another potential market.

Events for individuals

Not all sporting events are for teams; tennis and athletics tournaments, for example, are often (although not always) for individuals. In such cases, the accommodation may be booked by the player's travel agency, sponsor, agent or by themselves. They may be booked through the organizing committee. The players' managers, coaches, family and friends coming to watch are also potential markets.

Supporters and spectators

Many travel agents set up packages for important matches, which include travel, hotels and tickets for the games. Many bus companies, anxious to fill empty coaches, set up special packages as well. The club secretary can normally tell you how it all works.

Most of this traffic is day trips but it doesn't have to be. If the supporters stay longer, the agent earns more commission. Over 300 schoolgirls booked into a hotel after a women's hockey international because the next morning the hotel arranged a brains trust, on the panel of which sat the international centre forward.

Don't miss the business for the more obscure events: the Student Championships, a lacrosse international, the Ice Hockey Cup. Their supporters are equally as enthusiastic about the game as followers of more mainstream sports.

Planning

You don't always know long in advance who is going to be playing in a match. For example, a cup final is between the two teams who won the semi-finals and until the semi-final matches have been played, you don't know who your potential clients are. You, therefore, have to do the same pre-planning on all four teams in the semi-finals, in advance. Considerations are: how the tickets for the final will be distributed and which travel agents or bus companies locally will be taking supporters to the game? What are the best local advertising media, and does the Supporters' Club secretary need help? Talk to the club manager about looking after the team and officials.

If it is an international competition, there will be airline packages rather than bus trips. Does your national airline have a sales executive who specializes in the sports market?

International competitions

For many of these events, the demand for hotel accommodation is very great. In such circumstances, you may be in a position to set down conditions on the length of stay: no one-night bookings, for example. The important thing is to keep particularly careful records of those groups which stay more than two nights.

French Rugby supporters coming for the Scotland match may decide to do some sightseeing and stay three or four nights. Next year the match will be in France. The year after, back to Scotland. Therefore, in two years' time you want to be able to follow-up on the four nights group, so make sure the correspondence can be easily found and the trace date is for two years hence.

The press

The bigger the event, the more the press need to cover it. If they're not based locally, they have to travel and then you can get the accommodation. The press can be contacted by ringing the newspapers in the countries in which they work.

Third Party Agents

Hotel booking agents will book their clients accommodation for any occasion. A 'Third Party Agent' is an agent who only finds hotels for organizations who want to book conferences. The agent normally locates three hotels and the client then decides which hotel to book. The service to the client is free as the Third Party Agent receives commission from the hotel.

Third Party Agents should be treated with exactly the same quality of service as a travel agent. They don't normally disclose the name of the client. As the agent normally gets three quotations, you have a two to one chance of not getting the business. If you send the Third Party Agent a conference pack, it will usually be passed on to the client. A good selling letter, though, usually will not.

Like some hotel booking services, some Third Party Agents like to suggest that, as they brought a client to you in the first place, you should not try to get that client back, except through them. They also suggest that, if the client does come back, they are still entitled to commission because they introduced the business. As I've said, such contentions are illegal under EC and British law. If they were accepted, they would restrict competition and they have, therefore, been outlawed.

Why do Third Party Agents choose one hotel rather than another?

Third Party Agents want a quick answer and efficient handling. Passing on the quick answer impresses their clients with their own efficiency. They are also influenced by the size of the commission they receive. If, however, you increase commission levels or offer over-riders to get business during quiet periods, the next hotel down the road will match it. It isn't worth it.

What do you want from the Third Party Agent?

You want the chance to get the client to visit the hotel and deal with you direct. If the agent does give you that opportunity before the client finally makes up their mind, the agent is entitled to commission.

Is there a way to get the client to come direct originally?

Third Party Agents deal with a considerable percentage of the conference market because they have worked hard on the clients. From the client's point of view, it's a free and efficient service. The best way to avoid dependence on Third Party Agents is to be more proactive in contacting clients at the time they want to book conferences. Get into competition with the agents, not with the other two hotels which have also quoted.

BUYERS AND CUSTOMERS

Tourist boards – local

A national tourist board differs from a local tourist board. It seldom owns any part of the tourism product it attempts to promote. It advertises everything from stately homes to tennis tournaments, but it doesn't own either the castle or the courts. A local tourist board may.

Take a town we will call Wortherham. The tourist board is part of the town council's attempts to sustain the economic activity in the town; it promotes Wortherham. The tourist board leader is a councillor on Wortherham Town Council who has the Tourism portfolio. The board has permanent staff in a Tourism Office. Wortherham has exhibition or concert halls, which the town has built over the years for the benefit of its citizens.

There are two main kinds of event:

- Conferences and exhibitions attracted to the town.
- Entertainment – concerts, plays, etc. – which local people attend.

Many towns, like Wortherham, may have staff to get conference organizers to choose the town. It would always be better for you to have a Conference Promotion Committee, including the hotels, rather than an exclusively town hall controlled sales force, excluding the hotels. You will then have an influence on what happens.

If they get the business, the Conference Office then ask the local hotels to provide an allocation at an agreed price. The delegates are told which hotels are on offer and what the price is. The hotels then wait for the delegations, or delegates, to make up their minds. If the Conference Office fills the allocation, the hotel is happy: if they don't, the hotel gets a cancellation and isn't.

It would be a mistake for you to contact the delegates direct and offer a lower price than the competition. That would simply lead to a price war. There is, however, no reason why you shouldn't contact the association or chapter or branches direct, and persuade them of your superiority over the hotels they are offered at the same price. You could telesell the delegations.

This very seldom happens. If you do persuade a local branch to choose your hotel, then you need to advise them to make the booking through the Conference Office and not direct; the Conference Office will not appreciate being bypassed.

Requests for information

Tourism offices produce promotional material in order to get *enquiries* from people potentially interested in coming to the town. Everybody who asks is sent brochures and information. The question is how many of the people who get information finally decide to stay in the town? Obviously the town cannot follow up every enquiry on the phone. Where you are really interested is when the town is asked for information by a group; a sports club thinking of coming to play, a Masonic Lodge Ladies Night weekend enquiry, a Townswomen's Guild or a Gardening Club. You'd like the opportunity to do the selling job on that kind of enquiry by calling them direct.

Tourist boards – national

Obviously, you want to support the national tourist board. There are three main areas of opportunity:

- Sitting on their committees.
- Giving them money.
- Taking part in their events.

Sitting on their committees

Identify the committees on which hoteliers can sit and decide which you would like to join. Committees discussing the development of business travel, incentive movements, international conference promotion, etc. are all potentially valuable sources of future business.

What you seek is advance information on future events that might help fill the hotel.

If you are invited to join a committee, don't rush in with your ideas. Achieving objectives may take years rather than months. But then so it will for the competition if they want to change what you achieve over time.

Giving them money

Some expense is inevitable. There will probably be a membership fee. There are always a number of Tourist Board initiatives where they would like financial support from the private sector. You don't want to appear uncooperative but not all the initiatives will appeal to you, So, if you can offer support in kind instead – bedrooms, food and drink, etc. – it is cheaper for you than the equivalent money.

There should be some constraints on what you spend with them:

1 Avoid, if you can, expenditure on public relations exercises. Host a group of conference organizers, by all means, but not a delegation of city councillors coming to have a look around your city.
2 Avoid advertising in 'prestige' publications, such as the Annual Report, or some overseas country's Chamber of Commerce guide. If you advertise, be sure that you can judge afterwards how much you got back in additional profits.
3 If you decide it's worth advertising, make sure the advertisement is professionally produced. Remember, too, you have to decide whether the advertisement is worth more than supporting the board by going on a workshop, or taking space on their stand at a travel exhibition.

Taking part in their events

A lot of national tourist board events are well worth supporting. When the tourist board is the host, the trade are far more likely to attend.

The board's overseas offices can also arrange for the right

customers to be present. You do have an additional objective, however. You want to have access to the important clients whenever you participate. If there is a FAM trip coming, you want the decision makers to stay with you. If you're attending a trade lunch, you want to sit next to the people who can give you business. Try to arrange in advance that you are going to get close to the right people.

How else can a tourist board help you?

Tourist board data bases

The contents of a tourist board's data bases are available to everybody. Suppose you want a list of all the agents in a foreign country who specialize in walking holidays or golf holidays. It is the tourist board who have the responsibility in their brief for collating this information abroad. You can ask them for it. The quality of tourist board data bases varies considerably. At their best, they'll give you next open dates, decision dates, decision makers, and lots of other useful information.

Special Events

If you are trying to create a Special Event (these are dealt with fully in Chapter 12), the tourist board is often able to open doors for you and introduce you to the people you need to meet. They will also encourage those people to cooperate with you because it will help the nation's tourism. Always keep in mind, though, that the tourist board will provide whatever information they have to anybody – including your competitors.

Journalists

Tourist boards are always keen to get journalists to visit the country and write favourable articles about it. If the tourist board asks you to put up and feed journalists free, it's a very cheap way of getting positive publicity. If you want to promote a particular market, you can go for journalists who write for that market.

Overseas workshops

This is where the tourist board arranges an exhibition in a foreign country and hotels and other tourism products take stands. The tourist board office in the country issues invitations to the local trade to visit the exhibition. That's the standard format.

If you decide to participate, the essential thing is not to just be there on a stand and hope that somebody will pass by and call in. You need to have as many appointments as possible made with people you want to see in advance.

Travel agent advertised groups

This business doesn't actually exist until the public buys the travel agent or tour operators' packages. It is, therefore, absolutely essential that you keep in touch with the agents on a regular basis to monitor how the tour is selling.

If the booking is made for a peak period, the normal final release date is 28 days before the arrival of the group. You should at least contact the agent 42 days out in order to see how sales are going. If they are going poorly, try to reduce the number of rooms being held. What happens, though, if the booking is for dates when you are not likely to fill the hotel? Then allow the agent to keep trying to sell the space until the day of arrival! Don't ask for a release date at all.

With series groups, you will find that many agents, in order to negotiate better rates, offer dates in the shoulder months as well as in the peaks. You should always keep records of the performance of a series, in order to overbook sufficiently on those dates when the group is likely to be substantially reduced or cancelled. However, that last year's performance – even the performance of the past few years – is no absolute guarantee that history will repeat itself. For the performance depends, to a considerable extent, on the economic conditions in the home country. If the Mexicans have another currency crisis, it will affect the number of visitors to Madrid. If rising petrol prices adversely affect the manufacturing industry in Thailand, you'll get less Thais. One of the first things to suffer from economic problems is long distance holidays. Add those element to your calculation of the likely level of arrivals.

Trade unions

The trade union market consists of:

1 National conferences.
2 Local conferences and events.
3 Officer travel.
4 Visiting delegations.

National conferences

The decision on where to hold these may be taken in many ways; that it is the turn of a particular area of the country, that the union chiefs do the selection or that the union responds to invitation by union branches. If it is a question of responding to an invitation by an individual branch, you need to:

1 Identify if the dates would be helpful to you.
2 If they would be, persuade the local branch to issue such an invitation.

Local conferences and events

Arrangements for local events are made by local officials. They often take place at weekends. That is the best time for union members who have weekday jobs. The audience would be of shop stewards and union officials. Annual functions might well be arranged by the local social committee. Do the research.

Officer travel

This would be the same as any corporate account.

Visiting delegations

The union's Head Office would know who is coming. Visiting delegations are often very well entertained.

The university market

There are a number of elements of the university market. The main ones are:

1 Students
   - Student balls
   - Halls of residence
   - Clubs
   - Departments.
2 Sports teams playing against the university.
3 Girlfriends/boyfriends or family coming to visit students.
4 Graduation celebrations with the family.
5 Visitors needing accommodation for graduation ceremonies.
6 Academic
   - University conferences.
   - Academic visitors to the university.

Student business

The decision makers on students business change each year. The responsibility normally is given to students in their last year at the university and when they leave, the job is passed on to the next person.

The first task is, therefore, to identify the decision makers. This isn't easy. The key is to be in the same location they are and talk to them. The best opportunity is the Freshers' Week. This is an event for new students where the clubs and societies at the university try to interest them to join in their activities. So there is a hall where for a week all the clubs and societies take stands. You need to take a stand as well. The reason you should be allowed to have a stand is that the students may need accommodation for their friends and relatives, and you'll bolster Student Union funds by paying for the stand. You can then meet function decision makers on the other stands.

You should get the following information from the other stands:

1 Do they hold a function?
2 How many guests are likely to attend?
3 When do they hold it?
4 When will they make up their mind where to hold it?
5 What is their decision making process?
6 Who else do they know who holds a function?

When you have the information, tell them that you are holding a free lunch for function organizers at the hotel in November. They will hear how they can run their function successfully. All you need is their names and where to send the invitation.

The function organizer is often a complete novice, yet they want their ball to be better than their predecessor. You can tell them about solving the problems, help them with their in-house advertising, etc. You should be prepared to give them shell promotional material; blank posters except for your identification; direct mail letters to their members; advertisements for the student newspaper. If you get a function, identify who is going to be running it next year. Then, next year, do it all over again.

Individual student business

The best way to reach students is to advertise in the student newspapers or magazines. The space rates are usually very cheap and the students will see them. Alternatively, put up posters in the Students' Union building.

When do you advertise?

For accommodation bookings for visiting friends and relatives, any time is as good as any other. Except that advertisements for accommodation for graduation ceremonies should be towards the end of the examination term.

Academic business

To identify the academic business, it is best to get in touch with the university's administration department first – the Registrar's Department.

Your first objective is to find out:

1 Who needs accommodation?
2 How do you get in touch with them?

When you have that information, you would contact the secretary of the decision maker and find out:

1 What is the programme of events for which they will need accommodation?
2 When is the event taking place?
3 How much accommodation may they need?
4 When will they make a decision on which hotels to use?

University conferences may offer accommodation within the university to many of the delegates. You are interested in those delegates who want something more comfortable. And in the overflow.

The wedding market

Families put announcements of their forthcoming weddings in newspapers. The announcements seldom include addresses. How then do you reach the families? You have to start from the other end. Who are the families likely to contact when they're arranging the wedding? Car hire companies, morning dress hire companies, bridal dress makers, etc. It is the second best solution, but if you can't reach the families yourself, you need to be recommended by as many other companies as possible. And, of course, so do they. So, the solution is to form a Bridal Association in your town or local area. Get agreement that all the members will recommend each other. Then to hold a Bridal Fair each year – maybe twice a year – at the hotel. There should be a piece of promotional material for all the companies involved and these leaflets should be displayed and handed out in each member organization.

What is the process for forming a Bridal Association?

1 Select the best company in each segment of interest to a family with a wedding to arrange. The following list isn't exhaustive, but you could include:
   - Bridal dresses
   - Morning dress hire
   - Florist
   - Calligrapher
   - Printer
   - Car hire
   - Photographer
   - Wedding cakes
   - Bands
   - Entertainment
   - Travel agent
2 Approach the best company in each sector in your town to join you in forming the Association. Promise them exclusivity if necessary.
3 The advantage to them is the greater exposure their products are going to have to the families. The more companies, the cheaper the cost of promotion to each of them.
4 Agree a date for a Bridal Fair. You will provide the room free, the tabling for stands, the reception staff, the designer for the promotional piece and the PR. The other members of the Association will pay for the advertising and the printing of the promotional pieces; posters, banners, tent cards, local paper advertising, etc.
5 Advertise the Bridal Fair as widely as you can. Use PR as well.
6 Admission to the Bridal Fair is free.
7 When the day arrives, you need to get the names of the visitors and their addresses and telephone numbers. Plus the probable date of the wedding, if decided. Set up a Registration Desk for this purpose. Get the visitors to sign

in and monitor that all the details have been written down.

8 Provide the list to all the members after the Fair. Then follow up on the phone to get the families to call at the hotel again and sell it to them accordingly.

Dealing with wedding enquiries

It is often a tremendously time consuming task. If the demand justifies a full time executive, the ideal candidate would be the sort of person to whom the bride and her mother would turn, as they would turn to the grandmother in the family.

Remember that the two key objectives of the family when organizing the wedding are to impress the guests (perhaps particularly the 'other side') and not to exceed the budget. You need to reassure them on both points. The family may not have organized anything so large before. If that is the case, they may change their minds from time to time. Reassure them that this doesn't present a problem to the hotel. The family will, obviously, want to see the hotel, and entertaining them to lunch or dinner is a good way to win a better chance of getting the business. Be careful, though, that you don't become a free meal out for every family for miles around!

Summary

Effective selling involves you in understanding the customer; in being able to put yourself in their shoes and to understand how they think and what they want. It is simply inefficient to approach people at a time that suits you, and in order to get them to buy whatever you decide will be the product. So learn as much as you can about the markets and then tailor your products to fit in with their various needs. There is a great deal to understand and you never stop learning: I wish I knew more about the ground rules of Relationship Marketing in the Chinese communities!

Case study

This case study illustrates:

- The sheer variety of opportunities there are for filling hotels.
- The varied kinds of approach there can be to getting business.
- The necessity of spotting opportunities faster than the competition.

If you were looking for some extra business in 2000, you might have considered the effects of the civil war in Sierra Leone. Transport aircraft were flown in to evacuate the expatriates from the war zones. They were taken to their countries of origin, but via the UK. When they landed in Britain, they would have to make onward arrangements to get to their homes. So would the Britons themselves. A lot of them would need hotels. Where would they stay?

I first came across this market at Grand Metropolitan Hotels when the Syrians blew up the pipelines of the Iraq Petroleum Company in the 1950s. All the expat employees of Iraq Petroleum were thrown out of the country and finished up at Heathrow Airport one freezing November night. It was one of the best pieces of off-peak business I got in those early days. Then when the Dutch were thrown out of Indonesia, the Indonesians wouldn't let the Dutch airline land in the country. So British Airways were asked to fly them out to Amsterdam. They came via London and I got another first class booking.

Of course, you have to consider the moral implications: you are benefiting from calamities. For example, we looked after some of the survivors of the sinking of the liner *Andrea Doria*. These people were lucky to be alive; a lot of the passengers they'd sailed with had perished. Should you reject the opportunities for the same reasons we all hate vultures?

The fact is, however, that somebody has to look after

survivors. Somebody has to care for them and help them with their immediate problems: heat the food for the babies, settle the nerves of the very old, help them find relatives and onward flights, and provide everything from toothbrushes to warm coats. When the Turks invaded Cyprus in the 1970s, the holidaymakers had to be flown home. We got 5,000 bednights in July and August by setting up a hotel booking service at the RAF station where they were flown in. Embassies all over London wrote letters of thanks to us for stepping into the breach in the emergency.

Somebody has to help – and, in helping, you benefit from increased turnover, first class public relations and the warm regard of the organizations you look after.

From these experiences came the concept of the Disaster Squad – nominated executives whose task it was to be on the lookout for opportunities of this kind 24 hours a day, 7 days a week. The Turks invaded on a Friday. We got permission to set up the hotel booking service at lunchtime on Saturday. You have to be able to go into action any day and at any time. We were also allowed to run a booking service at Paddington Station and by 2 o'clock on Sunday morning we were getting tired. So I rang a couple of members of the Sales Department and they came down and relieved us – at 2 in the morning and without a word of complaint. (One of them eventually became Sales Director for Intercontinental.)

Some Disaster Squad opportunities are fairly easy to predict. If there's a national rail strike, then a lot of people stay in hotels because they wouldn't be at their office desks the next day otherwise. If there are floods, people may move into hotels until the floods subside. If there's a fire at another hotel, somebody has to look after the guests who are arriving tomorrow when their bedrooms have gone up in smoke. It is a fact that you seldom find anybody else from competitor hotels on the scene.

I once read a report in the *Sunday Times* Business Section which told of the government's concern at the decline of the village shop. The Minister had the problem in hand, we were assured. I rang a senior civil servant in the relevant government department. Did they really have the slightest idea what to do? No, the Minister had reacted to a question from the press and then left the problem in the civil servant's hands. I eventually had the Department set up a series of training courses around the country for village shop owners to help them compete with the area supermarkets. Alas, it didn't save a large number of the village shops, but it was the right solution and a hotel company made a great deal of additional profit.

Other opportunities are presented by, e.g. juries who can't make up their minds and have to be locked away in a hotel overnight, so that they can continue their discussions the next day; or a headline which reads 'US East Coast Airports closed because of blizzards'. Alright, you haven't got a hotel in America. But if the airports are closed, how are the flights to America from your local airport going to land? They're going to be delayed until the airports open again – maybe overnight. Then the passengers will need hotels. If it's a short delay, the airline may use local hotels. If it's 24 hours they may well prefer to have the passengers in town centres where they can amuse themselves better. That's where you might come in. Delayed flights are a godsend in dead periods.

The opportunities are all around you. Some disaffected group is going to lobby the government or the local authority. Then they're going to have to have a meeting beforehand to decide their approach. Where will that be held? Will they need overnight accommodation? What about the marches and the lobbying? Or government inquiries into major accident: who is putting up the expert witnesses, the lawyers, the claimants and the press?

The hotel industry exists to look after people who need overnight accommodation. Their reasons for needing it may stem from normal eventualities – holidays, commercial activity or social arrangements – or they might come

about from unexpected and exceptional circumstances.
Your job – as with any market – is to understand the complexities and to act before your competitors.

4 Face-to-face selling

Is there one right way to sell? Yes, there is. There will be many variations within the method, but the basic format always remains the same.

DIPADA

We remember it by a mnemonic – **DIPADA** – which stands for Define, Identify, Prove, Acceptance, Desire and Ask for the order.

Define

Why does the client want to spend the money in the first place? You get asked to quote for a dinner for 20. Suppose it is a goodbye for a fairly junior employee who is leaving to have a baby? Suppose, on the other hand, it is a dinner for a firm's top European buyers?

The quotation for the first event might emphasize your value for money, your informal atmosphere and your friendly service. The dinner for the major buyers might emphasize your high quality, your impeccable service and your ability to impress the guests with the hospitality. The bill is very important for the first party, but probably less so for the second.

Until you know why people want to buy the product, you don't know what aspects of it are going to be needed to convince them to use you.

Identify

When you know what they want to buy, you would, hopefully, be able to tell them that your venue is the best for their purpose.

Prove

Do you believe what every sales executive tells you? Nor does anybody else. Whether the client asks for proof or not, you should provide it. (For a full breakdown type of the kinds of proof available, see Presentation Books in Chapter 7.) Everybody is going to say that their product is marvellous. You have got to do better than that.

Acceptance

When you have finished talking about a part of the product, you want to move on to something else. If the client is still thinking about what you have said, or if still has questions about the topic, you shouldn't. The client will still be thinking about the microphones when you are trying to move on to the air conditioning. So you check with the client that it is alright to move on: 'Does that seem reasonable?', 'Are you happy about that?' 'Would that solve the problem?'

Desire

There are many good things you could say about your product. Some will be more important to the client than others. Your discussion with the client should identify those points of interest. Before you try to get the business, you should reiterate the factors which are in your favour.

Ask for the order

When you've made the perfect presentation, you can still lose the business if you don't ask for a definite booking. Not a provisional or tentative reservation, but a definite one. This is called *closing the sale* and it is, obviously, crucial to your success.

Closing the sale

There are a lot of different ways of closing a sale. It is like having a series of shots you can play at tennis or cricket. When the ball arrives, you choose which one is best suited to score. You, therefore, need to learn as many closing techniques as possible. There are lots of them and you need to decide which is the best one to use on each occasion. If the first one doesn't work, try a second – and a third and a fourth and a fifth – until you have run out of ideas.

So, we will deal with them one at a time, starting with closes to use in the face of the objection that comes up most frequently – price.

'I can't afford your prices. We haven't got that much money in the budget.'

A closing technique that may help you to overcome this problem is:

The Budget Close
'I appreciate that it's more than you budgeted for, but you do like the hotel. Couldn't the extra be found from another budget?'

Budgets are not always spent on what they were allocated for. If you have a budget yourself, you may well spend some of it on something else. So do your clients.

Or you might hear:

'You're more expensive than the other quotation.'

Then you could try one of these two:

The Plus Close
'That's true, but if you come here you get (this) *plus* (that) *plus* (that) which you don't get with the other quotation.'

The Minus Close
'That's true. But if you use the other place you don't get (this) and it's *minus* (that) and *minus* (that).'

You will notice, of course, that you have to know what you are offering that the other competitor isn't.

Another option is:

The Division Close
'That's true. But if it's £1,000 more and there are 100 delegates, it's only £10 a delegate. Is it really worth going to an inferior venue for £10?'

This isn't some form of confidence trick; it's absolutely true. If you are organizing a conference, you want each delegate to benefit from it. If you are holding an important dinner, you want each guest to enjoy themselves. Each delegate or guest may have a marked effect on the future prosperity of your organization. So it's perfectly legitimate to point out that your quotation is only a small amount extra for a better offer.

Let's look at some other closes, starting with one that works time and time again, but it is a strain on you.

The Silence Close
The client asks the price and you tell him. There is then dead silence while he thinks. Don't interrupt him. The first one to speak loses. If you don't say anything, the chances are he will finally break the silence and agree to the price.

If you have never tried this before, you won't believe its effectiveness until you do.

Then you might get the client who says 'I've been offered a lot of different places.' To deal with that, you need to move the client from this position – called the Principle of Maximum Choice – to:

The Principle of Minimum Choice Close
'Well, your choice here seems to be between the Emperor Room and the Princess Room. Which one do you think would suit you best?'

If you can get the client to look at the problem from that point of view, whatever the decision, you win.

Some closing techniques are not concerned with overcoming problems. They are just points in the conversation when you could close the sale. When they occur, you need to close the sale then. Don't wait till you get back to the office or take a seat in the lounge. When the moment arrives, try to close the sale immediately.

The Confirm Close
'Could we have a 4 course dinner rather than a 3 course dinner?'
  'Is a 4 course dinner the one you want then?'

You have moved the client past the decision point of 'Do I use this place or not' to 'What shall we have at this place?' Or you might be able to use:

The Guarantee Close
'Could you guarantee us the Princess Room?'
  'If I could guarantee you the Princess Room, would you like to make a definite booking?'

This is one of the most frequent positions where sales are lost. All too often the thinking is directed to whether to commit to providing the space, when it should be to closing the sale.
  Don't just show the client what you can provide. Use this next close and get her involved in making decisions about the event:

The Involvement Close
'So do you think you'd like the top table here or here?'
'Would you like champagne for all your guests or just for the top table?'

When the client answers questions, as in the Involvement Close, say:

The Note Close
'I'll just make a note of that'

as if it was part of a definite booking. You are moving from what might be, to what will be, i.e. beyond the decision. If the client queries this – 'I didn't say I wanted it', you respond 'No, of course not. But anything which is important to you, I don't want to forget.'

Sometimes you get clients who have a very high opinion of themselves. When they can't make up their minds, ask them:

The Negative Close
'Would you have to discuss where to go with your colleagues?'

Rather than admit they haven't the authority to make a decision, they will prove they have the right by giving you the business.

If the decision maker lives a long way away, use **The Guest Close:** invite him and his partner to come to visit you for the weekend as your guest, and see the product at first hand.

Sometimes you come up against the objection that what you are proposing isn't their company policy.

The Empathy Close
'I'm not sure we can come to you. We've held the event at the Intergalactic for the last 3 years.'

'I appreciate that. But you had to move it to the Intergalactic from somewhere else originally. So aren't you just moving it on again?'

One of the problems every purchaser has to resolve is whether the product is going to be good enough for the purpose for which it is needed. Of course, every sales executive, every waiter, every shop assistant is likely to tell you the product is just perfect. So, to be convincing you have got to do better than that. You can use **The Unbiased Expert Close:** get a couple of your best clients to agree that if a few people phone occasionally to ask for their unbiased opinion, they will tell them how good you are.

A variation of this is **The Similar Situation Close**. Identify a piece of business you have handled recently of a similar nature, and produce a complimentary letter from that client saying how well you did it.

The Stall Close is where you ask the client for a definite booking and he says he will have to think about it. This is often just another way of turning you down politely. So you have to go on selling to try to get him to change his mind and give you the business. You say:

'In my experience, Mr Fontaine, when you say you have to think about it, there are certain aspects of what I'm suggesting, with which you're not entirely happy.'

Of course, that has to be true. If he was happy about everything, he would give you the work. So he will reply:

'Well, yes, there are one or two things.'
   'Could you spare a few more minutes for us to discuss them?'

And he will probably give you some more time. Now you go through another set of steps:

List: 'So, tell me, Mr Fontaine, what aren't you entirely happy about?

Get a full list. Don't deal with the objections one at a time. If you do, he will just come up with more of them. Get them all out at the beginning

Confirmation: 'And those are all the points you're not happy with?'

He should confirm that.

Offer: 'If I could solve those problems for you, would you then be happy to make a booking?'

If he is the decision maker and you solve his problems, what else can he do? So now you:

Deal with the problems.

Confirm again: He agrees that you have done so as you go along.

Ask for the order: When you have solved the problems, ask for the definite booking.

But how do you solve the problems? You need to know how to overcome all of them. Take the problem of car parking, if you haven't enough. Among the solutions are getting a block booking in the nearest multi-storey car park, pointing out the fact that it doesn't affect people coming by train and plane, and suggesting the possibility of people coming together rather than separately, thus saving petrol and giving them the opportunity to get the car serviced while they are away. By the time you have finished, it should be almost an advantage not to have sufficient car spaces!

When clients can't make up their minds, there are specific closing techniques for that problem.

The Benjamin Franklin Close

'Well there's a lot to be said for both you and the other place. I'm not sure which to choose.'

'Yes, it is a problem. You know, when Benjamin Franklin had to come to a similar conclusion, he used to take a sheet of paper and draw a line down the middle. On one side he used to put all the reasons for doing it and on the other the reasons for not doing it. Why don't we try that?'

This was, indeed, the way Mr Franklin dealt with his problems. So if the client agrees, write down all the reasons for using you. She will think of some, you add the others. Then say:

'Now what about the reasons for going somewhere else?'

Only this time you don't help. Aim for about 15 reasons for using you and the client will probably only come up with

about half a dozen reasons at most for going somewhere else.
Then say:

> 'Well, there are 15 reasons for coming here and only 6 for
> going to the other venue. So, on balance, it looks as if this
> is the best choice.'

A word of warning: judge carefully who you use this with. A
lot of professional buyers know this technique, but not many
ordinary members of the public.

So, there are 16 different closing techniques from which you
can choose the right one. And if that one doesn't work, try
another. As I say, a lot of sales are only completed after the
fourth or fifth closing technique.

When you have got so many closing weapons to fire, you
need to choose which one is most appropriate and if it doesn't
work, you move on to the next one. This is technically known
as *bridging*. For example, you try to close the sale by asking
whether the client would like to make a booking if you could
guarantee what he wants – the Guarantee Close. The answer is
'Well, I'm not too sure if we can afford it.' Then you'd say 'Yes,
I can see that's a problem.' That's the bridging phrase. Then
you could go on 'Well, might it be possible to take the money
from another budget?' – the Budget Close.

You can see the vast difference between providing information and selling the product. There is a psychological reason,
however, why so many people prefer to just provide information. If you are trying to sell the product and the client eventually turns you down, you have failed. You may feel that you
have been rejected, even humiliated by this failure. If, alternatively, you see your job as purely to provide information, when
the client leaves with all the information they needed, this can
be seen as a successful interview. That is also a reason why, on
so many occasions, the Banqueting Coordinator or the
Advance Booking Reservationist is quite satisfied with accepting a provisional or tentative booking. If they get one of those,
they don't feel they have failed. If the client subsequently
cancels, they have still put off the evil day.

There is a substantial benefit from appreciating that every
sales executive, no matter how expert, fails on many occasions

to get the business. This doesn't worry them for a moment, any more than a squash player expects to win every time they go onto a court. They do their best but realize that there will be occasions when their best isn't good enough. The reason they try to close the sale is because they want to win. If they don't, and they did their best, there will be other opportunities in the future; the game can be played again and, next time, they may be successful. They look forward to the next occasion because they enjoy playing the game.

When the client does say 'yes' every sales executive gets a buzz. Everybody enjoys winning. Naturally, when you start, you may not win all that often. As you get better at it, though, success comes more frequently. The essential thing is to enjoy playing the game.

Buying signals

You now know to try to close the sale at any point in the conversation. There are better times than others, though. One way to spot the right time is to keep a constant look out for the *buying signals*.

Typical buying signals occur when the client gives full approval to what you're suggesting; 'that would be great', 'that's just what I need', 'yes, that would solve the problem'. When you hear those magic words, try to close the sale.

Body language

Another way of spotting when to close the sale is by watching the client's body language. When you first consider the subject, body language makes no sense. How can the gestures made by somebody in India mean exactly the same as those made by somebody in Brazil or in Yorkshire? The answer is that the gestures do not relate to a nationality or a culture. They go way back to the behaviour of primitive man. If a Neolithic man wanted to show a compatriot that he had no aggressive intentions, the simple way of proving it was to put up his hands. When you see people do that today, the message is still 'it's the truth'. It is perfectly possible that you won't believe that body language works – until you try it.

In discussing body language, there is one caveat at the beginning. It is possible with body movement that the thinking of the client and the body language mean different things; that it *is* just coincidence that a piece of body language occurs when the client is thinking something quite different. For example, when someone pulls at their ear, this normally means 'I don't like what I'm hearing'. It could, however, simply indicate that the person's ear itches, although it is very unlikely that this is the case, that it's just a coincidence. In any event, you need to check, by asking further questions, to find out if the client is feeling the way the body language suggests.

So here are a wide selection of body movements, together with what they probably mean.

Fingers

Index finger up cheek; another finger crosses mouth; thumb supports chin	'I'm evaluating what you're saying'
Finger moves across upper lip	'Either I'm lying or I think you are'
Palm up	Submissive
Palm down	Attempting to take over
Hands clenched	Holding back a negative attitude. The higher the hands, the more negative the feeling
Steepled hands pointing upwards	'I want to give you a lecture'
Steepled hands pointing downwards	'I'm prepared to listen'
Hands gripped behind – palm in palm	A gesture of confidence
Hands gripping wrist behind	Frustration (Attempt at self control)
Hand gripping elbow behind	More aggravated

Body movement

Thumbs tucked under lapels	Ego trip
Hand over mouth and fake cough	Probably not telling the truth
Finger in mouth (pen in mouth)	Under pressure
Hand supporting head under chin	I'm bored
Drumming fingers/tapping feet	Impatience
Closed hand on cheek	Evaluating what's been said
Heel of palm supports head	Losing interest

Legs

Legs tightly crossed	'I don't like what you're saying and I disagree with you'
Sitting forward, hand on knee	Ready to say 'yes'
Foot pointing	If it points towards a person, they like them. If it points away, they don't like them

Arms

Arms crossed across body (Defensive)	'I don't like what you're saying and I disagree with you'

Head

Head and chin down	Hostile
Face covering	Deceit or lying. Doubt, uncertainty or exaggeration
Nose scratching	If the person's covering their nose when you speak, they don't think you're telling the truth
Ear rub	'I don't like what I'm hearing'
Neck scratch	Doubt or uncertainty
Collar pull	'I've been caught lying'
Chin stroking	Making a decision
Slapping back of neck	'I wish you hadn't corrected me'

| Slapping forehead | 'I'm aggravated I forgot, but I don't mind you having told me' |
| Hands interwoven behind head | 'I know as much about this as you do' |

Where an individual gesture may be a coincidence, a cluster of them indicating the same thing is a pretty certain guide. So, if a client is sitting opposite you with his arms folded, his legs crossed, leaning backwards and with his head on his chest, this is not a good time to try to close a sale. If, alternatively, a client is leaning forward, her legs and arms are not crossed and her head is up, that is the time to ask for an order.

Office interviews

In the chapter on Banquet Sales (Chapter 7) you will find the format for entertaining the client in a hotel or restaurant. There will be occasions, however, when you will need to visit the client in his or her office. Now you are playing away from home; it will not be a location with which you are familiar and, if you're not accustomed to such negotiations, you're likely, initially, to be quite tense. The more interviews you have, the easier you will find it, but you have to reduce the tension you feel because it can lead to you talking too fast, to saying things you later regret and a nervous atmosphere is contagious. So try to follow the rules.

1 Before you set out, check that you are carrying with you all the promotional material that might come in useful.
2 Always arrive early. Plan to get to the appointment at least 10 minutes early. That way you won't be worried about not finding anywhere to park, or getting into a traffic jam, or not finding the building, all of which make you more nervous.
3 Be nice to everybody you meet; commissionaires, receptionists, secretaries, everybody. You never know when these people may be able to help you in the future. You also never know when juniors may get promoted and eventually become your clients.

4 Thank an assistant who takes you into the client's office and let the client hear you. It establishes your courtesy and backs up the claims you are going to make for the good service they will get if they use your product.

5 Don't sit down until you are offered a seat. If the client realizes you haven't been offered a seat, this is recognition that his or her own courtesy has been at fault. That means that the client has to be nicer to you to make up for it.

6 When you sit down, don't put your promotional material on the client's desk; this is a private area.

7 Always sit back in the chair and relax. Your physical relaxation will reduce your mental tension. Also, if you lean towards the client your physical position will be intimidating. If you are bigger than the client, that is an even more important point.

8 If the client has kept you waiting and apologizes, be gracious. Never show the slightest irritation. Keeping you waiting is discourteous and the client has to make up for that in his or her future treatment of you. Most clients don't want to feel inferior to you, so they have to behave as courteously as you do.

9 The process of selling is to fit your product to the client's needs. You, therefore, need to adopt the DIPADA approach again.

10 Watch the client's face carefully. When the client opens his or her mouth to speak, you close yours. The process of selling is for the client to fit in what they want to buy with what you're trying to sell them. The client who just listens is not buying. It is when the client starts to ask questions that they are trying to make the product fit their needs. That is exactly what you want, so make sure the client isn't kept waiting before they can make their comments. Just stop talking.

11 When you show the client a piece of promotional material, always stop talking as they study it. The client can't both read the material and listen to you, and he or she will be irritated if they find they have to try.

12 Your product is going to be much like the products of your competitors. One key to successful selling is to find out what clients perceive to be wrong with the products they

are buying at the moment. Does a client dislike buffets, or is the existing conference room he is using too noisy? Has a client had difficulty in booking rooms during peak periods? Has her car been broken into in the car park? If you can solve these problems, you are differentiated from the competitors' products.

13 Never argue with the client about anything. If a client says the sun rises in the West, that's where it rises. The client's views on anything, other than which product to buy, are totally irrelevant to you.

14 Never disagree with the client. The sales executive is always fighting on the defensive. Confrontation leads to rejection. You may be 100 per cent right but the client always has the ultimate weapon in any argument; they can say 'no' to buying your product. You can lose every battle in the discussion, so long as you win the war when the client says 'yes' to buying from you.

15 When you see a client for the first time, you want to know as much as possible about the business that client could give you. Market research is a most important part of the interview: and it is not just what he or she can buy from you. It is also about which of their colleagues could buy from you too.

16 Look and listen extremely carefully. The clues to the business you could get can appear at any moment. There may be a Long Service Award certificate on the wall. So is there a dinner when they're given out? The client might mention a company Social Club, membership of an Association, or a union meeting. It might only be in passing but you need to spot the clues.

17 Few clients will buy a hotel, a conference room or a ballroom without seeing it first. So your objective will be to get the client to call and see your product at first hand. If you are just selling bedroom accommodation for visitors, it wouldn't matter when the client comes. If, however, it is a specific event, then, of course you want the client to come when they are ready to buy. The decision date is a very important piece of information.

18 If you get an agreement to visit, when you've completed your market research, and when you have given the client

all the information he or she needs, don't overstay your welcome. Offer your thanks and leave.

Customer benefits

One of the key phrases in all kinds of selling actually refers to selling food. It's 'Sell the sizzle, not the steak.' Of course, what that means is that there's far more to the process of buying than the physical product. You sell fresh food and not refrigerators. You sell clean clothes for the children and not just a washing powder. You sell personal attractiveness and not perfume.

So when you sell hospitality products, you have to identify what are the major benefits the customer is seeking. Take a wedding: what are the main objectives of the bride and her family in arranging a wedding celebration? You work this out, as you always deal with any sales problem of this nature, by putting yourself in the position of the client. So, say you are the bride's parents. What are your two main objectives? Well, your daughter is marrying into another family. You want that family to think well of your family, for your daughter's sake. So you want to impress the bridegroom's parents with what a beautiful wedding you have arranged. (You may feel impressing your own family isn't quite so important – although sometimes it may be more so!) Your second concern is not to have to take out a second mortgage on the house to pay for the wedding. The budget you have agreed mustn't be exceeded.

There will be other objectives, of course, but I think we can agree that these two are important. Now in the light of this, look again at your promotional material for weddings. Do you tackle either concern? Does the brochure say 'You can be quite sure that if you choose the hotel, all the guests, *from both sides of the family*, will be impressed' (my italics). Or 'If you choose the hotel, it will be our responsibility to make sure you don't spend a penny more than you've allowed for the party.'

Customer benefits obviously cover an enormous number of possibilities. The essential thing is to identify which are the ones to put before the client first. It is no use waxing lyrical at the start of your letter about your 15 acres of landscaped gardens if you are selling a conference. The average conference organizer is, primarily, interested in the conference room. Talk about that first.

Consider that conference organizer again, though. Now we will assume that it is a very important conference. The organizer's boss will be there. So what is his main objective for the conference now? Not to impress the delegates, but to impress his boss. And if his boss is staying in the hotel, to be sure she consistently gets VIP treatment.

Here are just some of the customer benefits which can make clients decide to spend more on your product than they originally intended.

1 Trust in you. When you consider the lack of brand loyalty as clients use many different kinds of hotel, restaurant or banqueting house, it illustrates that this trust is not as great as it is with toothpaste, beer or washing powder. They trust the devil they don't know more than the one they do.
2 They can't be bothered to shop around; it's so much easier buying from you. Consider a PA who has to make a last minute booking. If she rings your hotel, she knows you answer the phone within 3 rings, she will be treated as a friend rather than just as a client, if you are full you will find her the accommodation at another hotel and confirm the booking to her, which saves her writing to you. Why use a hotel where you hang on for ages, where they don't know you, where, if they are full, they will leave you to ring other hotels, and where they want a confirmation? The price may be higher but the service is far better.
3 They feel important when they're in your surroundings; they belong, they're a member of the club.
4 What you're saying sounds so attractive that they buy it on impulse.
5 You'll offer them extended credit. So long as you are sure they will pay in the end, 6 months credit equals a 3 per cent reduction in your price (assuming that bank interest is 6% per cent).
6 They believe that, if they use you, they will finish up congratulated by their colleagues and peers.

You always have to look behind the scenes at what really matters to the client.

There's nowt so queer as folk

In the hospitality industry the customers come from every kind of cultural background. Their judgement of you and your product may be based on a totally different style of behaviour from the norm in your own country. Do you normally blow your nose and cross your legs? That is extremely uncouth behaviour – in Japan. When you meet clients, the last thing you want to do is give them the impression that you are ignorant, unsophisticated, bad mannered and insensitive: use first names with a German client, fail to shake hands with a Frenchman, or call Britain 'the mainland' when you are with an Irish client, and you can do just that.

It is obviously, impossible to give you a full breakdown of everything to avoid and everything you should do with every nationality and culture. The best way for you to deal with the problem is to talk to people who come from those different backgrounds and get to understand them better. What you can't do is ignore the problem. You can't be 'one of us' to everybody, but you can show that you are on their side.

For example, New York taxi drivers have a poor reputation for civility. I had a particularly surly individual one day until I said to him 'When did you come from Haiti?' He asked how I knew that. I told him that on his licence was the name Toussaint Lecroix. He was, therefore, obviously named after the great Haitian statesman, Toussaint Louverture. The driver was really happy that a passenger knew the high spot of his history. He would have done anything for me from there on in.

It is not possible to deal with every culture. But the same personality types appear with every nationality. Every client is different; laid-back, aggressive, charming, unpleasant, organized, disorganized ..., you will meet them all – and a great many more. You can't treat them all in the same way. What goes down well with one is a disaster with another. You can share a joke with one client and the next is strictly business. Consequently, you have to select the right approach for each customer.

It is a truism in selling that before the clients buy the product, they first buy you. Therefore, they have to like you but they are all different. How can you appeal to everybody?

After all, if they don't like your personality, what are you supposed to do about it? The answer is to select the personality they would like and to use that one, because you have a lot of different personalities: you with your partner and you with your old head teacher; you at a sports match and you at a funeral; you with very elderly people and you with small children. All of those – and many more – personalities are genuinely part of you. So you can genuinely project the personality which suits the client you are dealing with.

Introversion and extroversion

All of us are slightly extrovert or slightly introvert. Some more so than others. The personality traits for each are as follows:

Extroversion	*Introversion*
Sociable	Less sociable
Active	Less active
Impulsive	Cautious

Look, listen and try to understand which your client is and you will see the different approaches that are necessary; that's empathy. If an extrovert says 'I'll have to think about it', it goes against the impulsive element in their nature. It is more likely that what they really mean is that they are not going to buy your product. If an introvert says that, though, they are just following their natural bent. An extrovert is likely to be happier in a social atmosphere than an introvert. So you would take an extrovert into the bar before lunch, but you would ask an introvert if they would prefer a drink at the table.

The big question, of course, is how do you tell the difference between an extrovert and an introvert? As a general rule, extroverts like plain colours and big patterns. Introverts like small patterns. Extroverts like chunky personal jewellery. Introverts prefer smaller versions.

If you haven't come across this concept before, you won't believe it until you have tested it thoroughly. You will find exceptions; he's an extrovert but he's wearing the small patterned tie his grandmother gave him because he's visiting her this evening. She's an introvert, but she's wearing a plain colour dress because that's the fashion for this season. You will still find that, in the vast majority of cases, it works out.

Notice the importance of deciding which of the two types your client is. You take them into a room with a very plain decor. If they are introverts, they probably won't like the style. Knowing that in advance, you are ready to praise its natural light, how lovely it looks when set up for the dinner, etc.

Summary

1 Your selling approach should be in the right order – DIPADA.
2 You should select the appropriate closing technique to secure the business.
3 Watch for the buying signals.
4 Watch the client's body language.
5 Identify the right customer benefits for each client.
6 Sell to each client, according to their personality.

Case study

This case study illustrates:

- The need to think deeply about the needs of the customer.
- The creation of customer benefits which can get you the business ahead of even superior competitors.
- The application of the appropriate hotel facilities and skills.

Radisson Edwardian Hotels asked for my views on their new promotional material. Specifically, they had been asked to quote a cosmetic company for a series of training courses. These would be held over a period of 6 months and the total budget was about $400,000. There would be 20 delegates on each course and they would assemble on the Sunday evening and leave the hotel on the following Friday evening.

The company's promotional material was of a very high quality; thick paper, beautiful graphics, leather binding and expensive envelopes. I reported back that the material was alright but that they had only dealt with the points they knew about. I said that I couldn't respond to the enquiry properly until I had asked the client a further 20 questions. My point was that all the other hotels who wanted this $400,000 contract would know as much as I did. I therefore wanted to know a lot more. I wanted to offer the client far more reasons for using the hotel. (Of course, the client would be more likely to spare you the time for these questions in a face-to-face interview than they would on the phone.) To identify those customer benefits, I would have had to put myself in the position of the cosmetic company's Sales Trainer before I met him or her and work out what additional advantages would interest them.

Right, you're the Sales Trainer and it's 5 o'clock on Friday afternoon and you've got a problem. What is it? Well, the next conference starts on Monday morning and you don't want to take all your surplus hand-outs, equipment, staging, etc. home for the weekend. So the hotel had better offer the organizer free, secure storage.

Now you're a delegate. It's 5 o'clock on Friday evening and you've got a problem too. You've been handed all this material, the bottles and posters and displays and how are you going to get them home? The hotel should offer free, secure car parking.

You're a delegate. Who employs you? It could be the company. It could be a drug store. So what's the difference? If you work for a chemist, you may be on another course in the future, run by a different cosmetic house. You'll compare the two. Who offered you the better presentation, the better hospitality? The client cosmetic company wants the answer to be that they did. If the delegates are company staff this is, of course, not a problem; the delegates are stuck with you. So you'd better find out because then you'll know just how important it is for the client to impress the delegates.

If they do work for chemists, the organizer wants them to remember this company and this course. You'd better come up with creative banqueting ideas.

Now, who sells cosmetics? Can we agree it's most likely to be attractive, young women. So what are you going to emphasize? Computer locking on the bedroom doors and the security of the hotel.

Will there be any VIPs coming to represent the company? If there are, you need to emphasize how careful you are to look after VIPs.

What are the delegates going to do in the evening? If the answer is homework, you can talk about the power points for computers, the room service at 11 o'clock at night and the good lighting if the delegates are studying in their bedrooms.

Is this the first time the Sales Trainer has ever run a course? Hardly. And this is a very big series. Why isn't the organizer going back to a hotel they have used in the past? Alright, you may have been recommended but it's still a risk using a new hotel for something this important. You ask: 'These courses are very important. If you could create the perfect hotel in which to hold them, what would it be able to offer.' The answer usually pinpoints what the last hotel didn't offer well enough.

Are the delegates senior or junior? If they're senior, the organizer is going to be prepared to spend more on them.

And where do they come from? If they come from abroad, will they have any dietary needs? How good is your international cuisine?

That's 10 questions, producing 10 customer benefits your competition may not be able to offer. Not because they couldn't, but because they don't know they *are* customer benefits.

What's the purpose of the sales training? To launch

their new product, Black Carnation? Now you can order black carnations from the florist to decorate the bedrooms. Will there be a social programme? You can come up with lots of good ideas for them to enjoy themselves outside the meeting. But perhaps there is also a need to improve the *ésprit de corps.* Then you can come up with teamwork exercises ideas. Are the speakers all experts or would some advanced audiovisual aids, like an autocue, help the weaker presenters to do the job better? Are there any guest speakers who have special needs?

That brings the questions up to 15.

Would the organizer like an office in the hotel if they're moving in for 6 months? Will the organizer need secretarial services you are very willing to provide to keep his or her HQ office going while they are away for so long?

Would it be helpful if you put the promotional material for the course into the bedrooms of the delegates before they arrive?

Are the delegates eating in the hotel every night, because you can come up with all kinds of themed menus to vary the experience?

Well, that's 19 questions. You can come up with the twentieth – and a few more as well – because there can never be too many customer benefits when you're trying to persuade a client to use you. When the client compares what you're offering with the stereotyped letters from your competition, you have a far better chance of winning the contract.

Notice that you still haven't asked at what time the organizer would want tea and biscuits! The answers to those kinds of questions seldom produce customer benefits.

5 Telephone selling

Potential clients may get in touch with you by telephone, letter, fax, email and in person. When they get in touch with you by phone, they are often handled by relatively junior staff. Yet, whether they buy the product or not depends on how good those staff are at selling on the phone.

It is standard practice to do test calls to check on their competence, but these have serious shortcomings:

1 They are spasmodic.
2 The results can only be discussed well after the events.
3 It is difficult to discuss them one-to-one.
4 They are not immediately followed up by another call where the improved technique can be practised and monitored.

There is a better alternative. The airlines and central booking offices have had a better system for over 30 years. The manager has the ability to listen in to both sides of the conversation at any time. If your present phone system doesn't incorporate this facility, such equipment is commercially available.* When you have sorted out the capability, you should always tell the staff that you are able to carry out this work. You are trying to help them improve their performance.

---

*Phonecoach (telephone: 01268 274 317). A Phonecoach telerecorder costs about £220.

The hospitality industry is in some respects not the same as others. We will probably have done business with some of the callers before: regular guests, Travel Agents, travel departments, Third Party Agents, etc. These people have to make enquiries as part of their jobs. As we have discussed before, they need four specific services to make their lives easier. So remember:

1 They need to be able to get through.
2 They would like to be recognized as more valuable clients than those who ring once in a blue moon.
3 If they are ringing to make a booking, they would like to be able to make one.
4 They would prefer not to be involved in any paper work.

How do you measure up to those needs?

- Can your clients get through? The acceptable standard for departments taking orders in companies like Unilever is to answer the phone within three rings. Your problem is that if the phone isn't answered, the client may ring off and then you have lost the booking. They just ring another company which does answer.
- Are they recognized? Is there a list of VIP customers in your departments, so that you can give them a more personal response? 'Hello, Jenny, how nice to hear from you again.'
- What happens if you are full? Do you find the client what they want somewhere else? If you adopt such a policy, the client is far more likely to phone you. They are often more concerned to get the space or the tickets rather than to bother about where they book it.
- When you take a booking, do you ask them to confirm it? That involves them writing to you. If you confirm to them, it doesn't.

Now, if you have to make a booking, which company would you ring? One where you can get through, where you are recognized, where you can be sure of a booking and they will confirm to you. Or one where you usually have to hang on the line, where they don't know you from Adam, if they are full they just say 'no' and where you have to confirm to them. It's no contest.

Increasing the percentage of productive calls

In addition to taking calls, you are obviously going to make outgoing calls. The higher the percentage of sales calls, the better. These are, however, the more difficult ones. The temptation to make less emotionally stressful calls is considerable. For example, a lot of Banqueting Departments always make a call to the client after the event is over, to find out whether they were satisfied or not. These are, normally, public relations calls. You don't get any more business, but it is a pleasant, hassle-free call. Yet if you ask the same department why they are not chasing up old business, you are told that there isn't enough time.

So cut out the PR calls and spend the time on chasing old business instead. Following up after an event is poor selling technique anyway. Immediately after the event, the client can remember every detail of what went wrong; a roll missing, a cracked glass, a defective bottle of wine. By the time the client wants to make another booking, however, those minor problems will have been forgotten. All that will be remembered is that a lot of the guests congratulated the organizer on how well it went. At the decision-making time, the call can be more productively made. You need to find the time to make as many selling calls as possible.

How do you answer the phone?

As with all other aspects of selling, the correct technique involves you in putting yourself in the position of the client. Right, you are the client making the call. What's the first thing you want? To get through without being interrogated. So, if a client wants to talk to you, your only concern is that they may change their mind. Here is potential business. The telephonist should never ask the caller's name or organization. Why does that happen anyway? Because there are people you don't want to talk to. Even so, you shouldn't treat potential clients like unwelcome callers. Treat the unwelcome callers initially as potential customers. You can always realize your mistake quickly and put the phone down as soon as possible.

If you were the client, what sort of person would you want to speak to? You would want them to be somebody senior and an expert. You want to be able to trust them to tell you the truth and to deal with your request in a competent manner. After all, you have got senior people coming to your event and you are going to be held responsible, even if it is the hotel or restaurant that doesn't do a good job.

And what is the normal response you get: something like 'Banqueting Department. Julie speaking. How may I help you?' You immediately know that the person you are speaking to is a junior. Anybody senior answers with both their names – Julie Smith. Incidentally, when they sign their letters with the title 'Conference Coordinator', you get the same message. If they signed the letter 'Conference Administration Manager' you would, again, think they were senior. Expressions like 'How may I help you?' are merely a repeated formulaic phrase. Why? Because, in real life, nobody ever says 'How *may* I help you'. You say 'How *can* I help you?' Formulaic phrases exude insincerity. Cut them out. Let the speaker talk naturally.

As we have seen, selling starts with DIPADA (see Chapter 4). To handle an enquiry successfully, you normally need far more information than you are offered initially. The client asks about the availability of a room or a table on a date. Behind that request may be far more important factors. Do you have an efficient microphone system because, at the last place, the microphones didn't work well. Can you provide Punch cigars for the Chairman? Can they get a motor car into the room? Listen carefully for clues and let the client lead the conversation. You need to know why they want to spend the money and then prove to them that it would be best spent with you.

Calls come through when you are extremely busy, as well as when you are quiet. Clients should never get the impression on the phone that they are anything other than the high spot of the day for you. The message is, in the middle of a boring day, you have finally perked up because they are on the line. Clients want to feel they are important to you. Don't let the rush of the day lead you to give them any other impression.

Sometimes the clients ring you and, with the best will in the world, you can't help them. Sound genuinely sorry. You may be the tenth hotel they have tried. You may be condemning them to try many more before they get fixed up. They deserve your sympathy and they will remember if they got it from you, and a curt regret from your competitor.

If, by chance, you identify that the client is having a difficult day, discuss it with them and give them some more sympathy. Most clients have jobs to do and nobody wants to listen to their excuses for failure. So you be the one who listens – and agree that they have a very difficult life.

Lead the conversation

You know what you want out of the phone call. You should make a list, if necessary, of the information you want before you pick up the phone. Now the objective is not to put the phone down until you have got everything you need. The client will only give you a limited amount of time. So you have to guide the conversation onto the right lines. If the client goes off at a tangent, you need to bring the conversation back to the points you want clarified. Do it gently and always listen to what the client *is* saying. A clue to a major piece of business you didn't know about may be forthcoming: 'I don't want to consider what AVs we need at the conference at the moment because we have the Annual Dinner coming up.'

Success is putting down the phone with all the information you wanted; and more besides.

When should you telephone?

There is no good time of the day to phone. You can make the excuse that the clients open their post till 10 o'clock, are in meetings throughout the day, apart from lunch, and sign their letters after the meetings, not wishing to be interrupted. Then there would be no good time to ring. So ignore all of that and phone whenever you have the time.

Research calls

The first question, of course, is who do you need to speak to? If you don't know, don't ask to speak to the Social Club Secretary or the Sales Director or whatever. Tell the telephonist that you are writing to the Social Club Secretary and would like his or her name. This is good business manners, and so the telephonist will usually provide the name. Get the spelling right at that time as well: 'Is that Stephen with a ph or with a v?' Then ring off, ring back when you are ready, and now ask for the person you want to speak to by name. You are far more likely to get through if you can use the name.

If you are trying to identify new business which may be available to you, you need a 30 second approach. Clients taking calls from strangers don't want to waste a lot of time. Thirty seconds is about all the time they will give you before they get irritated. So bring them into the conversation as soon as possible. Try something like:

'Good morning, Mr **Jones**. My name is **Harry** Brown, from the Stretched Out Palms **Hotel**. We've **done** a fair amount of business with you **in the past**, Mr **Jones**, but, as far as I can see, we've not looked after your **National Sales Conference**, and I wondered if **you held one**.'

Now, obviously, you wouldn't mumble this introduction. But for the client to understand what you are saying, you need to emphasize the key words; just like a TV newsreader. I have put the key words in bold letters in the example you have just read. If the client listens even half-heartedly – and he may have all sorts of other important things on his mind when he picked up the phone – he will get the key points. It's someone called Harry who is from a hotel which we've used in the past, who knows my name and wants to know if we hold sales conferences.

With most organizations, you will, indeed, have had a guest using your product at some time. The importance of establishing this is that it means the client doesn't have to try something entirely new. If anything goes wrong in the future, he can always point out that he was just following in the footsteps of other colleagues. This insurance may be necessary to him.

If the client says he does hold a conference, then you need to find out how many attend – can you cope? – when it is held, and when he makes up his mind about the venue. When you have that information, you can ring off.

'Thank you very much for the information, Mr Jones. I won't take up any more of your time now but, if I may, I'll ring you again when you're ready to make a decision.'

The client is delighted. You are leaving him in peace. But when you ring again, at the decision making time, you can say to the secretary 'Mr Jones suggested I ring him.' He may remember the call, but if he doesn't, always say to him 'You'll remember ...' before you tell him what he has forgotten. (The same approach applies to telling clients what they don't know: 'As you know, Mr Jones, the 1989 vintage was the best of that decade.' He hasn't a clue, but you aren't giving the impression that you are superior.)

Now, if the client sounds as if he isn't too busy, you could do a little more market research.

'Could I take one more moment of your time, Mr Jones? Could you give me the name of your colleague who looks after the overseas visitors who come to see you?'

When you go back to the client at the decision-making point, the objective of your phone call is to get him to come to see the product. Always know before you pick up the phone what your main objective is. Don't just call and give him the set presentation. If you want a conference, don't start with 'the hotel is only 3 miles from Junction 74 of the M93'. The client will be far more interested in 'the conference room is air conditioned and has natural lighting'.

If the person you want to talk to is constantly badgered by sales people in your industry, then you may have to get past their personal assistant, who is there to filter calls. 'Mr Jones is in a meeting at the moment. Could you send us some details' is normally a polite way of saying 'Would you please get off the phone and stop bothering us.' Of course, you could do your

TELEPHONE SELLING

research calls with the PA, who may have the crucial information you need.

If you must speak with the client personally, one of the best ways is to get their mobile phone number. Then there isn't a PA available to hold you up. You could say to the telephonist, 'Mr Jones needs me to ring him but he's out of the office. Do you have his mobile number please?' This normally produces the mobile number without further enquiries. You might feel that this is dishonest, when the person hasn't asked you to call, and you would have a point. But then consider that the poor client is wasting so much money using a product that gives inferior value to your own, that you are actually doing him a favour getting through to him.

If you can't get the mobile number, then try phoning when the secretary or PA may not be there, like early morning or after 5.30pm. Secretaries do work long hours as well, but seldom as long as their bosses.

Always remember that when someone has to buy a product, they have to talk to someone. If you are on the phone at that time, they are saving themselves the problem of finding someone else. It is more convenient to talk to you.

Preparing for sales calls

Selling on the telephone is like playing chess; you need to concentrate all the time. One false move and you can lose the game. Every word needs to be carefully checked to see if you are using the right one. It sounds an intimidating prospect, but the first thing to do is isolate yourself as much as possible. If you can arrange to be in a room all by yourself, that's best. If you are with others, ask them to keep the noise down. If you feel more at ease with your feet on the desk, so long as no clients can see you, put your feet on the desk. Whatever makes it easy for you to concentrate is legitimate.

We all hope we are lucky. In selling there are two sayings about luck. 'It's amazing how my luck improved when I started working more efficiently.' And 'Luck is when thorough preparation meets an opportunity.' Trite, perhaps, but a cliché can be an eternal truth.

So are you properly prepared when you make a sales call on the phone? Surround yourself with all the information you might logically be asked to provide. About the product, about the district, about the costs and the distances and the sizes and capacities. When a client asks a question, you need to give a straightforward, accurate answer in an unhesitating voice. Don't er and um.

Are you being asked to set a standard which is higher than anybody else's? Absolutely. The competition may have lots of advantages over you, but they can't stop you selling better.

The voice

Remember to be enthusiastic about your product on the phone. You are not giving a technical lecture on a scientific experiment. You are persuading a client that your product will satisfy her needs. Not 'The restaurant will seat 75 on tables of 6' but 'It's a lovely restaurant which is fine for 75 guests and the decor is really very pretty.' That enthusiasm comes out in your voice.

What is the relationship which is established by your voice? Are you servile, fawning, obsequious, aggressive, flattering? Unless you have any reason to do otherwise, your voice should imply that this conversation is between one good organization talking to another: you are worth your salt and so is the client.

How quickly do you speak to the client? That depends on the client's voice. If they are speaking ponderously, don't go at it hammer and tongs. If they are speaking fast, then you do the same. The speed of voice of the sales person is more normally dependent on how nervous the sales executive is. The more nervous you are, the more you speed up. Gear it instead to the voice on the other end of the line.

An enthusiastic voice at the speed of the client – and a smiling voice. Nobody wants to hear the voice of doom. Or the voice of a robot. Get a smile into your voice and keep it there, no matter how annoying the client may be.

The tone of voice also needs to be flexible. If you are speaking to a client with a military background, they will be accustomed to dealing with brisk, alert voices. If you are approaching a senior citizen's club, something gentler will probably go down better. Flexibility is the key point.

How loud should you talk? The simple answer might be don't bellow and don't whisper, but you do need to take into account the age of the client – if you can – and the background noise level where the client is listening to you. The older the client, the worse their hearing is likely to be, although it is embarrassing for the client to say they can't hear you. It is far more likely they will say they are busy at the moment and could you send details.

Overcoming objections

When a client starts raising objections, she is starting to buy. Look upon objections as a help in your selling process. At the outset, you are telling her about the product and she's listening. She's just wandering round your information shop. When she starts to raise objections, though, she's trying to fit what she needs with what you are telling her. That's great. Overcome the objections and you have a good chance of getting the business.

That applies to objections about price as well. The client doesn't like the price because he doesn't want the product badly enough – yet. The more customer benefits you give the client, the more reasons for coming to you, the more the price recedes into the background. Sales people don't really sell; buyers buy.

To learn of those objections, though, to have a conversation rather than give a lecture, you must be ready to stop talking when you get any inkling that the clients wants to talk themselves. It is easier in person because you can see their mouth open. On the phone you must listen very carefully; the slightest noise on the other end of the line and you break off in mid-sentence.

Whoever is filtering the potential client's calls is not your enemy. They can be a very useful ally. They can tell you when it would be a good time to phone. That's very important because, at a good time, the client may be more receptive to your presentation. The filterers can provide you with information about decision-making processes, problems with your proposal, etc. So treat them with the utmost courtesy and try to get them on your side with a light-hearted comment or two. Try to jolly them along so that you stop being just another caller and become someone who makes the day a bit brighter. It needs always to be a pleasure to speak to you.

You also want them to believe that their boss would really benefit from talking to you. One way to do that is to be able to say that one of the person's colleagues has suggested you call. That's why it is much easier to get more business from an existing client company than a new one; you can be recommended within a company with whom you already do business.

Often the filterer knows a good deal about the way the business you want is handled. They will know what the other hotel *isn't* doing well. They can give you all sorts of good advice, so that your presentation, when you finally reach the decision maker, is geared to the right needs.

Dealing with complaints

When people want to complain, they will very often ring you. If you don't deal with the complaint to their satisfaction, they can take their business away from you.

There are four steps in successfully dealing with a complaint. They are:

1 Listen
2 Let them know – or see – that you are making notes.
3 Apologize.
4 Agree with them what you are going to do about it.

So, first you listen. Don't interrupt. Like a steaming kettle, let it all get out into the open. Let the person know you are still listening with the occasional 'uh, huh' but don't interrupt except to say at one point early on 'This is inexcusable. Let me just make some notes.'

When the complainant has finished, apologize. This isn't always easy because you may be entirely in the right. If that's the case, apologize for the fact that things they are complaining about weren't made clear at the outset. No client wants to be proved wrong when they complain. If you prove it up to the hilt, they may grudgingly excuse themselves, but you are still less likely to keep their business. If you apologize, they may well be mollified.

Then agree with them the action you are going to take to see that it never happens again.

Getting the right answers

When you ask a client for sensitive information, you may encounter resistance to providing it. Ask the client, for example, what his budget is and he may not want to tell you. He feels that, if you know the budget, you will quote higher prices than if you don't. In such cases, you always have to provide the client with a good reason for telling you the facts. That reason has got to involve a benefit for the client. Put yourself in the client's shoes again. What benefit would he get from telling you his budget? Simple:

> 'Mr Jones, at the Stretched Out Palms we feel that it's our responsibility to make sure that you don't spend one penny more than you've allocated for the event. Tell me, Mr Jones, how much have you set aside?'

Notice the word 'budget' isn't used. That word triggers alarm bells in his mind. You are right that the last thing he wants is a bill higher than his budget. If he gets one, he may punish you by not using you again, but he still has to explain to his boss why he overspent. So the benefit is a very real one.

You even have to be sensitive to the effect of a single word. One of the most important things you have to find out is who is the decision maker. You are talking to a member of the organization and you want to know if he's the one. If you say to him 'Do you make the decisions yourself, Mr Jones, or aren't you important enough?' the client's *amour propre* will demand that he says 'Yes, I am', even when he isn't. He also won't like the question put that way at all.

The right way to identify the decision maker is to say to your contact:

'Will you be deciding on the venue yourself, Mr Jones, or will you be delegating that to one of your colleagues?'

Notice that beautiful little word, 'delegating'. You can only delegate downwards. So you are asking the client, not whether he's important enough, but whether he's *too* important. That's your best chance of getting the truthful answer because he doesn't lose face: a definite advantage to him.

One final example of this need to ask questions to include a customer benefit. You want to know what business they have for you in the quiet season – the depths of the winter, for example. If you say to the client 'We're very quiet in the winter. Could you give us any business then?' the client would think 'I don't care what they need. It's what I need that interests me.' So how do you manufacture a benefit? You say:

'Mr Jones, looking at our records, there were occasions last summer when the town was very busy, when we weren't able to look after you.'

It opens the floodgates. The client tells you about the shortages, about how long he had to wait on the phone, about the inadequacy of the treatment he received. You sympathize right along the line. You then continue:

'That's terrible. We really do want to improve on that. Tell me, when do you have your largest need?'

And he says 'for the national conference in February' or 'for the Annual Dinner in December'. Given a choice, most of the major events are held in the winter because it is difficult to get everybody together during the summer holiday period.

You have identified the information you were looking for, and you have done so by asking the wrong question. If he can't get what he wants during the summer, the right question would seem to be 'what do you need during the summer?' You asked what was his largest need. It appears to be an attempt to help him with his problems – and you are going to try to do that anyway – but it is really aimed at identifying the business you want.

TELEPHONE SELLING

Open and closed questions

The more a client talks, the more you learn about his or her business. Therefore, you want to ask questions in such a way that you get the maximum amount of information in reply. Consider the question 'When do you want lunch?' The answer is '1 o'clock.' That didn't help much. We call that a closed question. Supposing you'd asked 'Is the lunch a major part of the conference or just a question of taking on 1500 calories?' Now the client can talk about the lunch in general. That's an open question.

Brochure and Tariff request calls

When people ring and ask for your brochure and tariffs, it is normally because they are thinking of buying your product. You need to do more, therefore, than simply send them the material.

You can send it and then follow up on the phone. If you do that, don't start the call by saying that you are just checking that the material has arrived. As neither Red Indians nor Highwaymen have attacked a mail coach for some years now, the client expects the mail service will deliver the letters. So they know that you are making a poor excuse to try to make a sales call. Therefore, tell them in your covering letter that everybody has different requirements and you will ring them to give them more specific help. When you have provided the help, you can try to close the sale.

Because of the increase of sales calls to private homes in recent years, even this genuine offer of help often doesn't go down well. We are all programmed to pick up the phone, find out that somebody is trying to sell us something, and put the phone down as quickly as possible. The best time to get a booking from someone asking for a brochure and tariff is when you take the initial call. Get into a conversation with the caller. 'Oh, you're thinking of coming down here for the weekend. How nice. Are you planning to see the sights or is it a celebration ...' As you chat, you are really making a sales presentation. Notice you have started with the D in DIPADA again. If you give callers all the information they need, a considerable proportion of them should be able to be signed up on the spot.

Summary

The more you practise selling on the phone, the easier it gets. You need to relax and concentrate. You need to put yourself in the position of the clients and try to work out what they want from your product.

Try to increase the number of productive calls, against those which are simply courtesy calls. Pay particular attention to the type of voice you feel will be most appropriate for the call you are making. Call whenever you have the time. Ask open questions.

Don't worry about sales calls. Nobody has ever been physically attacked by a client over the phone.

Case study

This case study illustrates:

- The type of market for which telephone selling is particularly appropriate.
- The development of a teleselling campaign.
- The importance of correspondence research.

The Slieve Donard Hotel, in Newmarket, Co. Down, in Northern Ireland, is a nice hotel but the winters are very quiet. Now a hotel can easily justify being empty but, of course, very few good hotels are ever totally empty. Therefore, the thing to do is to find out why the clients you do have are booking the hotel and then see if you can get some more from the same source.

You need a bright receptionist to do this, and a very able person was given ownership of that responsibility in the Slieve Donard. One day in November she got a letter from a client booking a single room for a Friday night in January. So, having been well trained, she rang the client and said:

'I got your booking this morning, Mr Farrell. We can offer you the room but, if it isn't private, could you tell me what brings you to the hotel on a Friday night in January.'

Mr. Farrell said, 'I'm coming for the dog show.'

The conversation continued:

'What dog show is that?'

'I breed spaniels and there's a big show in January.'

'Will many of you be coming?'

'Oh, I suppose about 70 of us.'

'And where might I get a list of spaniel breeders?'

'Well, if you ring the Kennel Club in London, they'll give you the list.'

So she rang the Kennel Club in London and the list arrived. Then she asked herself what dog breeders were likely to want from a hotel. Were the dogs going to sleep with the owners? Would they need any form of feeding? What sort of exercise do you give a dog before it parades at a dog show? Do they need to be kept separate from all the other dogs?

She wrote down as many questions as she could think of and then rang the first name on the list. She didn't ring to get a booking but to get answers to the questions and to find out if there were any points she'd missed. The breeder was helpful. Most people are if they are asked for advice. They like to show off their expertise and, if you are polite and grateful, you can get the information you need without too much trouble.

When she had all the information, she settled down to ring the 70 breeders. It soon became obvious that there were times when it was easy to get hold of them and other times when they were busy and didn't want to be bothered.

There's a lot of teleselling going on these days. People ring and try to sell you double glazing, mobile phones, new kitchens and goodness knows what else. The reaction of a very large percentage of the population is to get the sales person off the phone as fast as possible. This was different though. The people she was talking to had to get themselves a hotel somewhere. What was more, they had to do it soon because the show was only a couple of months away. Timing is very important indeed. If I want to sell you Christmas cards, should I ring you in October, November or late in December. When do you buy them? And some people buy them in the sales in January.

Of course, not everybody was in when the receptionist first phoned. She had to find out when they were likely to be in and then ring again. One potential client she had to ring seven times before she finally made contact.

At the end of the exercise 40 breeders had agreed to stay at the hotel. It was a remarkably good result – but it still wasn't enough. If you are going to do the job properly, you can try one more possibility. The receptionist had found out where the dog show was being held, so she rang the Booking Office and said to the manager:

'Do you have many dog shows at the hall?'

'No, not many. It's mostly weddings, football club annual dinners; that sort of thing. I don't suppose we have more than – oh, about 15 a year.'

'15?'

'Yes, you know: Dachshunds, Great Danes, Borzoi.'

All she had done was pick up one letter where she couldn't understand why the guest should want to come and stay. From that one letter she had identified a new market which could help the hotel 15 times a year.

Of course, you can go on from there. Where are the judges staying – and the press, the enthusiasts and the overseas buyers. There was an Aberdeen Angus Show in Perth in Scotland where the buyers used to come from the Argentine. It still doesn't stop; will there be a dinner for the breeders, an Organizer's Committee Meeting, entertaining by the dog food manufacturers? Was there a Northern Ireland Spaniel Club which would like to have its annual dinner in the hotel, to coincide with the show?

When you find a new source of business, you have to examine it from all angles.

Why the telephone? Why not just direct mail the breeders? Because you can throw a letter in the waste-paper basket far more easily than you can get rid of a pleasant voice on the phone.

What would the initial approach on the phone be? Something like:

'Good morning, Mr Neill. My name is Sarah Brown from the Slieve Donard Hotel in County Down. We already have a number of spaniel breeders staying with us for the show in January and I wondered if you were going to be looking for hotel accommodation as well?'

Then you go on from there. Nothing more complicated than that.

6 The shape of things that came – the technology

Modern technology has been devised to help you win the battle for business against your competitors. For a great many executives in the hospitality industries, this fact might well recall the famous words of the Duke of Wellington about his army; 'I don't know what effect [they] will have upon the enemy, but Lord, they terrify me.'

If that is how you feel about the technology, take comfort from the fact that you are about as alone as the grains of sand on the seashore. Everybody anticipates trouble because these are still early days for much of the technology, and mistakes abound.

Fundamentally, the technology is not that difficult to understand. The problem is that it is made difficult by the abyss, the chasm, that seems to exist between the customer and the manufacturer when it comes to the language they use. When that is simplified, as I hope to do, you should have fewer problems.

The main elements of the new technology are Global Distribution Systems (GDS), the Internet, email, Property Management Systems (PMS) and Yield Management Systems (YMS).

Global Distribution Systems (GDS)

Travel agents used to have to use the mail or the telephone to make bookings on airlines, with car companies and hotels, etc. The airlines decided that they could provide a better service than that and they developed global distribution systems (GDSs). These enabled the travel agent to learn more about the airline's services on a computer, identify whether space was available and book it. There are today four main GDSs – Sabre, Amadeus, Worldspan and Galileo – formerly operated by airline companies but now on their own.

Sabre is very strong with travel agents in the USA. Galileo is strong in both the USA and the UK. Worldspan is strongest in the UK and Europe and Amadeus in Germany and Europe. Most travel agents are only using one of these systems because they are all expensive.

For the travel agent, this took care of the airline bookings but it didn't help with hotel bookings. So a number of the major hotel companies financed the creation of a company that would tell the GDSs what hotel space they had available and enable them to book that. The alternative for the hotels had been to tell the then six GDSs separately, which was also very costly.

The company was called Thisco (which changed its name to Pegasus Solutions). Later, Avis car rental developed a system for telling the GDSs what cars they had available and how to book those. Avis then decided to accept hotels onto their system as well. The Avis company was called Wizcom. Both Pegasus Solutions and Wizcom are called Switch companies because they enable the travel agent on GDSs to 'switch' on the information about a hotel's availability and price and to make bookings. Both companies will handle other kinds of hospitality industry bookings as well.

So, to put your information onto the four specified GDSs – there are smaller companies as well – you could make an arrangement with a Switch company. There are two kinds of message on GDSs; one is faster than the other and called Seamless. It also has more information, but it costs the hospitality company more, though not much. The other kind is called Type A. They both give the travel agents answers in 7 seconds.

There are, of course, major hotel representation companies as well. In the hotel industry you have organizations like Utell International (which is now a division of Pegasus Solutions as well), Trust (Germany), Lexington (US) and VIP (Canada). They represent hotels all over the world. They originally enabled travel agents and the general public to make hotel bookings, by calling a telephone number in their own country, instead of having to contact the hotel direct, possibly thousands of miles away. From your home in New York, you would ring Utell's office in Omaha, Nebraska, to book a bedroom with a hotel in Tokyo.

Today, of course, these companies take the traditional bookings over the phone and direct electronic bookings through their automated systems. You are linked via Pegasus Solutions or Wizcom to place your information onto the GDS. You know the sort of thing: 'You have three options. For resort hotels in Tibet, press 1', etc.

So let's take a simple example. A travel agent in Wyoming who wants to book a hotel in Bournemouth, gets in touch with his GDS with his request. The GDS passes the request through the switch company to the hotel or to the hotel's agent – a central reservations system, a hotel representation company or a hotel consortium booking office. Whoever is called either takes the booking, if the space is available, or rejects it. Often the call is dealt with by a computer which has the information on whether there's space. Then nobody human is involved in the booking at all. It is a much faster and cheaper system for the travel agents and more and more bookings are made by this method.

Most hotel representation companies are now only taking about 15–20 per cent of their bookings over the phone. The rest come through electronic means and the telephone bookings get fewer every year.

To get bookings, though, the hotel representation companies do need the space to be available. You are able to tell the agent that, because you are busy, the space may be available or it may not; that's being 'on request'. Except in a period of really peak demand, however, the result of this will be to make sure the agent tries another hotel. 'On request' is a serious turn-off for the agent.

In addition, a hotel representation company will handle your bookings on a 'private label' representation if you pay for that. Then you are separately listed, rather than being one of a host of options.

A hospitality company that trades in the global market place and still has to be contacted direct, rather than through a GDS, is now at a severe competitive disadvantage in the main tourism and commercial markets. Also, almost all the major corporate customers in the hospitality industry and the business house agents that represent them, demand that transactions are now primarily done in the way described above.

Most of the GDS bookings do tend to come from companies, but there is a percentage which comes from the leisure market. As most of the bookings are corporate, they are normally worth more than those in the leisure sector. Remember, though, that there are a vast number of minor markets where you can still do business over the phone or by letter, although they do diminish every year.

If you are linked to GDSs, you have to pay particular attention to keeping the information updated. There is nothing that aggravates a travel agent more than having the booking rejected and then, on phoning the hotel for the client, finding that the space was available after all. Time is one of the travel agent's most precious possessions.

You can also vary your rates, so that if you are in a quiet period, you can make special offers of lower prices. There is plenty of flexibility in the system but you have to use it well all day and every day. Remember also not to block off multiple night bookings if you can avoid it.

Of course, you have to assess whether it is worthwhile being on a GDS. If you are a small operation and you are in a small provincial town, it may just not be worth your while. Don't spend any money just to be like the big wheels.

Well, all of this is an excellent service for the travel agent. The snag for the hospitality company in the GDS booking system, is that everybody has to be paid for their part in making the booking. Suppose the booking comes from a travel agent through a GDS, through a switch company and a hotel booking service. Then a different level of commission has to paid to the four organizations. Between them, they can collect

20 per cent of the price you are getting for the product. What is more, apart from the commission on each transaction, you may have to pay an annual fee to the hotel representation company. That's why the public may often only be offered rack rate at hotels if they use such a system. Of course, when the man in the street books direct with you on the Internet, you cut out all the commissions.

There are companies who will load your information onto the GDSs cheaper. One is called Hotkey and it is in competition with companies like Utell. It is cheaper because it loads the information less expensively, often manually. That makes it a slower process than Utell's automated Netrez system but cost will, obviously, come into your final decision.

There is one other company which matters here, called the hotel Clearing Group. It facilitates the collection of commission by travel agents. The way it works is that it transmits commission from the hotel to the travel agent. It doesn't charge the hotel for this service but it charges the travel agent commission on the commission. From the travel agent's angle, it ensures that they get their money and that they get it in their own currency, thereby avoiding bank charges for clearing cheques. For hospitality companies, it is worthwhile doing business with the agents that way. If agents can be sure of getting their commission, hassle free, if they book with you, then you are as good for them as any chain hotel.

The Internet

The Internet, as you know, is a vast collection of information on every subject under the sun. You could add to its store of knowledge by letting people who have access to the Internet know about you. They could call at your Internet shop (website) and get the information. They could make a booking. They could give you their names and ask for more information. It also enables you to provide far more information than you can on a GDS. The whole approach is what is now referred to technically as B2C – Business to Consumer – communication.

So, they might get in touch with you on the Internet. If they can do that, it will be for one of three reasons: because you have your own website, because you are represented by a hotel booking service, or you may be a member of a chain of hotels – Relais & Châteaux, Best Western, etc. – and they have a website. You may have your own website within theirs as well. Then the public can ask about your availability online. The enquiry is passed through the web to you or your agent and the public can make a booking. Customer to website, website to your agent or you, and back to the customer. Both you and the customer have a booking.

The major difference between a booking through the Internet and a booking through a GDS is simply a question of cost. You can afford to offer a better deal on the Internet because of this. The cost of distribution – how much it costs you to take a booking – is much reduced. You also can cut out the costs of print and postage. The fact is that Internet bookings are, potentially, a great threat to the financial viability of travel agencies in the years to come.

The challenge, of course, is generating the traffic on your site, so that your reliance on your agents reduces. As, however, most of the major companies in the world now use large business house agents to negotiate rates and book travel on their behalf, such agents are likely to dictate the way they do business for a long time yet.

Creating a website

We have identified that if people want to know about your product and buy it on the Internet, then you need a website and a booking system. We have also recognized that the latter could be your own or that of a representation company. So, how do you go about creating your own website and how do you get people to book your products on it?

1   If you are able to access the Internet on your computer, you have an agreement with a company that provided you with that access. Such a company is called an Internet Service Provider (ISP). That's the first necessity.

Be well Dined at Art's!

Welcome! Our aim is to make sure that your experience at ART'S is one that will ensure that you will return time after time!

Setting the Scene. Select your favourites from our dazzling array and create your own masterpiece! Your choice of pates, terrines, pies, charcuterie, smoked fish and fresh crisp salads. Seeing is believing!

The Main Subject You may create this from a varied selection of Hot Roasts of the Day, Home Made Pies, Fish, Pastas and Vegetarian Specialities, blended with other exotic delights created by our chef to tickle your palate! If you fancy something and you can't see it, tell us - if we've got it in stock, its yours!

The Cost

	Lunch	Dinner
3 Courses with Coffee	£12.30	£15.50
2 Courses with Coffee	£9.50	£12.50
Main Course with Coffee	£6.50	£9.50

Children
Under 12 - half price

Finishing Touches Fresh Berries and Fruits, Hot Pies and Jellies, Luxury Ice Creams in splashes of exciting and exotic flavours Raspberry, Rhubarb, Greek Honey and Stem Ginger - The Impressions will linger and delight!

The Signature Your choice of freshly brewed Tea or Coffee with Sweetmeats

Individual Masterpieces For a supplement of £5.00, our Chef will accept individual commissions based on any of the following dishes:

Fresh Market Fish of the Day Please ask for today's catch and we'll cook it to your liking

Noisettes of English Lamb Pan-fried and served on a rich Madeira sauce, garnished with woodland mushrooms

Breast of Wild Duck Oven roasted, served pink with and orange and Grand Marnier glaze, garnished with orange fillets

Medallions of Venison Dijon Pan-fried roundels from the saddle, accompanied with a pepperan sauce and presented with pears and redcurrants

Grilled Fillet Steak Cooked to your liking, served with Tomato, Mushrooms and Straw Potatoes or accompanied with one of Chef's freshly prepared sauces: Red Wine & Shallots/ Brandy & Blackpepper/ Whisky & Mushrooms

All prices are inclusive of VAT. Service is not included, and is at your discretion

New thinking can emerge on any topic. A menu doesn't have to be a boring card (*Source:* Jarvis Hotels)

2   Then you need to create the material you want to put on your website. It is obviously true that you could do this for yourself without paying anybody to do it for you. But then you could also ask the Hall Porter to cook dinner for 500 after reading the Repertoire de la Cuisine. It is difficult, under those circumstances, to guarantee the quality of the dinner.

3   The process of putting your words onto a website involves translating them into a language called HTML. You can learn how to do this by buying a software package which explains the whole system. Something like Microsoft Front Page. That will

teach you how to create a web page and, if you are prepared to master the subject, then that is a perfectly acceptable commercial route.

4   Not surprisingly, there are also companies who will produce a website for you. They are called *web agencies*. Just as an advertising agency produces advertisements for you, so a web agency produces web pages for you. Most advertising agencies now have website design staff too.

5   If you use a web agency, they can often arrange the space you need on the Internet to display your information. So to get onto your website, the public need an Internet Service Provider for themselves, and you need the space for your information, which is located on a *server*. This server can be yours or, again, on a representation company website. If you are part of a representation company website, they will also make bookings for you. They will, of course, charge you commission.

You could have a website which enables you to take the bookings yourself. There are companies, like all-hotels.com in Edinburgh, who will provide you with free software to enable you to build that facility into your website. The way it works is that the client can book through you because you are linked to all-hotels.com. They too can make bookings for you, if your clients contact them direct. They will charge you a small commission for each booking, but it is likely to be much less than the hotel representation company or your consortium.

6   How does the client find you? Say you are with one Internet Service Provider and the client is with another. ISPs can communicate with each other through what are known as *search engines*. If you want to know about something you call up search engines like www.excite.com or www.yahoo.com and they will put you in touch with almost anything.

There will be a charge made by your Internet Service Provider. Probably for a single company, a few hundred pounds would cover that. The search engine is free.

7   The cost of the web agency's work is, obviously, a lot more. How much depends on how large a website you want; how

many pages, how complicated. Again, for a single company, you are probably talking about a few thousand pounds for a website that only provides the public with information about your product. If you want them to be able to buy it as well, you will need a *booking engine* – a way to book. This can either be tailor-made for your own needs or be in association with someone like all-hotels.com.

8 Talk to a web agency to find out about the cost. Shop around. Your Internet Service Provider can come up with suggestions as well.

9 The customer can now carry out two actions:
   - Get the information about the product.
   - Buy it.

The process of getting to the page you want in different circumstances is known as navigating the website. The more complex the necessary navigation, the more expensive the bill from the web agency.

You should also take into account that the website has to be updated if you want to take bookings. You will also change prices, for example, and then the website will have to be modified.

10 What goes onto the website is words, pictures and graphics, just like any other piece of promotional material. You need powerful headlines, enthusiasm, calls to action and testimonials from happy customers. In fact, the rules for promotional material which you will find in Chapters 9 and 10 apply. There are two which apply with even more importance.
   - Like an advertising agent, the web agency will try to carry out your instructions, but they won't necessarily know anything about your business. So you have to brief them very carefully.
   - Because there is so much competition when the public use the Internet, it is even more important that your website is easy to read. If they don't like your brochure, there may not be another immediately to hand; but if they don't like your website, there is.

Make sure the letters are large enough, the lines aren't too long (plenty of margin space) and that your message is very easy indeed to understand. The most important page is, of course, the first one – known as the *home page*. If that isn't as clear as crystal, your site visitor will just leave and look for another site.

Let's now look at the rules for a successful website.

Design

1   Keep it as simple as you can. If it is difficult to use, it won't be used. One of the things that makes the website look difficult to use is if you pack the screens with words – and use small type as well. The more margins there are, the easier it looks.

2   Remember that colours and typefaces reflect the product. Use those which best reflect yours.

3   Make it easy to navigate the site. And remember; they may want to go back as well as forward. Make that easy too.

4   Concentrate on your home page. It is critical. If they get what they want from that, you have a much better chance of them going on.

5   Make the navigation instructions on your home page comprehensive: how to find the information, the special offers, the rack rates, etc. Put the navigation instructions on each subsequent page, so that they can see immediately how to take the action they want next.

6   Make it as 'sticky' as possible. That's the new buzz word for making the website attractive, to keep the potential client interested.

7   Suppose the main attraction is a theme park near you. Have the details of that theme park on your website too. Have a click box (that's the hand signal rather than the arrow on the screen), showing them how to get the information on the other attraction. See that the information on the attraction is comprehensive.

8   You need a phone number where they can reach you on every page as well. If they run into difficulties, they can always ring you. You can answer their questions on a website too. For more information on that, take a look at www.humanclick.com.

9   Remember to have your email address on every page of the website ; if they can't book, they can still email. And if they want to phone you, you could give them an 0800 number, which is cheaper than the normal rate. You can also introduce a Call Me button. If they click that, they will be asked for their phone number and you will be told that somebody needs help. Then you ring them.

10   Make sure that your server can handle the contents of your website; that it can bring it up quickly and clearly.

11   Give your site the simplest name possible. If the public want to find it, they won't know the name of the website initially. They will find it through a search engine. So if you are the Empire Restaurant, Leconville, the sensible website name the public is most likely to try is empirerestaurantleconville.com. Not chipswitheverythingleconville.com. The latter might be cleverer but it is far more difficult to locate. A single typing error in looking for a website will mean the search engine can't find it; so the shorter your name the better. The search engine will identify you to the surfers because you fit the key words they have used to try to get the information they want – 'Restaurant' and 'Leconville', for example.
   When your website is produced by the search engine, there will be a descriptive paragraph about you. This paragraph is produced by the search engine by reading your website and picking up key words which form the eventual paragraph. So make sure those key words are in your website: Chinese, barbecue, buffet, 120 wines, etc.

12   What you are attempting to do all the time is learn more about your potential Internet customers. To understand more about their needs, who they are and how they react to your

message. You don't want to try to be all things to all people. It is difficult to be better than your competitors if you try to please every segment of the market.

It is going to be a long haul learning about all these points, but the Internet is likely to be an extremely valuable source of business for those who make the effort.

Rates

13   Even if customers can't buy the space on your website, still put the prices in. Then the public are told why they should buy it and also what it would cost them. That's called One Stop Shopping.

14   Explain the terms of any rates which are conditional *before* the customer tries to make a booking. Let's say you (as the website visitor) are told that the cheapest price for the product is £50. So you decide that's the one you want. You navigate yourself onto a page where you can make a booking, only to find that this price is only available if you pay in advance and don't alter the booking in any way. So you have to go back to the beginning and find another price you consider suitable. Only you might be so aggravated, you decide to try somewhere else instead; disaster for the website owner.

15   Don't have too many rates. Hotels have to quote for single and double rooms. Theatres are selling both stalls and the dress circle. The problem arises for the customers when they have a jumble of choices for rooms facing the garden, rooms on high floors, Superior rooms, weekend rates, special offers, corporate rates, rack rates, matinees, standbys, twofers, etc. The temptation to try to find a screen where it is simple to make up your mind is very great.

16   Ideally, you shouldn't try to promote any rate for a particular date unless the system knows that the room is available. Otherwise the client goes through the entire process of booking, only to be told at the end that the room isn't available. Of course, this is only possible when your website is

linked to your live inventory – what your booking position is at the moment.

Upkeep

17   Update the website regularly. Nothing looks worse than to find an offer on the website which expired a week ago.

18   Which raises another very important point. The people who use the modern technology expect a far faster service than of yore. The days when they were satisfied if the post arrived a day or two after the information they wanted was dispatched, are long gone. If people don't get a fast service now, they go where they *can* get it.

The main argument for all computer communications is speed and simplicity. If you are a travel agent in Kuala Lumpur and you want to book some opera seats in Milan, why bother to phone or fax when you can get the information on a computer screen in front of you, and confirmation of the booking as well? In another age, they used to give messengers money to make them hurry with the information: 'To Insure Promptitude' – TIP. We still appreciate better service.

19   You can alter a website's basic information at any time you want, but it does involve you in extra cost if you need to do it through a web agency. You can learn how to update the website yourself and not need to use the agency again, but if you update it without the same degree of style and elegance, you will be spoiling the ship for a ha'p'orth of tar.

20   Ideally, you want to know what happens when people log on to your website. Do they like it? Do they never get beyond the home page? Where do they come from? When your website is first created, you can ask for the facility to monitor this to be included. If you discover that 57 per cent of visitors to your site get to page 3 and then abandon hope all they who entered there, you need to do something about page 3.

Is the cost going to be worthwhile?

This is the £1 million question. And the answer is probably not today, but almost certainly tomorrow. The growth in the use of websites is very rapid. At the moment about 0.5 per cent of visitors to a website make a booking, but in 5 years' time that could easily be 5 per cent. If you are getting a 2–4 per cent response from direct mail shots, you can see that this could be a far better marketing option.

It is a matter of timing. The big companies need to be on the Internet now because they rely on the world of travel agents. Also it is a good way of getting rid of space at the last minute; that's what lastminute.com are all about. But the popularity of buying on the Internet is growing very quickly: I know one hotel at Heathrow which took 20 bookings over the Internet in August 1998 and 200 in August 1999.

Email

Email (the e is for electronic), is a new way of communicating with people. Just as the penny post distributed mail more cheaply and efficiently from 1840 onwards, just as the fax improved on the post in recent years, so email improves on the fax because it is faster and cheaper. Business done over the Internet by email is part of what is known as ecommerce.

A great many people on the Internet have an email address. Therefore, you can send them direct mail letters. Many companies, however, also use the Internet for internal communications. This internal mail system is called an Intranet and often includes the email address of all those on it. You can write a report for 10 people, attach it to an email copied to each of them and the job is done. Much quicker, no paper. If they want the report, they can always get it run off through their desktop printer. Your company can, therefore, not only communicate through a single Internet email address, but also to the various contacts who are on that company's Intranet if it covers their email as well.

If you send material via email, your client will get it as fast as a fax but cheaper. It doesn't cost you anything to send an email except your telephone time on the Internet at local rate. That's to anywhere at any time. They also get the original document and not a photocopy. So long as the client checks that they have email, they will get your communication as soon as they do so.

Even better, everything you send or receive can be filed in the disk space. It is a very simple filing system. To send email, all you need to do is identify the email address in a Mail File, key it in and click 'Send'. So the main task is to build your client database of email addresses. One way to go about that is to offer them an incentive to register their email address, such as a competition with a worthwhile prize. Get them to tell you whether they need you for business, leisure, Christmas or whatever. Then when you want to send them information, you can distinguish one segment of the market from another.

It is possible for the public to avoid getting email by making a legally binding statement that they don't want it from you. So you need them to register to say they do want to get it. Once you have someone on your database, you can contact them in the same way as any other client for direct mail. You have to keep on the right side of the Data Protection Act, though, so it might be an idea to get a bit of legal advice about how you are intending to use or store such data.

With the new technology, you are normally going to develop your promotional efforts with three distinct steps:

1 Provide an electronic brochure on the Internet.
2 Obtain bookings through the Internet and through ecommerce.
3 Improve your relationships with your customers, using the medium of sending them emails. If they want to buy because of the email, the next task is to get them to book again when they need you. Speed of response becomes a key point; people don't like to be kept waiting.

Computer programs

There are a considerable number of software products available for Reception and Banqueting Departments – Fidelio, Delphi etc. But as they're all different, you really need more detailed instructions on them than this book can offer to understand how they work.

What can be identified are some of the major problems that can crop up when you move from a manual to a computerized system.

1　In taking bookings, most junior staff members are motivated to say 'no'! You may think they're there to take bookings but just consider. Supposing you take a booking when you shouldn't have done so. Inevitably you will get into trouble. Now contrast that with what happens if you say 'no' if you are in any doubt about whether you should take the booking. Nothing will happen because nobody will know.

If that's always been the case, it becomes even more serious if the junior staff don't understand the more complicated computer systems. If in doubt, it becomes even safer to say 'no'.

2　Make sure that you are not dependent on a few executives who can work the system.

Enquiries can come in at any time. You need to be able to deal with them competently. It is no use saying 'Could I take a message?' or – even worse – 'Could you ring back?' When customers want to spend money, you want to take it, not turn it down because nobody knows how the IT works. You need people on duty who can do that, at whatever time of day it is reasonable to expect you might get an enquiry.

3　Not all systems are state-of-the-art.

You naturally assume that the systems are created by people who know everything there is to know about your industry. That isn't the case. The first computerized reservation system had lists of bookings where you couldn't distinguish between a provisional and a definite reservation. You still need to think for yourself. If you simply follow the instructions without thought, you can miss some important points.

For example, there is space on most programmes for the personal details of the decision maker. The space is, however, normally inadequate and seldom used. Yet you can't possibly remember every personal detail about every client. You need to have it on record though. When you next meet that individual and you say 'A Plymouth Gin and Tonic, Mr Jones?' he realizes that he's not just profit fodder for the company; he's an important customer, and your relationship blossoms from that realization.

4   Remember that the question is not 'is the space available?' but 'is the booking desirable?' Can you do better than take the booking on offer? There have to be clear instructions on the systems, besides the simple question of what's been sold and what hasn't. If there's no space on the system, then there will have to be notices on the walls.

5   Don't conceal the fact that you don't know how to use the systems. Plato said of Socrates that he was the wisest man in the world because he knew he knew nothing. We are all idiots. So if you don't know how it works, get someone to teach you. You can't have responsibility for company policies placed in the hands of staff whose only qualification is that they know how to use the IT. If you go into what is happening in detail, you will often find horror stories.

Property management systems (PMS)

These are hardware and software packages that help you to operate every aspect of your business better. Fidelio is a typical example. PMS don't just help you with sales and marketing; they enable your administration, purchasing, accounts and almost everything else to be tightened up. On the information the PMS provide, you can set up a *yield management system* (YMS). Also there are solely sales and catering systems, like Delphi.

The problem is that a PMS is normally very expensive for a small company to install. Equally unfortunately, it is nearly impossible to run a good YMS without a PMS downloading the information it collects and collates onto the YMS.

Of course, there is no reason why you shouldn't collate the information with a pen and a ledger; there was a world before computers and the information you needed before making up your mind was identical with what you need today. The point it that a computer can do the statistical work for you very much faster. And it can take into account almost every conceivable element which will affect your conclusions.

Yield management system

So, there are a number of computer software products you can buy which will help you achieve the optimum level of yield management. It is a very grand phrase, but all it means is that you set out to get the most money you can from selling your products. That has, of course, been the objective of landlords since time immemorial.

The principle is that you decide in advance, for example, how many bedrooms you want to sell at what price on every day of the year. You may look after travelling businessmen and Short Break holidaymakers, tourists from overseas and FITs (foreign independent travellers). Some guests may be prepared to pay rack rate, and weekend prices are usually – but not always – lower than midweek. The problem is that prospective guests book at different times in advance.

In the spring you may get offered, say, a group of American tourists who want to visit you in the summer of the following year. Do you want them at the price the travel agent is prepared to pay? Well, not if you can get better business from your corporate market on the same nights. Can you get better? Well, if for the past 10 years you have been full on those nights because it is the middle of the Agricultural Show, you may well be able to do so. But have you kept the records? If not, it is more difficult to make the right decision.

The YMS is really a large and complicated calculator. It encourages you to keep all the records and take into account a number of factors in addition to the state of play last year on the same day. The demand then may have been affected by residential conferences which may – or may not – occur again. It may have been a very wet Easter that year, or business was very good from Italy and now the lira has crashed, so the Italians can't afford to come now in the same numbers. The one thing we'd all agree is that few sensible people run a hotel on the basis of first come first served. You have to plan, and the more detail, the better.

There may be a pattern in the number of non-arrivals you receive and you may get similar numbers of people leaving unexpectedly. You may have patterns in cancellations, and some agents may never perform well in filling their allocations in the shoulder months, or on Monday or Thursday. All these factors need to be taken into account in deciding your policy. The YMS makes this possible by doing all the statistical work for you.

But, remember, yield management doesn't work unless there is sufficient demand. You may decide that you will sell half your rooms at corporate rates, 10 per cent at rack rate, and 40 per cent for bus and travel agent groups. So you have now sold the 40 per cent of the rooms for bus and travel agent groups and you get offered some more. Do you take it or not? You turn it down if you think you can fill the rooms at higher rates. You take it if the computer screens for future bookings on the nights in question tell you that it is very unlikely that your original plan is going to work. There is, undoubtedly, a great deal of profit wasted by making the wrong decisions. Your records may show you that the higher priced business only comes in within 7 days of arrival. The bird in the hand is there, but the birds in the bush aren't late yet. You may well have to take the risk and turn down the bird in the hand.

The YMS can tell you the pattern of bookings, but re-member the proverb about lightning striking twice. You may have a favourite Japanese travel agent whose tours are always up to numbers. But will they automatically be next year? Probably not if the Japanese stock market collapses. It is the economies of the countries from which tourists come that affect the level of traffic flows. You need to watch their economic positions.

There will be many occasions when the situation will change. You will plan on the basis of what you expect to happen, but somebody will start a revolution, or it will be the worst winter since 1712, and you will have to think again. Alternatively, demand may be beyond your wildest dreams and you will be able to stop taking the cut-price business. You make the decisions, but the yield management system gives you the good advice you need to make the right ones.

Good yield management requires a lot of monitoring. Here's a salutary example. A hotel had to outbook a client. They offered it to a hotel with a very advanced yield management system at £100. The yield management system gave the response that the booking could be taken, but only £65 should be charged, because it had worked out that was the best the hotel was going to achieve that day!

What we can definitely see coming in the future is a new programme on the World Wide Web which will enable you to collate all your information without the need for a PMS in-house. Instead of the cost of the in-house hardware, software and servicing charges, your terminals will simply be connected with a service provider within the web. When? About 2003 is a good guess. This will solve the problem which has been well described as islands of technology, where there are all manner of computers doing various jobs, but they can't talk to each other.

Summary

The new technology has got to be mastered. It is going to be the way we do business in the future. What proportion? We don't know. But as it is quicker, simpler and easier when you get the hang of it, every year is likely to see its popularity with customers grow.

It is almost inevitable that the elements of the technology will get cheaper as time goes by. You only have to think of the original cost of videos, computers and answering machines, and what you can get them for now, to see that this will happen. If you can delay buying without endangering your competitive position too much, it might be worth waiting. But the early bird catches the worm and if your competition gets too far ahead of you, you will never catch them up.

Certainly, the key to understanding the new opportunities is not to be ashamed to admit your ignorance. We all have a lot to learn, and always will have.

Case study

This case study illustrates:

- The difficulties of the learning curve with the new technology.
- Some of the problems to be avoided with websites.
- The difference between the public's perception and that of the hotel.

One of my clients is a major international hotel chain and more and more of their business is coming through their website. They have spent a great deal of money on developing their technology and it's a very attractive screen to call at on the Internet. These are, however, still early days in the development of effective websites and so, if you don't mind, on this occasion I won't tell you which company it is.

To see how their website worked, I decided to try to book a room at a major European hotel on a Friday night in June. I brought up the website and when I specified the date and the type of room I wanted, the screen filled with no less than 35 options! There were rooms overlooking the lake, the mountains, and the swimming pool; there were standard rooms, and rooms on Businessmen Floors; there were suites and penthouse suites. Then each category was divided into different options; Special Value, Corporate Rates, Rack Rates, Special Offers and the Banqueting Guest Rate. Incidentally, the prices for the lake- and mountain-view rooms were identical.

Well, what would you do with such a choice? It's very likely that a lot of people would go for the lowest price – let us say £100 for a standard room. So I tried to book that Special Value rate and the appropriate screen told me that such a bedroom was certainly available. The only thing I should know about it, said the screen, was that if I decided later to cancel the booking, I wouldn't get my money back.

I think we can agree that a lot of potential customers wouldn't like to take the risk. I mean it may well happen that there is a need to change your plans. So I went to another screen and asked for the next lowest rate, which was the Corporate Rate. That was available too – so long as your company actually *had* a Corporate Rate. Assuming that I was a private customer – very likely for a weekend booking – that wouldn't be any good either.

So I tried a third option. But would you? Isn't it far more likely that you'd switch off in frustration and try another hotel? So what's the solution? That the Home Page warns you of the restrictions which apply to the various rates. Don't let the customers find out when they go to the trouble to move on to the appropriate screen.

There also seemed – even with 35 options available – to be a category missing. Where was the Weekend Rate? So I rang the hotel and spoke to the relatively junior member of staff who had the responsibility of loading all these rates onto the Website for every day of the following year. I asked him where was the Weekend Rate? He told me that as he didn't have that many rooms left for the Friday night, he had decided – good Yield Management – to leave out the low Weekend Rate and hope to get higher priced business. How much would the Weekend Rate have been, I wanted to know. He told me £200. Then why was the Special Value £100 rate available, so long as I didn't cancel it? He thought for a moment and confessed that I had found the obvious mistake in their system!

We talked about the confusion that 35 rates were likely to create in the customer's mind. Why were the Rack Rates all listed? Because the customers should be shown what excellent savings they were getting, he suggested. Then you have to balance the value of that with the creation of confusion through a plethora of prices.

In my opinion, it really isn't wise to leave websites to junior staff without adequate managerial supervision. One reason why this might happen is that management could find itself very swiftly out of its depth if it gets involved; or takes the view that it is better to leave oneself with the insurance of being able to blame somebody else if things go wrong. However, this is not a very professional approach. One way around this would be for the managerial staff to just go back to school and keep up with the state-of-the-art.

In selling, we know that it is always necessary to keep the case for buying the product as simple as possible. It may seem cynical to say that you should never underestimate the stupidity of the general public, but I would definitely include myself in such a description of the general public. After all, we do have a saying 'If all else fails, read the instructions' and most of them I don't understand for a minute. Can you get the best out of a video machine? Then, in my opinion, you're brilliant.

So keep the website simple, because a bemused client can always end an unpleasant experience by turning to another supplier. The other thing we know is that the Internet is changing people's attitudes. Because you can buy things so quickly on a good website, the public is becoming more impatient when it doesn't work as quickly as they have experienced with other organizations.

Some major hotel companies run their websites on an international basis, making it possible for, say, a client in Brazil to be able to book a hotel bedroom in Thailand. But their input is controlled centrally. A lot of reservation systems are based in Omaha, Nebraska and the international approach works very well. As long as the company realises that although English may be the international language, not everybody speaks it. You can find a hotel reservation website in Germany for an American chain which is entirely in English! Not surprisingly, there are many clients who will turn off and look for a website in German.

The key to getting your website right is to look at it from the point of view of the average customer. In that guise, would you understand precisely what was on offer? Can you read all the information or is some of the lettering too small? Is the wording set out in clear colours? Books are printed in black lettering on a white background, because that is easy for the eye to read. A website with the occasional section of a page in orange lettering on a red background is almost impossible to read. So the average client will not bother to do so.

The fact that hotel reservationists know precisely what is meant by the material on the website is no guarantee that this will apply to the public as well. We used to say that you should check understanding by using a 14-year-old guinea pig; an average child. The problem with websites is that the 14-year-olds probably know more about them than their parents and grandparents!

7 Banqueting sales

Every Conference and Banqueting (C&B) Department gets enquiries from the public. The best guess at the national average for converting those enquiries into definite bookings is a figure of around 33 per cent. For every three handled, the department loses two. So, there is plenty of room for improvement.

Converting enquiries

To maximize your success in converting enquiries, you first need to have a control system to establish how well you are doing. You, therefore, need an Enquiry Book.

If you introduce a Conference and Banqueting Enquiry Book the efficiency of the department in converting enquiries can be easily identified. The enquiries are put into the book as they come in. There should not be a separate page for each date. When one date is completed, the next one should start automatically. In this way, nothing can be left out.

A typical set of entries would look like this:

FEBRUARY 17th

Company	Type & No.		Date	Sales Exec.	Result
SHELL	CONF.	50.	May 18	A.B.	Conf.
IBM	DINNER	120.	Sept 13	C.D.	Canc.
ICI	PRESS CONF.	40.	Aug 12	E.F.	N/A
BP	LUNCH	170.	May 10	A.B.	Conf.

FEBRUARY 18th
etc.

When do you produce the results? Not on the first of the month following, because the record for the month of February might read like this on March 1st:

Enquiries	120
Confirmed	18
Cancelled	14
Not available	35
Provisional	53

This gives you no picture of the actual performance of the hotel because the provisional bookings may be confirmed in the future or they may be cancelled.

The position on May 1st will be different. It might then read:

Enquiries	120
Confirmed	44
Cancelled	40
N/A	35
Provisional	1

Now you can work out the conversion rate. It is 44 out of 85.

N.B.: The rate is not 44 out of 120. You cannot hold the department responsible for getting bookings where the space wasn't available and the client wouldn't change the dates. The conversion rate is, therefore, in this instance 51 per cent.

The procedure for maximizing enquiry conversions is as follows:

1 If the enquiry comes in by letter or fax, you ring the client back immediately to start the sale.
2 You must try to get the client either to (a) visit the hotel, OR (b), if the business is valuable enough, see a sales executive. Sending details should be considered a failure to sell effectively.
3 You also want to know what other business the client may have for you.
4 What bedroom accommodation could you get with the banqueting?

If a client comes for a showround, the chances of getting the business go up to about 70 per cent. If they come for lunch or dinner, up to 80 per cent. So you need to decide at what level of profit you want the client entertained – lunch or dinner.

The Telephone Call Report (TCR) provides your working sales document.

Prepaid reply cards (PPRCs)

At many functions, more bedroom bookings from guests can be obtained by persuading them to accept prepaid reply cards.

Two types of PPRC should be printed: one for wedding guests and one for other banquet guests. Examples of the two types are attached as Appendix A at the end of the chapter. PPRCs should never appear to have come from you. They should always appear to have come from the client. Anything that spoils this impression reduces the chances of obtaining bookings. If it comes from you, it's an advertisement. If it comes from the client, it's a recommendation. Hence the wedding PPRC is phrased as the hostess would write it. The other PPRC core wording should be overprinted – as illustrated in the Appendix – with:

- The name of the event.
- The signature of the organizer.
- The crest of the organization.

Customer benefits, to be used by the sales executive promoting the cards, are:

- No cost to the client.
- No postage cost to the guest.
- No paperwork for the organizer, as the cards are returned to you.
- (Slightly) reduced tariffs for the guest.
- Non-arrivals are not the responsibility of the organizer.

To make the importance of bednights even more apparent,

every Banqueting Department should have an annual bednight target.

Bringing back the old business

This is fully discussed in Chapter 1 on the marketing plan. If there is nothing definitely planned for the future, you need to contact the client quarterly to see if things have changed.

From a sales point of view, you discuss the last function when you contact the client to try to bring the business back. You do not do so on the morning after the function. If you do it then, any minor problems are fresh in the client's mind. At the decision-making time, the good and bad aspects of the last function will be in proportion. Normally, of course, the good will substantially outweigh the bad.

Even when you first meet or talk to the client, you can start on the market research. Certainly, when you have a definite booking from a client, you should be able to find time to ask about other business.

Selling aids

There are many aids available to you when you are selling conferences and banquets. You do not need to rely solely on your prices and the quality of your banqueting rooms. Indeed, these can suffer in competition with lower prices and more exotic banqueting rooms on offer from your competition.

Whenever you are having difficulty in securing a function, the necessity is to offer the clients sufficient additional advantages to sway their decision in your favour. We are back to Value Plus. So what are these additional advantages that could be used?

Creative banqueting

A birthday cake is the simplest example of creative banqueting. It differs from other food in that it is personal. It helps the organizers of the birthday party to achieve their most important objective; to make the guest of honour feel that something has been done just for them.

Creative banqueting does not have to be expensive for the client. It does take a deal of imagination from you. If your own chefs are too busy, or not sufficiently experienced, to produce the creative banqueting items, you can usually find a craft teacher in your local Hotel School who will be happy to do the work for you.

Here are just a small selection of creative banqueting ideas:

- Something different from coffee and biscuits – small Florentines, Eccles cakes, doughnuts, shortbread, etc.
- The use of frozen carbon dioxide for smoke out of funnels, making cold dishes colder while giving the impression of getting hotter.
- Alphabet rolls – spelling clients' names on side plate rolls.
- Alphabet soup – spelling names out in pasta letters, e.g. IBM, ICI.
- Coloured ice cream – using a liqueur like blue curacao.
- Macaroons – company names on rice paper on the bottom: 'Eat your own words'.
- Sugar work, ice work, butter work or working in chestnut purée.
- Crests and names in: gelatine (oeuf en gelée), icing (cakes), pastry (boeuf en croute), coulibiac, cheesecake, custard (crème caramel).
- Flambé dishes – cerise Rothschild.
- Salade Mikado – with edible chrysanthemum petals.
- Client's crest or name on flags on masts on pineapple boats.
- Chickens paraded on swords.

There are non-food creative banqueting ideas as well:

- Unusual cabarets – wine tastings, horse racing films, mock casinos.
- Silk screening menus on serviettes.
- Dyeing carnations any colour.
- Condiments pouring from tins manufactured by the client.
- Dishes named after the client – Pêche Melba.

This stunning piece of creative banqueting only involved putting a pastry case over a leg of lamb to make a snail (*Source:* Crystal Cruises)

- Tablecloths and drapes in client colours.
- Different shaped menus – triangles.

Making the client a hero

When organizers book banquets, it is in order to achieve objectives. Often these objectives are far more important than the cost of the banquet; improving company ésprit de corps, getting important buyers into the right frame of mind, improving the image of the organization, launching a new product.

Why, then, do they make such a fuss about prices? Because they do not realize that you can do anything else to help them achieve their objectives. The client believes that one hotel is much like another. You have to prove that this is not the case. You can either do this when you talk to the client over the phone or in person, or you can do it when you write to them. It is often believed that the letters you send in response to enquiries are less important than the Conference and Banqueting Pack. This is not true. The covering letter is more important.

Better letters

Let's see how the rules for writing letters in the chapter on direct mail apply to banqueting. Look first at a simple letter which we can send the client in response to an enquiry (Letter 1).

Notice that the next action is left in your court; you will phone the client in a few days rather than wait for the client to phone you.

Many clients need more elaborate letters than this, though. They need more professional help from you. It is perfectly true that such letters take a good deal of time to construct. That time is well spent, however, if the result is a large piece of business. Letter 2 is the right standard of letter when you face this problem of the complicated function. In this letter, we have been able to do a great deal more to convince the client to use the hotel. Notice:

1 The importance of the letter to the client is the help it gives him to solve his problems. There is plenty of 'you' appeal. There are 32 'you' or 'your's in the letter but only 12 'me's, 'I's' etc. (If your charges include service, then it's 'your Head Waiter' and not 'our Head Waiter'.)
2 You have reassured the client you realize just how important the event is to the company: 'absolutely essential ...' (paragraph 1).
3 You have rubbished the efforts of your competition, where

Letter 1   *THE STRETCHED OUT PALMS HOTEL*
17 High Street, Warmington, Leicestershire

TNT/LASS   1st June 2000

Phil. E. Busta, Esq
National Association of Flint Knappers
17 Doddle Street
Fosschampton
Wiltshire

Dear Mr Busta,

As we discussed on the phone, I was delighted to see that you were thinking of using the Stretched Out Palms for a conference. This is, certainly, one of the most popular hotels in the district; in the last few months alone, we have looked after companies like Titanic Shipbuilding, Pompeii Construction and San Andreas Faults Inc.

Naturally, every conference is different and you will have particular objectives you want to achieve. A good hotel can do a lot to help; by careful logistics – keeping to timetables, providing the right food or the right visual aids at the right time, looking after the VIPs with the greatest care. Also by its imagination in creative banqueting. There are so many ways of getting over a message by use of the menu; a simple example would be to put the company's logo into a pie crust, on icing on a cake etc. What is more, it costs nothing to find out what can be done for your own meeting.

Another very important point for many companies is the necessity, particularly in these days of increased competition rates, to keep strictly to a budget. We specialize in making sure that you don't go one penny over the figure you have set aside.

You will find the hotel's Conference Pack enclosed with this letter. This gives you a lot of information about the hotel in general, but you would obviously want to see the rooms at first hand before making up your mind.

When, therefore, you've had a chance to consider the brochure, I'll give you a ring to see if you can spare the time to visit us. Alternatively, if you'd like one of our conference specialists to call on you to offer some additional help, I can arrange that as well.

Kindest regards

Toni Travers and
Conference and Banqueting Manager

Letter 2 *THE STRETCHED OUT PALMS HOTEL*
17 High Street, Warmington, Leicestershire

TNT/LASS   1st June 2000

Arnold J. Pudderwick, Esq
Samson Farming Equipment plc
Overunderwick
Shropshire

Dear Mr Pudderwick

It's good to know that you're thinking of using the Stretched Out Palms for a launch of the Green Gnome next year. Quite obviously, after such a tremendous investment in its development, it's going to be absolutely essential that the launch is a great success.

You will find details of the rooms we have available at the hotel enclosed with this letter, together with sample menus and a wine list. These are, however, only really appropriate for the everyday functions and that's hardly going to be suitable this time; your Chairman will want the arrangements to reflect the corporation in the best possible light.

Could we start with the Bush Room. You should have no difficulty getting the Green Gnome into the ballroom and we could provide you with a stage 60 feet wide, 6 feet high, and 30 feet deep. It can take weights of up to 2 tons, if necessary, and it has a proscenium arch and curtains, plus a wide range of lighting equipment. The microphones are available in many forms, depending on what system suits your speakers best.

Obviously, you will want your guests to remember the name Green Gnome. Here, you can take advantage of the skills of the hotel's Maitre Chef, Alfred Legrand. You could, for example, have a Green Gnome carved in ice work in the Reception Room, and this could be of almost any size. It should make a considerable impression. We have the time to have salt and pepper sets made in the shape of Green Gnomes for each table; they could also be souvenirs for the guests to take home. As you will probably want tables for 10 at the dinner, the words GREEN GNOME could be spelt out by getting the bread rolls made in the shapes of the appropriate letters, rather than in the round or plaited variety.

A model of the Green Gnome equipment itself could be made in butter work, chestnut purée and a number of other materials. Photographs of such models often attract the attention of the technical press, as you know. Another thought is that, if you decided to have a consommé in the dinner menu, we could put pasta 'G's in it – Consommé Samson, perhaps.

BANQUETING SALES

You'll want to know about costs. Could I make it very clear that the Stretched Out Palms is happy to take on the responsibility for ensuring that you don't overspend your budget. This could be seen as self-preservation; after all, you're not likely to ask the hotel to do another function for you if you're unhappy with the final account. Your budget is sacrosanct.

If you're not providing hotel accommodation at the expense of the company, the farmers will be making their own arrangements. If they did stay with us, there could be a reduction on your account. All that would be needed is to send your guests details of the hotel when you write to them in the first place. You will find enclosed a typical card we produced for IJI recently, along the same lines.

With a major launch coming up, Mr Pudderwick, you're, naturally, going to be extremely busy. On the other hand, you're not going to want to use a hotel without examining its facilities very carefully. Could I suggest that you visit the hotel and see for yourself. I'll give you a ring in a few days to see if a suitable time could be arranged. I'm sure there's a lot more that you'd like to know, and I look forward to meeting you.

Kindest regards

Toni Travers
Banqueting Manager

they have only sent a Conference Pack and a standard covering letter: 'only really appropriate for the everyday functions ...' (paragraph 2).

4 You have reassured the client that you do realize that the Chairman is involved in this one and that even more special care will, therefore, be necessary (paragraph 2).

5 You have said more to reassure the client of your skill, both in terms of audiovisual aids and creative banqueting.

6 You have come up with a lot of good ideas to get over the client's message.

7 You have reassured the client that, notwithstanding the importance of the event, you'll try to ensure his budget is not exceeded (paragraph 6).

8 You have tried to arrange for him to call.

9 Notice again that, throughout the letter, you could say every word to the client.

Presentation Books

One of the most important aids to selling is a good Presentation Book. This book should be used to prove the quality of the hotel and to illustrate aspects of the hotel's facilities which might otherwise not be visible, i.e. if a room is needed for a dinner and is set up for a conference when the client sees it, a picture of the room set for a dinner will be better than relying on the client's imagination.

This book should have the following material in it:

- Complimentary letters from satisfied clients.
- Favourable press comment.
- Pictures of creative banqueting.
- Pictures of VIPs in the hotel.
- Examples of prestigious menus, served to past functions, on the original printed card.
- Photographs of the rooms and floor plans.
- Sample menus.
- Details about the bedrooms.

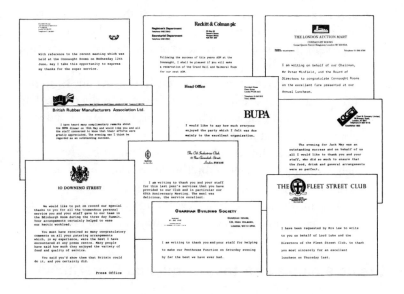

Is there another product in Britain endorsed by the Prime Minister's Office in 10 Downing Street? (*Source:* Connaught Rooms)

The books should not have any plastic material in them. The pictures should not be covered in plastic, nor should the cover. Plastic, in this form, looks cheap. The book should be large enough for the material to be attractively displayed.

Menu Selectors

Everybody has their favourite dishes. You have no way of knowing if the sample menus you are sending to clients contain dishes they dislike. A Menu Selector lists all the dishes you can serve with the appropriate prices. Clients can then select the dishes they enjoy. It often happens in such circumstances that a client will actually choose a menu which is more highly priced than they first intended.

Helping the clients sell tickets

Many clients – charities, clubs, etc. – sell tickets for their functions. Quite often, they have little experience in how to go about doing this. They know little about producing quality promotional material. If they fail to sell the tickets, it is your turnover which suffers. If they sell more tickets than they expected, the organizers would recognize that you deserve the credit if you help them to do so.

There is, therefore, a strong case for having shell promotional material available which can be given to the client. The type of material that would be needed is shell posters and suggestions for direct mail. If the client could increase the sale of tickets by some limited advertising, you might be prepared to help with the cost of this. You should see your contribution in terms of the profit you would make from additional covers.

A client who has a successful event is more likely to come back to you next year, to see how you can help them do even better.

Create a display for the Banqueting Department

The Presentation Book helps you to persuade the client that you are selling a good product. The whole atmosphere of the area where you're doing the selling should work equally well on your behalf.

Clients are often nervous in hotels. They find both the atmosphere and the staff superior and intimidating. Your objective is to get them to relax and enjoy their visit. For this purpose you need to discuss the event with them in pleasant surroundings; a special room for the purpose is ideal. In it there would be no desk; instead, there would be a coffee table and armchairs. The clients would be seated nearer the door; it makes them feel more secure. On the walls there would be further examples of the material you put in the Presentation Book.

Entertaining and showrounds

When the client actually comes to see your facilities, you have the best chance of getting a booking. Throughout their visit, you are working on two separate fronts: on the one hand, you want to make the best presentation but, on the other, you have to be on guard against anything going wrong. Telling the client that your service is wonderful if no brown bread has arrived with the smoked salmon, isn't easy.

Here then is your entertaining and showround checklist for making sure the visit is a success.

Checklist
1 Why are you lunching the client? Have your checklist with you.
2 Be at the door to greet him or her. (You don't want the client grilled with 'Do you have an appointment?')
3 Take your Presentation Book with you.
4 The client goes first. (You are not the great white hunter leading an expedition into the jungle.)
5 The client sits down first.
6 Always face the client.
7 Watch for the body language messages.
8 In the bar are there nuts, crisps, olives and gherkins set out?
9 Make sure the client has the right drink.
10 Is the glass dry? (Water dripping on the client's jacket doesn't support your claim of excellent service.)

11 If you are showing facilities, make sure that the lights are on when you get there.

12 Make sure there is a table in the room on which to put your Presentation Book.

13 The client goes first into the restaurant.

14 Does the client have a serviette and a roll?

15 Offer the à la carte as well as the table d'hôte: 'I'm sure you have your favourites. They'll be on the à la carte if they're not on the table d'hôte.'

16 Offer wine and mineral water.

17 Ask what the client enjoys particularly.

18 Watch for absentees – croûtons, mustard, sauce, vegetables, butter, cutlery, brown bread, etc.

19 Quickly correct errors of service.

20 Keep to business as long as possible. The client didn't come to enjoy your company.

21 Fill in the market research form as much as possible: e.g. Who else needs hotel space – other departments? When else does the client need hotel space – social, club, etc.?

22 Offer liqueurs and cigars.

23 If two clients appear to be ready to make a decision, leave them on some pretext so that they can talk privately.

24 Ask for the business whenever and wherever you spot a buying signal. Remember there are lots of ways of closing a sale.

25 Don't be afraid to make notes.

26 See them off when they leave the premises.

27 Get them a taxi or point them in the right direction.

Banqueting policies

Remember to decide:

1 Minimum numbers on busy days.

You sometimes make more money if you don't always take the first bookings available. On Fridays in December, for example, you want as near a full house as you can get.

2 Minimum lengths of days in busy periods.

There are certain weeks when the demand for conference space is very high. To take one-day conferences may prevent you from taking two- or three-day meetings. From your records of what you have turned down in the past, or from your general experience, you should be able to decide what minimum standards to set.

3   Days where banquets have to carry bedrooms.
As the profit from F&B is about one-third of bedrooms, you need to use the sales of banqueting rooms to maximize your occupancy whenever possible. There are times during the year when demand is sufficient to turn down non-residential conferences. You have to specify what those dates are.

4   Policies on conference organizing companies.
These are companies who offer conferences to the general public on various topics. If the public buy a place on the conference, the company runs the course. If they don't, the course is cancelled. Such business can be very costly to you if it is cancelled, because you may have turned down an alternative booking. What is your policy?

5   Photocopy the Banqueting Enquiry Sheets rather than retype the Weekly Function List.
Where the Weekly Function List is coming straight off the computer, it is not a very time-consuming job for C&B to produce it. Where it has to be done manually, it is: several hours a week, a couple of hundred hours a year. That time could be better spent on other sales tasks.

6   Do you put in the accents on the Kitchen French dishes? If the French words are not in capital letters, you should.

7   Many departments still create their letters by writing them out by hand and then giving them to a secretary to transcribe. This is terribly time wasting by comparison with the use of a dictating machine. It takes time to get used to a dictating machine, but the time saved can be used to much better effect. The letters sound far less formal as well; it is easier to write jargon than speak jargon.

8   What sort of language should you use for banqueting contracts?

The image you want to give is of a friendly, informal, caring, helpful company. The language of a banqueting contract is designed by lawyers to enable you to win in court. Your friendly image is often shattered by the tone of the contract. This isn't necessary. You can protect your rights perfectly easily and still use pleasant phraseology.

Banqueting checklist

Here is your Conference and Banqueting Department checklist to make sure C&B is selling efficiently.

Checklist
1   Banqueting Enquiry Book:
   – Is it being kept up?
   – Are the statistics being produced?
   – Are there too many old enquiries which have yet to be converted?
2   Are there Telephone Call Reports on the walls for:
   – All the enquiries you want to convert.
   – All the old business you want back.
   – All the bookings you had to regret or which were cancelled.
   – Is the work up-to-date, i.e. the trace date for the top sheet of the TCRs should be for tomorrow's date. Today's you should have removed to work on.
3   How many companies have accepted PPRCs for their functions? Look at the diary and the Enquiry Book and identify enquiries where PPRCs could have been sold.
4   Has the Reception Manager been checking the Banqueting Diary to try to identify bookings where you could have sold bedrooms? This is different from (3) because the Banqueting Diary includes rebookings which may not have been entered in the Enquiry Book.
5   Have you produced a banqueting policy?
   – What are the minimum numbers during peak periods for the rooms?

HOSPITALITY SALES AND PROMOTION

  - When will you only take residential conferences?
  - When will you take anything?
  - When do you want two, three or more nights long bookings rather than individual days?
6 Have the Banqueting Department personnel been given a bednight target to achieve? If so, how are they getting on in trying to achieve it?
7 Is the staffing sufficient for the selling job to be done properly?
8 After entertaining, you should complete as much as possible of the market research form. (See Chapter 2, Organizing a sales office.)
9 Is there a proper Presentation Book? Does it have the right material in it?
10 Do the selling letters contain:
  - Customer benefits?
  - Correct spelling, grammar and punctuation?
  - Do you suggest that a member of the sales department could call?
  - Do you suggest the client comes for lunch?
  - Is the next action in your court?, i.e. 'I will ring you in a few days ...'
  - Do you talk of the client's objectives?
  - Do you make any creative banqueting suggestions?
  - Do you mention bedroom accommodation?
11 What action is being taken to bring back the old business?
12 How is the research programme progressing, as far as old business is concerned?
13 Have you a display where the banqueting clients are talking about their functions?
14 Are you holding weekly provisional review meetings?
15 Are you now dictating onto recording machines, and not handwriting your letter? Sales ability is more important than fast typing.
16 Are the correct accents on the French menus?

Summary

Effective banqueting selling involves the maximum understanding of both selling techniques and product knowledge.

The function organiser is looking for an expert and, therefore, whoever is selling the banquet has got to be able to answer all the questions which the client will be throwing at them.

As the public have difficulty in distinguishing one property from another, it is important to come up with fresh ideas, fresh wording in the sales letters and to have a clear understanding of the client's objective and needs.

You cannot maximize your success in this area by treating all the customers alike. It is when customers recognize that they are not seen as so many mouths to fill, so many people to seat and so many guests to sleep that they warm to you.

Appendix A

Prepaid reply cards (PPRCs)

These cards are serrated in the middle and the bottom half can be detached and sent to the hotel. One side of the bottom half has the name and address of the hotel. The other side has a booking form.

The third side talks about the prices; e.g.

Wessex Flint Knappers Annual Dinner/Dance
Stretched Out Palms Hotel, 14th November 2000

We have arranged for the following prices to be available at the hotel:

Twin Bedded or Double Bedded rooms:	£45.00
Single Rooms:	£35.00

All the bedrooms have private bathrooms and the prices include English breakfast and VAT.

(The card comes from the Honorary Secretary or the Director General, not from you. So, notice that they would talk about 'prices' and not 'tariffs' and refer to 'private bathrooms' and not 'en suite bathrooms'.)

The fourth side carries the message from the organizer.

Obviously, the wording has to be approved by them and the signature of the organizer of the function lends even more credibility to the card.

The message from an organization or association might read:

Wessex Flint Knappers Annual Dinner/Dance
Stretched Out Palms Hotel, 14th November 2000

I have made special arrangements with the Stretched Out Palms Hotel for a number of rooms to be available to members at reduced prices. If you would like to take advantage of this, you need to complete the form, which is pre-addressed with the postage paid, and send it to them. The hotel is very attractive and I'm sure that they will look after our members very well.

Charles Fortescue
General Secretary

A message from the bride's mother to the invited wedding guests might read as follows, with the second paragraph added, if you would also like to fill some more rooms on the Friday night. The hotel pays for the champagne.

Bedroom accommodation if you'd like to stay
overnight

I have made special arrangements with the Stretched Out Palms Hotel for a number of rooms to be available to our guests at the wedding at reduced prices. If you would like to take advantage of this, you need to complete the form, which is pre-addressed with the postage paid, and send it to them. The hotel is very attractive and I'm sure that they will look after us very well.

It does seem a shame that we are only all together for weddings and then for such a short time. So I thought that it would be a nice idea to have a Champagne Breakfast on the Saturday morning for all of you who are staying on the Friday night. I've taken care of the champagne and I hope to see you then.

BANQUETING SALES

Case study

This case study illustrates:

- The necessity to try to offer something different from your competition.
- The importance of Creative Banqueting.
- The importance of making the product personal to the client.

The installation of a new Archbishop of York is a very important eccelesiastical event. On one occasion the guests at the dinner after the installation were served part of a marzipan model of St. George and the Dragon for dessert. The year? 1466! Creative Banqueting has been part of our traditions for a very long time. Can't you see that Outside Caterer going up to the Bishop's palace and saying 'If you give me the business, I'll make your guests a marzipan model of St. George and the Dragon'?

Another great artist in Creative Banqueting was the French chef, Carême, who served George IV for a few years during Napoleonic times. Carême produced the most fantastic models in a variety of food products. I know of no more powerful weapon when you're competing for important banqueting business.

Certainly, getting business from a hotel doing an already really good job for its client is the ultimate challenge. An example is the lunch for 350 given by the London Evening Standard to present their Drama Awards. Large functions in January are hard to come by in London and the prestigious Grosvenor House had really put itself out to do a first class job the previous year. Staff enjoyed serving film, theatre and TV stars, money was no object to the newspaper for this important occasion, and everything had gone beautifully in the Grosvenor House's lovely ballroom.

The problem was to get it away to my hotel, which was

really not as good, though just as expensive? I arranged an interview with the Editor of the paper.

'The key to this function,' I told him 'is that we shouldn't serve petits fours after the dessert.'

'Why aren't we serving petits fours?' said the Editor, intrigued. He was an elegant, sophisticated man who knew his food.

'We should serve macaroons.' I said 'On the bottom of the macaroons there is rice paper and on the rice paper I would propose to stamp the words "Evening Standard" in vegetable inks; perfectly safe to eat. Then when you make your speech, you can invite all the judges, the ones who voted for the Best Actor, the Best Actress, etc. to eat their own words!'

The Editor loved it. A good literary joke, linked specifically to the function. He couldn't resist the idea of making the sally at the microphone. And, indeed, it got a big laugh. He moved to my hotel. You will normally find that if most organizers buy into a Creative Banqueting idea, they'll give you the business, even though they could get their existing hotel to do exactly the same thing for them.

On another occasion, I sold a moderate hotel for a dinner where the bill came to the present-day equivalent of £100 a guest. For £100 the client could have gone to the best hotel in the city, so why did he choose to give the business to me?

The function was to celebrate the launch of a new lighter; I'm sure Dupont still do something similar. When I had identified this information, I said to the client 'If we could give that party, I'll make you a model of the lighter in Chestnut Purée and we'll parade it before the guests. And where the flame usually is, we'll insert a candle and then the lighter will come on lit.' The client couldn't resist that either.

Equally impressed was the organizer of a Naval academy graduation dinner in New York. On that occasion, the kitchen came up with an ice cream model of a warship, but with a difference. Inside the funnels the chef put some dry ice, which is frozen carbon dioxide and inexpensive. Before parading the ship in front of the guests, the chef poured a little water on the dry ice; the result is that it melts and, in melting, it smokes. The ship was paraded with smoke coming out of the funnel.

The football team I support plays in a blue and white strip. We once won a minor league championship and the Chair decided to have a dinner to celebrate. The decision had almost been made to use a very expensive hotel when I saw the opportunity to sell my own first.

'As we play in blue and white,' I suggested to the Chairman 'we should have a blue and white dish in the menu.' How would you go about that, I wonder? Not blue flowers, artificial colouring or table linen, but in the food. I suggested that we make ice cream footballs and that half of them should be made with Blue Curacao, a liqueur which tastes of orange, and the other half with Orange Curacao, which is white and also tastes of orange. Blue and white ice cream. We got that one too.

Creative Banqueting must always be genuine, though. My relations with IBM as a client were always warm and friendly. They're a very nice company. One day we were given a 1,000 delegate conference by an IBM executive who had never organized a darts match in his life! For the next eighteen months until the conference took place, I did my sheepdog act, trying to keep the client from getting himself into dangerous situations.

One day he asked me for a German menu for his 350 German delegates. I made the case against this idea: 'If I was in Germany, I don't think the average hotel would make a very good Irish Stew or Yorkshire Pudding. The delegates would compare the dishes with the best they'd had at home and find them wanting. You'd do better to let the chef produce a delicious menu of the dishes he does do well.'

'I don't know,' said the client 'I asked another major hotel for a German menu and they didn't make the same objection. Here's the menu they're suggesting.' I looked at the menu from the other hotel.

'How much did you say your budget for this menu is?' I asked.

'$50.55.'

'I couldn't do this menu for that', I said.

'You'd be more expensive would you?' asked the client.

'No.' I said 'I could only charge you $35. It's not worth more than that.'

Total collapse of the case for the other hotel. They'd seen an inexperienced organizer and set out to pull the wool over his eyes. When he knew the truth, he wouldn't go near the opposition with a barge pole. We got the business and it wasn't a German menu.

The importance of Creative Banqueting was illustrated on another occasion when a luxury hotel in Paris was offered a piece of business by a major Museum for the first time. They were overjoyed at getting such a famous organization to give them a chance.

The catering management, together with the General Manager and the Head Chef, sat down for a long meeting to plan a fantastic menu. When everything had been agreed, one of them said 'Why don't we have the side plate rolls in the initials of the museum. Like "L" for Louvre, or "P" for Prado.'

'That's one of Derek's ideas', said the General Manager. 'Still, it can't do any harm.'

So they agreed on that and I saw the General Manager after the lunch had taken place.

'How did it go?' I asked.

'We were rather disappointed' said the General Manager 'We produced an absolutely fantastic menu and the only thing they talked about were your damn rolls.'

But then my damn rolls were the only part of the menu that had anything to do with the client.

8 Direct mail

Where potential clients organize large conferences, it is worth your while talking to those clients personally. They are going to spend a lot of money and the profit will more than pay for your time. Where potential clients are only going to spend money on eating out with their partner, going on a Short Break Holiday occasionally, or joining a Leisure Club, however, you can't stop every man or woman in the street and try to persuade them to use your product.

This is when you need *direct mail*. It is the cheapest way of reaching a large number of potential clients. As this is also the case for any number of other sectors of the economy, there has grown up a direct mail industry to serve them, and the firms involved have spent untold fortunes learning what works and what doesn't work. Every tiny detail has been monitored, tested, argued over, researched and refined. As a result, it is possible to lay down tried and tested rules for the successful construction of direct mail campaigns.

There are two stages; planning the campaign and writing the direct mail.

Planning the campaign

When you start to produce your campaign, you need to ask yourself six questions.

1 Who do I want to send it to?

2 How am I going to find out their correct names and addresses?

3 What am I going to say?

4 When am I going to send it to them?

5 How can I get it to look right?

6 How will I know if it worked or not?

Who do I want to send it to?

Over 90 per cent of direct mail normally finishes up in the waste paper basket. *If you send it to the wrong people, the percentage of waste simply increases.* So target your market. If you're trying to get more business people for lunch, it probably isn't worth sending the promotional material to former Short Break holiday visitors. The idea that 'sending out direct mail can't do any harm, even if they're not interested' is only true if you stop thinking about the effect on your bank balance.

Don't try to fool the client that the letter is personal if it isn't. If you send it to someone by name, that's fine. If you can't, don't start 'Dear Sir ...' or 'Dear Guest ...' because that still doesn't make direct mail personal.

How am I going to find out their right names and addresses?

Building up a mailing list takes preplanning.

Existing users

You could, for example, ask a guest who pays the account in the restaurant with a credit card if he or she could give you their address: 'Would you mind if I put down the address as well, sir?'

Few promotions in the restaurant are sufficiently dramatic to attract guests who might have to stay overnight in a hotel. So those guests who ask for the account to be put on their hotel bill are not right for mailings for Mother's Day lunches or St Valentine's Day dinners.

Direct mail letters can be used, for example, for those people who announce engagements to be married in the newspapers. Or collecting business cards for a prize draw will produce a good mailing list over a period of time.

Registration cards are an excellent source for your mailing list. Use the information when you're selling Christmas or Easter programmes. Remember, though, not to include on the list overseas visitors. They're not likely to come from that far away for the event.

When guests come for Christmas lunch, book for Easter, or bring parties for New Year's Eve, put their names and addresses on *separate* mailing lists. Then you can be sure to write to the correct market. You can decide to add people from other lists as appropriate.

It is important to try hard to keep your mailing list up-to-date. Changes of address may be notified by the Post Office, clients may move on to different responsibilities. Keep cleaning (updating) the list.

Buying mailing lists

It is always possible to buy mailing lists from mailing list companies. The quality of these lists, however, differs alarmingly.

When you buy a mailing list, make sure that it is:

- Addressed to the name of the client, and not just to a job title: i.e. 'Dear Mr Jones' not 'Dear Managing Director'.
- That it has been recently updated. You don't want a list that hasn't been used for 5 years. Potential guests change addresses and jobs.

Additional sources for lists

You can buy a Kompass Register which lists all the companies in each town. The information normally includes the names of the directors of the companies.

Many Year Books for associations have lists of members. These can also be used for specific promotions.

Keeping the list

Ideally, you should keep the list on a computer. Have the names and addresses typed onto the computer in such a way that printing them out can also give you a set of labels.

Envelopes

When you send the direct mail out, it is worthwhile overprinting the envelopes. Have a coloured frame in the centre so that the label looks part of the design. Also put a headline on the left hand side that sums up the main advantage of the offer.

> 'Take your sweetheart to dinner on St Valentine's Day'
> 'It's time to say "thank you" to Mother'

If you're sending out material that is larger than normal post, don't squash it into the size of envelope you usually use. The material will arrive creased and unattractive. In such circumstances, you need cardboard backed envelopes. They're much more expensive but they ensure that when the material arrives, it looks as good as it did when it left your office. If you're in any doubt, send the material to yourself first and see how it arrives.

What am I going to say?

Whatever you're going to say, remember two vital points. When the potential clients have finished reading what you have sent them, they must:

- Understand what you are selling.
- Understand how to buy it.

*Don't worry about how long your direct mail letter is. It doesn't matter if it's two or three pages, **as long as it remains relevant and interesting.***

In writing good direct mail, what takes the most time?

As much as 90 per cent of the time you devote to a direct mail letter may be taken up by deciding what you want to say and in what order you want to list the customer benefits. The other 10 per cent of the time would be enough to actually write the letter. What you're going to say is what matters.

So, how do you start to write good direct mail? Ask yourself the following questions:

1   What does the customer need that the product can satisfy and what are the most important needs, in priority order?

Remember that emotional needs are often more important than physical ones; saying 'thank you' to Mum is the reason to take her out for a Mother's Day lunch, not the calories. Successfully concluding a deal with their guests is usually more important to a business person entertaining than the quality of the wine list.

2   What's your Unique Selling Proposition? Why are you better than your competitors?

3   What benefits are you offering? You could try, for example:

- Overcoming shortcomings: e.g. Why spend money on a directors' dining room at the office when we could do the same job for you at the hotel.
- Avoiding breaking the law: e.g. Stay overnight and don't risk the breathalyzer test.
- Improving profits: Spend the extra money on a really good conference room and you'll achieve your objectives more easily. (A good conference room is what it *is*. Better profits for the organizer is what it *does*. Always say what it does, rather than what it is.)
- Incentives to staff: e.g. Get a better performance from your staff by spending money on some aspect of our product.
- Value for money. There are good marketing people who believe that the price should go into the direct mail letter early on. Others think it should go in later. All agree it should go in.

4   Can you make a good offer?

5   If not, can you say something of exceptional interest?

6   Are you using the name of your product often enough in the copy?

When am I going to send it to them?

You need to create a programme for your direct mail campaigns. Obviously, some direct mail action will be created as a result of new ideas. A number of the mailings, however, you can anticipate because they are annual events.

If you plan well in advance, there is less chance of errors arising because you are pressed for time. You, therefore, need a plan that will include:

1   What types of mailing are you going to send out?
2   When do you need the first draft?
3   When are you going to approve the final draft?
4   When are you going to print it?
5   When are you going to post it?

How can I get it to look right?

Obviously, the most important thing is to make it easy to read. Here are some ways to achieve this:

- Make sure there are wide enough margins.
- You could divide the letter up into columns – like a newspaper.
- Use a serif typeface.
- Keep the same style of typeface throughout.
- Break up the long blocks of copy with crossheads (small headlines).
- When you make your points, don't use 'and ... and ... and ...'. Use asterisks, number the points, or use circles or bullets.

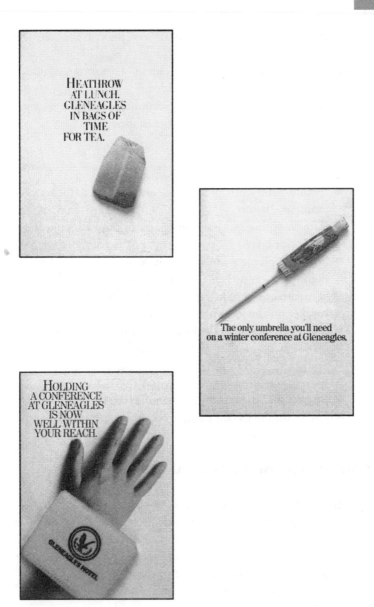

Here is some of the best direct mail produced in the industry over the past 10 years. The first piece was used to say the hotel wasn't far from London and had a real tea bag on the front. The second publicized a new Leisure Centre with a real cocktail umbrella. The third linked the conference potential with the leisure facilities, using a real tennis sweat band (*Source:* Gleneagles Hotel)

DIRECT MAIL

- Indent the paragraphs, i.e. don't start them at the side of the page.
- Make sure that if you use a coupon, it's easy to cut out.
- Make the coupon look valuable.
- If you are producing a flier as your direct mail piece, vary the size of type, the colours and the shapes.
- Cartoons get the most attention.
- Don't forget the headline.
- Photographs are more convincing than drawings.
- 'Before' and 'After' pictures are very convincing. (For example, 'Before' = hurrying with luggage from a train. 'After' = sitting in a comfortable bedroom with your feet up and a drink.)
- 'Reward' pictures are better than 'problem' pictures. (For example, a 'reward' picture might show the client being congratulated. A 'problem' picture might show him watching a speaker on the lectern in the conference.)
- One large picture in the flier is better than lots of small ones.
- People staring out of pictures attract attention.
- Something odd in the picture attracts attention.
- Extreme close-ups attract attention.
- Be sure that the illustration demonstrates the product.
- Use testimonials (the complimentary comments).

How will I know if it worked or not?

We don't know all the answers when it comes to direct mail. We know it ought to be sent out three times. *If you have the option of sending direct mail three times to 1,000 people or once to 3,000 people, you will get better results from sending it three times to 1,000 people.* Of course, the wording is different in each of the three mailings, but the message is, fundamentally, the same.

Successful direct mail involves a lot of patience. It is the classic example of 'if at first you don't succeed, try, try, try again.' KEEP trying to improve the quality of your direct mail. KEEP trying by writing to your potential clients again and again.

We don't know how lavish the direct mail piece ought to be

in every case. Sometimes a simple letter is fine. Sometimes it may be better to send a leaflet or a flyer. Only experimenting will prove what is best in each instance. Therefore, it is very important to keep records, so that your successor has the advantage of your experience. Make a record. It should include in the folder:

- The method you adopted.
- An example of the material.
- The results you obtained.

Of course, this means that you have to have some way of knowing whether the promotion worked or not. These can include:

- Application forms.
- Records of phone bookings kept by the executive responsible for taking them.
- Comparative covers, compared to the previous year, or the previous period.
- Vouchers handed in.

You will know if it worked or not by the number of bookings you get as a result. Notice that the criterion is bookings . If you ask the recipients to send you back a coupon for more information, getting thousands of coupons shows you the direct mail shot certainly aroused a lot of interest. If, however, you send the information and not enough people book, the whole effort will still have been a failure.

It means, of course, that two things have to be right:

1 You need to make sure that there is a means of measurement every time you send out direct mail.
2 If you ask for a response, you need to know in advance how you're going to deal with it.

It is no use getting thousands of coupons and then having one or two people to dispatch more information. If the potential clients want more information, they want it quickly. Preferably by return of post. Requests that arrive in the morning, should be dealt with *that day*.

Knowing how many bookings you received as a result of the mailing is the first step. The second is to know whether you made an overall profit at the end of the day. If a reasonable response won't give you a reasonable profit, it may well be a good idea not to start the campaign in the first place.

Test marketing

Sometimes there may be disagreement on what is the best way to phrase your message. Two, or even three, headlines look attractive. There is no harm in trying all three approaches, so long as you can test which of them produces the best results. For example, send one approach to all the people on your list in one city, and the other to the list for a different, but similar, city. Then see which draws the most business.

Back winners

A lot of advertising doesn't work in spite of all your efforts. The money which is lost is considerable. So, if you do get a winner, keep doing the same thing until the success starts to taper off.

For example, if a flyer (small leaflet) produces a larger response than an advertisement, keep sending flyers till they begin to tail off. Then consider a different approach for another flyer, as well as the alternative of an advertisement.

Last thoughts on the planning

Right, now finally ask yourself these questions, and answer 'yes' to all of them, if your direct mail is as good as it should be.

1 Have you included every possible reason for the recipient to do something?
2 Have you taken nothing for granted?
3 Have you made it as believable as you possibly can?
4 From the very beginning did you give the impression that it was urgent that the recipient took some action?

5 Do your words say what your pictures show?
6 Is it simple to buy the product?
7 Have you made your message absolutely clear? Another way of saying this is 'sedulously eschew obfuscatory hyperverbosity or prolixity'. It still means make it clear.
8 Have you shown it to your friends and asked them to criticize it?

Writing the direct mail

There are 39 rules for writing good promotional material. You need to know them all and practise them every time you construct a campaign.

Content

1 Before you write anything, make a list of:
- What are the advantages of what you're selling to the customer?
- Which are the most important to them, in priority order?

2 Be sure to have all the details you need. When, what, why, how much, and what's included?

3 Take the most important advantage and turn it into a headline. For example: People are afraid that drinking alcohol is bad for their health – hence 'Guinness is good for you'. People want clothes to look clean after washing – hence 'Persil washes whiter'.
   You can't make people do what they don't want to do. You can't change the benefits in order to offer them something they don't want. Even if it's a speciality of the chef, if the public won't eat it, they won't.

4 The headline say what the product does. Not what it is. They're not selling refrigerators; they're selling fresh food. You're not selling a restaurant; you're selling mouth-watering food.

DIRECT MAIL

5   If you possibly can, get the word 'you' or 'your' into the headline. (In the 100 best advertisements ever written, the words 'you' or 'your' appeared in 45 of them. The next most frequently used was 'how', with only 18.)

6   When you write your letter, the group of words 'I', 'we', 'my', 'us', 'our' and 'me', should be outnumbered by the words 'you' and 'your' by a ratio of 1:4.

For example: You don't say 'I am enclosing the brochure and we pride ourselves on the quality of our cooking and the professionalism of our staff' *but* 'You will find the brochure enclosed and you can be sure that you'll thoroughly enjoy all your meals and you can rely on the professionalism of the staff').

7   Give the reader facts, not generalizations, and don't lump all the benefits together.

For example: You don't say 'We have the latest audio-visual equipment and we can offer superb cuisine' *but* 'You can have every kind of audio-visual equipment from back projection and Autocues to OHPs and a stage 15 metres wide, 4 metres deep and 2 metres high. You should also enjoy the cooking because your Head Chef, Albert Street, has many medals won in culinary competitions.

8   Remember you're writing for a single reader. Not 'Guests can enjoy ...' *but* 'You can enjoy ...'.

Style

9   Write the way you talk. If you wouldn't say it, don't write it.

For example: just try *saying* 'The facilities you require are detailed in the brochure which I enclose for your perusal.'

10   Be consistent in the tone you use. It is confusing to the reader to sound chummy in the letter and then sound like the Old Bailey in the Terms and Conditions.

'You'll have a great time and it should be a brilliant evening. A

£10 non-returnable deposit is required per guest and must arrive before December 1st.' That is an example of not being consistent!

11   If you are using a quotation, get it absolutely right. Otherwise, don't put the quotation in inverted commas.

For example: the quotation isn't 'A little knowledge is a dangerous thing', it's 'A little learning is a dangerous thing' (Alexander Pope).

12   Use endorsements whenever possible, rather than the reader having to rely on the hotel's description of how good it is.

For example: Don't say 'The hotel is renowned for its superb cuisine' if you can say 'The Mayor was kind enough to say recently that he was very impressed with the dinner'.

13   Get plenty of enthusiasm into the copy.

For example: Filet de sole Veronique is not 'Poached fillets of sole in a white wine sauce with green grapes'. That's the recipe. It's 'Delicate poached fillets of fresh sole in a delicious white wine sauce with succulent green grapes'.

14   Avoid tautology, i.e. don't say the same thing twice.

For example: '... serve her a complimentary meal free of charge'.

15   Good writing is concise. Don't use unnecessary sentences. Nor unnecessary words. Make every one tell.

16   Use bullet points.
   ● A
   ● B
   ● C
not 'and ... and ... and.

17   Use guile to keep people reading.

For example: '... and then there's a special offer of ...' – but the special offer is on the next page.

18   Make it sound easy.
'All you have to do …'

19   Don't use hospitality industry jargon.
For example: 'you would like your guests to pay for their drinks before dinner', not 'there will a cash bar for pre-dinner drinks'.

20   Don't order the clients about.
You should never say 'you must …' or 'we require …'. It should be 'we'd be grateful if you would …'.

21   Don't use 'from …' as in 'from £40'. Use 'about £40'. If you say 'from …', most people believe there won't be anything decent at that price.

22   Use simple English language terms. Say 'a guest', not the Latin word '*per* person'.

23   Use 'carrier' words and phrases – '… and then there's more …'

24   Use the present tense whenever you can:
For example: You should say 'The bedroom is lovely' *not* 'The bedroom will be lovely'.

25   Don't lie.
'A special introductory offer' in the depths of the winter doesn't fool anybody. 'The New Year's Eve Gala costs £75, including a free half bottle of wine with dinner' is, equally, not a credible claim.

26   Ideally, not more than 25 per cent of the words you use should have more than five letters in them. Short words are simple to understand. (You will find they are easier to spell too.)

27   Don't use the same large word twice.
For example: Not 'accommodation … accommodation … accommodation', *but* 'accommodation … bedrooms … rooms').

28   Don't be negative if you can be positive.

For example: You don't say 'we cannot guarantee your rooms will be available before 3pm' *but* 'we can guarantee your rooms will be available after 3pm'.

29   Don't use words you don't understand. If in doubt, use a simpler one.

For example: If you write a menu dish explanation as 'sole complimented by Tartare sauce' you are saying the sauce admires the sole. You mean 'sole complemented by Tartare sauce'. So, in this case, you can't go wrong with 'sole with Tartare sauce'.

30   Don't use the words 'persons' or 'people'. You should refer instead to 'guests', 'visitors', 'delegates', 'holidaymakers' and 'tourists'. They're warmer words.

31   Don't use the telegrammic style, as in 'complete attached form'; it should be 'complete the attached form'.

32   Don't hype up the product unless you can live up to it.

For example: 'Superb cuisine in a magnificent ballroom with impeccable, professional staff' is a tall order for anybody!

Lay-out, punctuation, grammar, spelling

33   Indent the paragraphs; your letter will be much easier to read that way.

34   If you are writing a long letter, use cross heads (small headlines).

35   Punctuation makes it far easier to understand what you are writing about. Use it properly.

36   Get the accents right on French menus. (The best book for this is *The A–Z Gastronomique* by Sharman & Chadwick. Sadly, at the time of writing, it is out of print but you might be lucky enough to find an old copy somewhere.)

DIRECT MAIL

37   Keep your first sentence to no more than 13 words. No sentence should have more than 24 words. Over 24 words, only 4 per cent of the readers understand the sentence the first time they read it. Use short paragraphs too. Remember, this is for writing direct mail. Books have different rules!

38   If you use different lengths of line, it will make your letter stand out.

39   Restate the most important benefits before you end the letter.

The personal selling system applied to direct mail

The personal selling system we discussed in Chapter 4 applies to direct mail as well. Now let's write a letter and see how that works. This time the acronym is slightly different: **DIPDA**.

Define

'Much as your guests may enjoy the result, nobody brings in caterers for fun.'

Identify

'You may be raising the *ésprit de corps*, entertaining VIP clients, strengthening the company's image or marking an important anniversary or a special event.
   When it matters like that, you need Outside Catering which will work hard to help you achieve your objectives.
   You need the team from the Splendide.'

Prove

How good is the food?

'Between them, our chefs have 116 years' experience.'

How good is the service?

'Well, we're very proud of the fact that, in 2000, the hotel was chosen for the Rutland Trufflers Dinner. Not to mention the Ochester Hospital Ball and the Ancient Order of Bedmakers Luncheon.

What's it going to cost?

'Everybody has a budget. So will you. The best is never cheap, but then achieving your objectives is worth a lot as well.'

Desire

'We're extremely flexible. You can have any kind of food you enjoy All we really need is a reasonably equipped kitchen on your premises. Though we've coped without one before.

You can either provide your own equipment, china, cutlery, glass, etc., or it can all be brought to you.'

Action

'Why not come and have a chat? Or, if you'd rather, we'll come and talk to you. Just give me a ring on (09999) 322 3622.'

In what sequence do people read direct mail material?

The important points in a direct mail letter are not dotted around in a haphazard manner. Research has proved that the majority of people look at direct mail in the following way:

1 They read across the top
2 Glance down the right-hand side
3 Read the PS (if any)
4 Glance up the left-hand side

5 Look at the crossheads
6 Then, if they're still interested, they read the whole letter

This means, of course, that your headline, PS and crossheads are very important. They have the best chance of being read and, if they capture the client's interest, the rest of the letter is more likely to be studied.

Building the business lunch market

You might well like to fill your fine restaurants more at lunchtime. One obvious sector to approach is the business lunch market – clients who are entertaining their guests with the intention of achieving an important objective, such as selling their products, dealing with their suppliers, investors, officials, etc.

Suppose you were trying to persuade a bank manager to give your company £1 million. What sort of facilities would you want the restaurant where you were entertaining the bank manager to provide? You would want:

- Quiet.
- Privacy.
- Unobtrusive service.
- Your guest greeted warmly.
- Your guest's favourite food on the menu.
- Your guest's favourite drinks available.
- A bill as high or low as your guest rate.

So what sort of a direct mail letter might you produce to get over all those advantages to a potential client? An example would be the letter opposite.

There are a number of points to notice about this letter:

- It has a headline that encapsulates the main customer benefit.
- The first line will get the client saying 'yes'. That's important too. You need the client to agree with your first statement. Colleagues do make fun of executives who do a lot of enter-

IF BUSINESS LUNCHES ARE A MILITARY EXERCISE, HOW GOOD IS YOUR ARMY?

A lot of nonsense is talked about Business Entertaining. All those jokey remarks about long lunch hours and feasting at the company's expense. You know – and I know – that Business Entertaining is a very serious exercise. I make no apology for dealing with one of your most effective management tools at some length.

You've got a couple of hours to make your case without interruptions. A short time to gain agreement on matters often vital to your company. Two hours concentrated work, where a single slip can lose you the case, the contract, the compromise or the profits of winning.

So how much help is your present restaurant? Certainly, the food and wine will be good. They'll greet you warmly and serve you efficiently. What more can any restaurant do?

The back-up

At The Boulevard Restaurant , a very great deal more. Let's agree the essentials first. The restaurant needs to be quiet enough for your guests to listen to your case with ease. If a restaurant is too noisy or if the music is too loud, your guests can't hear themselves think. Then, it's got to offer you a degree of privacy; we've plenty of tables where you won't feel you're being overheard.

What sort of service? Few restaurants come up with the right answer. You want unobtrusive service. When you're coming to the crunch, you don't want to be interrupted by a waiter asking 'Is everything alright, sir?' at the crucial moment. If you don't want to stop talking, my waiters will come back when you're ready; no diversions to force a cease fire.

Your guests

There's more to the back-up your battle plan will get from here. Tell me the name of your guest, and he or she will be greeted like a long lost relative – or less effusively, as you brief me. Give me a ring in advance and tell me what you want. If the guest feels comfortable and relaxed, it's going to make your life easier. If your guest has a favourite dish, likes a particularly obscure drink, we'll produce it; just say when you ring.

Both the food and the wine here are first class. The bill, though, is your decision; there's a good *table d'hôte* for £12 if you're budgeting carefully. There's also some Corton '47 for £250 a bottle if the game is worth playing for high stakes.

What do you do now? Come and meet me at the hotel. Try the restaurant out. Mobilize the army, and see how much help you can get to win your next battle. When you need back-up, come to a restaurant that really understands what it's about.

Kindest regards

Emile Latour
Restaurant Manager

taining all over the world. The potential clients you're writing to will agree with the first statement – and read on.

- Developing the point, you show that you understand the importance of the entertaining process.
- You haven't criticized the competition. To do that is to query the client's judgement.
- You have broken up the copy with crossheads – the small headlines – to make the amount of copy look easier to read.
- You have carried on the military theme in the headline – 'cease fire' and later 'battle plan'.
- You have got plenty of 'you' appeal in the letter. There are 36 'you' and 'your's and only 10 'me', 'we' and 'I's.
- There is a call to action at the end: 'ring me ...'. Which means that there is a way to measure whether the letter works or not.

Either they ring or they don't. Either you suddenly do a lot more covers or you don't.

Two last points here:

1 Like all direct mail, you need to send three letters on the same subject. They will all give the same message, but they will use different words. In this instance, send them about 2 weeks apart.
2 Be sure that the restaurant phones will be answered whenever the clients ring, and that whoever answers knows what you've offered.

Getting all this right may seem a pretty hefty task. It will all seem worthwhile, however, when those positive replies come in.

Case study

This case study illustrates:

- The development of a direct mail campaign.
- The rationale behind the construction of a direct mail letter.

In many countries school teachers mark the end of the school year with a party. Before the British hotel company, Stakis, was taken over by Hilton, there was a very successful direct mail exercise developed because of this. It started with a single enquiry to the Banqueting Department for a party in July by a school. The General Manager, who wasn't accustomed to doing business with schools or to getting much banqueting work in the height of the summer, identified the reason for the enquiry. So often this doesn't happen. You get business when you expect to be empty, but don't meticulously find out every time why it is being offered to you. If you are offered business by Division 8 of the Meat Traders, where are Divisions 1–7 going?

So the market for school teachers' parties was identified. Now a database was needed. How do you get a list of schools in the district? From the Local Education Authority. You say you have moved into the district and would like to know more about the available schools. Could you have a list please.

Now you have your list and have to decide when to send the letter. Logically, a party for the end of the summer term isn't going to be organized in the spring term. For many reasons, schools organize events at comparatively short notice. So the beginning of the summer term seemed the right time to write. And that's when the hotel had got the initial enquiry anyway.

Remember, you should write three times – at, say, weekly intervals. The same product but a slightly different message every time. So, first, second and third weeks in May.

Now you need to turn to what to write. What are the parameters?

1 This is a party for fun. It isn't a serious exercise.
2 For this market you can use a wider vocabulary and perhaps more sophisticated humour.
3 You don't want the letter to sound too commercial. Commercialism and the school market don't mix very well.
4 Teachers treat direct mail like anybody else. Most of it goes into the waste paper basket and you only have 4 seconds to get their attention. So a powerful headline is important. You will have an advantage, though, over a lot of direct mail efforts in that you're writing at the right time and the teachers are going to buy the product – though, not necessarily, from you.

So, the illustration shows the letter that was sent in this case.

About 20 parties were booked as a result of sending out this letter. You can't prove why this happened but the thinking behind it is easy to explain.

The headline is an adaptation of a phrase which comes from *Through the Looking Glass*. Lewis Carroll's two 'Alice' books are among the most popular books in the English language and, therefore, the first reaction of the reader should be warmth and affection. You've allied yourself with a friend of the reader.

The second point is that the letter is fun. The teachers are organizing an enjoyable event rather than an educational one. It's important that they recognize that the writer isn't stuffy and formal because they don't want the party to be like that.

The letter also is literate. Teachers are literate and people like to work with organizations where they can feel there is common ground. The letter also illustrates some understanding of the school words, with references to government demands and the stress of exam

Hilton
Croydon

The end of term - Oh, frabjous day! Calooh! Callay!

Admittedly, the quotation celebrates the end of the Jabberwock rather than the end of term. Nevertheless, the sentiments are apt and you will, no doubt, be rejoicing.

We do rather a good line in rejoicing at the Hilton; for example, if your party is for more than 10, you'll have a free bottle of champagne. A seriously well cooked 3 course repast is £9.95 and you should then be past caring about the exam results, further government demands and whether public hanging could be reintroduced especially for that hulk, Jones, in the Upper Fourth.

These celebrations – either for lunch or dinner – are extremely popular at the Hilton. We had the pleasure of looking after many such gatherings last year and while it would be a pleasure to look after you as well, a little advance warning would be much appreciated.

Could I suggest, therefore, that you give me a ring, so that you can consider the various cornucopiae (I'm presuming that cornucopia is first declension) and nectars which are on offer.

Kindest regards

results. The reader can feel that the hotel isn't a distant stranger.

The letter is full of mild jokes; 'rather a good line in rejoicing' and 'public hanging for that hulk, Jones'. It even has a mild Latin joke – which may be the only Latin joke ever used in direct mail – and contains unusual words like 'apt', 'sentiments' and 'advance warning'. Not to mention describing the food and drink as cornucopiae

DIRECT MAIL

and nectars; words that you don't often find in letters from hotels. There are seven 'you's in the letter, so that the reader recognizes that you're interested in them, as personalities, and not just in 'guests' or 'persons'.

In no way is the letter what is often described as 'hard sell'. It is informal, jocular and friendly. It is a letter specifically aimed at the market it is approaching. You wouldn't use anything like it if you were trying to attract the gatherings of mourners from Funeral Directors.

9 Advertising

If you are unhappy about the results of your advertising efforts, you could well say 'But I'm not an advertising agent', 'I'm not a graphic artist' or 'I'm not a copy writer'. You may not even be working in your own first language. So the temptation is to try to muddle through, or depend almost entirely on the skills of advertising agents.

Unfortunately, advertising agents may know all about advertising, but most know very little about advertising hotels and restaurants, banqueting and bars. To make matters worse, as your budget is likely to be comparatively small by their standards, a lot of them are tempted not to put their best people onto your account.

We have fooled ourselves about the results for years. We have not bothered too much about whether the money we spent on promotion came back in increased profits. We have often told ourselves that the publicity would have a cumulative effect, that if this or that promotion was not particularly successful, it would still lead to better turnover in the future.

But advertising costs too much money to settle for that. Also, there are tremendous financial advantages if you are the first in your area to get your advertising right. But how do you go about it?

You have to learn the rules of good advertising. Yes, advertising has rules , just like the *Guide Culinaire*, and you ignore them at your peril. Disobey the rules and the advertising is very likely to be a total waste of money. Like any other aspect of your business, to be successful with your advertising, you have to try very hard to get everything right. That isn't easy. As Benjamin Franklin said, 'Perfection is made up of little things. But perfection is not a little thing.'

To be successful you should take account of these 10 vital points:

1 The average reader only sees three advertisements in a newspaper or magazine. Therefore, yours has to be powerful.

2 The first objective at the beginning of an advertisement is to win the reader's attention. For this purpose, you need a good headline and, whenever you can afford it, a good photograph. *Research shows that the reader gives you, on average, 4 seconds, to achieve this.* No, there is not much room for error!

3 Don't generalize. The more facts you tell, the more you sell.

4 Never waste an inch of space or a single word in an ad. Who needs the post code for a restaurant ad? Leave out the 00 in 10.00. An advertisement always benefits from having plenty of white space; don't waste that white space on unnecessary words.

5 If you can't say it, you can't write it. There are NOT two English languages, one for talking and one for business letters. There is only one.

6 The three most important elements in an advertisement are the *headline*, the *picture* and the *caption* under the picture. Four out of five readers never get beyond the headline!

7 When you are trying to write copy for the guests, imagine you are talking to a typical member of that market: jazz freaks, connoisseurs, gourmets, drinkers, etc.

8 In advertising, telling the truth isn't enough. You have to get the reader to believe the truth. Believability leads to conviction which leads to sales.

9 The effect of your advertising should always be to get the reader to do something, to take action.

10 Your overall objective is to move the reader through a number of stages: unawareness – awareness – understanding – conviction – action.

Planning an advertisement

There are three elements to planning an advertisement:

- Before you start
- Image
- Measuring success

Before you start

Decide
- What image do you want your advertising to convey?
- Will the potential clients see the advertising at the time they are making their decisions?
- What are your USPs (Unique Selling Propositions)?
- What are the customer benefits for the type of business you are going after?

Remember
- All advertisements *have* to answer the questions when, where, how much and what does it include?
- You are always writing copy for a single reader. It is personal to the reader. Queen Victoria disliked her Prime Minister, Gladstone, because 'He always addresses me like a public meeting.'
- It doesn't matter how long an advertisement is, so long as the copy remains relevant and interesting. You may have to tell the readers a great deal about the product, or it might be very simple to explain. The amount of copy will vary accordingly.
- The effect of your advertisement must be to get the reader to *do* something; to take action.

Image

What image do you want to portray? There are all kinds, so let's keep it simple; you want the readers to believe that your operation is:

- **Friendly:** Formal language, rules and regulations drawn up in stiff, legal terms, together with phrases like 'you must ...' or 'we require ...', are not friendly.
- **Clean and hygienic:** But is all your promotional material absolutely clean? No marks on your posters, the glass and frames kept polished, no stained menus?
- **Efficient:** If the material fails to give the client all the information they need – where, when, how much, etc. – it isn't efficient.
- **Professional:** That means the spelling, punctuation and grammar are always perfect.

Check and check again that you are maintaining your image.

Now, when you come to check the material, if you have planned your advertisement properly, *you should be able to answer all the following questions.*

1 Is the advertisement aimed at the consumer or the trade?
Remember the customer is less sophisticated than the trade.

2 Which target audience are you going for?
Whichever medium you use, there will be lots of people reading/seeing it who are not interested in your product. Those readers are known as *waste circulation*. You want to keep them to a minimum because you are still paying for them as readers. So decide who you are trying to reach, and then choose the method of getting to them with the least waste circulation.

3 When do you want the business?
A lot of restaurant advertising only results in more guests coming when you may well be busy already – Sunday lunch or Saturday dinner. The real benefit, of course, is if you can increase the covers when you are quiet. Linking the advertising to special attractions is, therefore, often a wise move.

4 How far in advance do you want the advertisement to appear?
Plan the advertising campaign well in advance. That way you won't be rushed into decisions because of a lack of time to change them. You also won't be too late to attract the market.

5   What is your advertising objective?

6   What are your customer benefits?

7   What could you advertise as a benefit that your competitors don't?
   Not that they *couldn't*, but that they *don't*. For example, few hotels quote favourable press comment in their advertising. They seldom mention the awards their chefs have won in national competitions. Yet these are more credible examples to the public of your quality than just telling them you think you're marvellous!

8   Is there enough time to produce it?
   A lot of advertisements fail to produce results because they appear too late. The clientèle has made up its mind already.

9   If you are producing the advertisement in cooperation with another organization, have you remembered to plan what you have to put into the advertisement for *them*?

10   Can you afford it, and how are you going to measure the success of the advertisement?
   We need to know far more, all over the world, about the volume of advertising which will produce the best additional profit. So you must know whether the advertising is successful or not. Failure is inevitable on some occasions; not all advertising works, no matter how carefully planned. You must learn more about it, though, and that means finding a way of measuring success. We will come to that in a while.

11   Will there be a coupon in the advertisement?
   Coupons can be returned and this gives you some idea of the interest your advertisement has aroused. It does not tell you how much of the product you've sold. Only statistics on the coupons converted into definite bookings tell you that. Coupons do involve the reader, which is good. Before you coupon an ad, ask yourself 'who is going to deal with the coupons?'. There is nothing worse than receiving coupons clipped by clients and then not getting the material to them

quickly enough. As the coupons come in, the material should be posted the same day.

Coupons should be put at the bottom of the advertisement, on the outside edge, highlighted with a large bold border, and given a code which identifies to you that they came from that particular advertisement.

12   Does the magazine have a Reader Card which can be filled in and sent to you?

13   Is it possible to use reprints of the advertisement for other advertising purposes?

For example, if you get reprints of an advertisement for your restaurant, these could be used as a direct mail shot for your Regular Diners list. Find out from the publication how much reprints would cost you. Remember that there isn't likely to be a great deal of additional cost if you take large numbers; the difference between 1,000 and 5,000 run-ons should be quite small. Sometimes, if you want a comparatively small number, you can get them free by asking the publication for overruns.

14   Are you going to make a special offer?

15   Have you assessed the dangers of dilution?

Say you offer a low price for a dinner. Because of the number of people who buy the offer, you don't have enough tables for the guests who would have paid the normal higher price. Those lost profits from the higher paying customers are what happens when you 'dilute the market'.

Measuring success

The question that needs answering is this: *How much money is it worth spending on advertising the product, in order to maximize the profit?*

If you completely sell out the product – restaurant promotion, Special Event, etc. – you will make an extra profit. Some form of advertising will take you nearer to that complete sell-out. But the advertising will cost money.

What happens if you spend too much?

Suppose that you can always rely on 100 guests for the New Year's Eve Ball. Suppose that your ballroom can take 200 guests. The extra 100 guests are not guaranteed by previous results. Suppose the profit from that extra 100 guests would be £1,000. (And don't forget that the profit does not have be reduced by the cost of the band or cabaret. That should be paid out of the revenue from the 100 guests you are certain to get.) In these circumstances, it would be foolish to spend £1,001 on advertising. Even if you filled every table, you would still lose money on the advertising.

So how much do you spend?

If you spend £1,000, you have to fill every seat. Somewhere between £1 and £999 is the best answer you can give at the moment.

In this instance, we are saying that an extra cover means a £10 extra profit. You obviously wouldn't plan to spend the whole £1,000 extra potential profit on advertising. You might start with £100; if you get another 20 covers = £200 extra profit minus £100 advertising = £100 extra profit nett. If you then spend £200 you might get an extra 40 covers = £400 extra profit minus £200 advertising = £200 extra profit nett. At some point you will maximize your extra profit. Your job is to find out where that point is.

Are there exceptions to this rule?

There is one. But don't say it exists if it doesn't. The exception is when there is a lot of increased competition. Now, you could be advertising in order to make sure that you are still going to get those 100 guests you normally attract. This is known as *defensive advertising*.

And how do you prove it was a success at the finish?

Whenever you finish a promotion, you need to produce a Profit and Loss Account on it. You need to list all your expenses and the additional profit from the extra income. Only in that way can you really know whether the promotion worked or not.

Promotion budgets

Let's take, as an example, a budget for promoting your restaurant.

It starts with monitoring the number of covers you did last year. Let's keep it very simple. Supposing the position looks like this:

	1999	*2000*
Jan	500 covers	450 covers
Feb	560	510
Mar	600	540
Apr	700	630
May	800	
June	900	
July	950	
Aug	950	

As you can see, you are running 10 per cent down on last year. Suppose, therefore, that in May you spend £2,000 on promoting the restaurant in the local newspaper, over a period of 4 weeks.

Now suppose the figures continue like this:

	1999	*2000*
May	800	790
June	900	920
July	950	920
August	950	870
Sept	900	840

What does this show you? Where, before you advertised, you were running 10 per cent down, you got back to last year's figures during the period of the advertising, and then you beat last year's figures in June. When the advertising was finished, there was still additional business in July but the position was back to almost the same as before in August. *But not quite.* You finished doing slightly better than your performance before the advertising. This means that you finished at a level slightly above what you could have expected if you hadn't advertised.

(When business continues to improve after the advertising has finished, we refer to an 'echo' effect.)

Now, of course, this is a very simple way of assessing results. There are a number of additional factors we could have taken into account:

● Bookings associated with an event taking place in the locality or the hotel either this year or last year. (Suppose, for example, you had a large exhibition in town last year, but not this year. Or vice versa. That is going to affect the figures and you need to analyse the covers each week to identify these special situations.)
● The weather can have an effect. (For example, if the weather was very bad and people stayed at home last year, but it was much milder this year, then that will have an effect.)
● If you had a Special Event in either year, this will have an effect.

If you are able to identify this additional information, so much the better. If you haven't got it now, remember you will need it the next time you try the same promotion.

Let's assume, though, that the two years were identical. Now you work out the additional profit you made from the additional covers. Don't put staff costs into your figures because you won't have employed any more staff to handle the additional covers. It is just the food and drink cost. Let's say, for the sake of argument that your average spend is £20 and your profit would be £10. Now the figures look like this:

	1999	2000 (with advertising)	2000 (without advertising)
May	800	790	720
June	900	920	830
July	950	920	855
Aug	950	870	860
Sept	900	840	820

We can estimate that your covers increased by a total of 255 – 70+90+65+10+20. If the additional profit was £10 a cover, then you have made an extra £2,550 for an outlay of £2,000. That would be satisfactory; you are building a market for your restaurant.

Now, in fact, most other industries would expect the pay-back to be over a much longer period. You have to consider the position where a restaurant is losing a lot of money. Unless you do something about it, this situation may well continue. Therefore, your investment in advertising will not only improve matters today but will also have a long term effect on the profits in the future. This can only happen, though, if you keep up the effort. Otherwise, the business will go back to the normal 10 per cent decline.

As the business starts to go back to the previous position, therefore, you need to have another advertising campaign. Let us suppose that you decide to spend another £2,000. Let's include the figures you would have had before you started to advertise again in August.

	1999	2000 (with advertising)	2000 (without advertising)
May	800	790	720
June	900	920	830
July	950	870	860
Aug	950	1010	860
Sept	900	1000	820
Oct	850	940	765

You have the same echo, but you started building your business from the higher base provided by the first advertising campaign.

See how the profits have now moved. Between May and July, inclusive, from the first advertising campaign, you did an extra 170 covers. At £10 profit a cover, you made £1,700 pounds profit against your £2,000 investment. From August to October, inclusive, however, you did another 505 covers – 150+180+175 – at £10 profit a cover, and that equals £5,050. Getting onto a higher plateau can make that much difference.

Records

It is essential that accurate records are kept of the restaurant business. Only in that way can you properly assess the results of your advertising. Here are the factors you should take into account:

- Any special events in the city or hotel.
- Any special events in the restaurant.
- The weather.
- The number of residents in the hotel. (The larger the number of residents, the more likely you are to get additional restaurant business.)
- Any tours in the restaurant.
- Any special celebration parties.

All these factors count if you are trying to compare like with like.

Promotional campaigns

Any advertising needs to promote a consistent message. They told us Guinness was good for us for 50 years. Your restaurant advertising needs to follow the same rule whenever possible. Stay with it till it stops working. All too often there are just one-off promotions. It's a 'Peruvian Gourmet week' this time; 'All the tagliatelli you can eat' next time; and 'Enjoy a free half bottle of wine' for the third effort. You need to decide a strategy for your advertising. What are you going to concentrate on? What is the USP?

There are many possibilities. Here are a few:

- The best T-bone steak in town.
- The best chefs in the country (because you won the championship).
- The Guide's favourite restaurant (with suitable quotations from restaurant guides).
- The best restaurant in which to entertain clients.
- A better standard of living ('Gracious living starts with dining at the Buckingham Palace restaurant').
- The prettiest restaurant in town.

The important thing is that you *have* a USP in mind and keep advertising it. If you try to please everybody, if you don't tell the public the Unique reason for visiting your restaurant, you

The headline must always include the most important Unique Selling Proposition, preferably in a striking way. You won't find a better one than this for the Mermaid Hotel in Rye in Sussex, Southern England (*Source:* Mermaid Hotel)

are going to have great difficulty in getting them to remember you.

Why should anybody read your advertising?

> 'A hotel is a place where they charge you $150 a night and call you a GUEST!' (Shelley Berman)

When people read advertisements, their sole interest is in the advantages to them of buying the product. They are not interested in the slightest in a hotel's high opinion of itself.

Customer benefits

You should not spend money on advertising to say how good you are. You should spend it on advertising how much you can do for the guests. Tell them what are the *customer benefits* to *them*. So you don't say 'Feast on our Austrian buffet' *but* 'Feast on a spectacular Austrian buffet'.

Distinguish between benefits and features

'24 hour Room Service' is a feature; whereas 'You can have something delicious to eat in your room at any time of the day or night' is a benefit. And benefits can be *emotional* as well as physical. Among the emotional benefits which have proved powerful attractions in getting business are:

- Belonging
- Approval
- Love of family
- Superiority
- Sex
- Food and shelter
- Self indulgence

ADVERTISING

Benefits differ according to the market

The customer decides what the benefit of the product is to him/her. You can't make the clients do what they don't want to do. If they have decided what the benefit is to them, that is the one we must try to satisfy. You can't sell a 'weight-watcher' puddings, but you can sell them calorie-controlled dishes. This still leaves you with the need to decide what the right benefits are. Thus:

All:	Complimentary comments from satisfied customers.
	VIP functions which have been with you for many years.
	The thousands of people who have enjoyed your hotel.
Weddings:	Making a good impression on 'the other side'.
Organizers:	Keeping to budgets.
	Keeping to timetables.
	The organizer will be congratulated.
	Their colleagues and peers will be impressed.
	We take orders from our clients, rather than give them.
	Helping them achieve their objectives.
	Making the client a hero.
Organizers and gourmets:	Awards won by your restaurants or kitchens. Use the chef's name where appropriate – 'Chef Solo Mio (6 gold medals at Hotelympia) recommends ...'

Make conditions into benefits

If there is no charge for children, or an extra night for 50 per cent of the normal price, those are benefits not conditions. Tell them what's special, in terms of fact.

USPs (Unique Selling Propositions)

Anybody can say they offer 'superb cuisine', 'a wide range of audiovisual aids' and 'magnificent service'. But if your chef won the Gold Medal in the Gobi Desert Haute Cuisine competition, other chefs can't always say they did too. If you have back projection facilities, others may not have. If you provide a hotel coordinator for every convention organizer, many of your competitors may not. Against those competitors, these would be the USPs to promote.

Even if they have the same USPs, it is still possible they don't mention them in their promotional material. Convincing arguments, like complimentary letters, often stay in the files. Everybody can promise to keep to the client's budget, but how many do? If you use the right arguments and they don't, you become the more convincing product.

Writing the words for your advertisement

Always remember there is nothing that will *order* potential clients to read your promotional material. In fact, you start off with the likelihood that they won't. Consider how much direct mail you throw away without giving it even a first glance. You won't remember many of last week's advertisements in the papers either. The dice are heavily loaded against all advertisers. Therefore, you have to work very hard to gain the client's attention and then to hold it.

You gain their attention with a good headline. A dramatic picture would come second, but the body copy (the main wording in an advertisement) comes a very poor third. Only 5 per cent of readers finish the body copy. That doesn't, of course, mean that any old copy will do, just because hardly anybody is going to bother with it! That 5 per cent is the small core from which you may get enough business to justify your expenditure. The fact that it is only 5 per cent just highlights how easy it is to fail completely.

Any rules that help you reach 5 per cent – or get all the way

ADVERTISING

up to 6 per cent – are vital for your success. Those rules are:

1 Make the copy easy to understand.
2 Make the copy lively and interesting.
3 Write good English.
4 Make it fun.

We will look at each of these rules below. There are two important points though, we should deal with here before we go on. Is English your first language? Is English the business language used in the country where the hotel is located? If the answer to either question is 'no' you need to take the following action.

1   If English is not your first language and you are writing the copy yourself, write it in your own language first and then have it translated into English. This is because you have a larger vocabulary, a greater choice of words if you write in your own language. You'll find it easier to choose the words you really want to use. If you then need to pay to get it translated by somebody who is bilingual, do so. The additional cost will be very small compared to the total cost of the promotion.

2   If the business language of the country where the hotel is situated isn't English, you have to ask yourself whether the recommendations I have made will be effective in the language of the country in which you work. This can also apply to pictures, colours, etc. Remember to check.

Before you start to write a word though, you need to know if your advertising concept is any good? The answer to this vital question is not a personal 'Yes, I like it' or 'No, I don't' (that constraint should apply to any executive, no matter how senior). Ideally, you should test the concept on a panel of potential customers – a Focus Group. They are the ones who really matter. This can be much too expensive, however, and in normal circumstances the correct approach is this.

Stage 1   Rough layout, concept and copy.
  Ask yourself, at this early stage, does the advertisement fulfil

the brief? (You know what you wanted to say and to whom. Does it?)

Stage 2   Comprehension and copy.

If you are using an agency and you can't visualize what the advertisement will look like, you can ask for a 'comp'. This is a very carefully produced layout, with the headline set in type, and the rest of the copy in 'Greek' type. That's a random mixture of letters, which say nothing but show you how the copy will appear. This is more expensive than making decisions based on Stage 1, but it lessens the possibility of 'surprises' at a later stage.

Stage 3   Visual.

Attend the meeting where the decisions are made on how to take the photograph and what will be in it. Then, ideally, be there when the photographing takes place. If you don't like the photo you are eventually shown, ask to see others taken at the time. If the photographs are no good because the photographer didn't keep to your brief, you can ask for a reshoot at the photographer's expense. If it is your fault, it may still be better to photograph again rather than to use a poor picture.

So, now you have considered how it might look, how it might read and what sort of photograph you will use. Now the words have to play their part in convincing the reader to buy the product.

Advertising copy checklist

We have already agreed that, before you start, you need to make sure that the advertisement:

- Maintains your image.
- Addresses the target audience.
- Addresses the client's objectives – the customer benefits are prominent.

If it is good copy, you need to answer 'yes' to all the questions in the following checklist:

1 Have you a good headline?
2 Have you answered the questions where, when, how much and what is included?
3 Have you included the right customer benefits?
4 Have you told the readers how to buy it?
5 Have you only used short sentences?
6 Is it in simple language?
7 Does the body copy back up the benefit in the headline?
8 Have you avoided all the meaningless phrases?
9 Have you avoided using the same large word twice?
10 Have you said what the product does rather than what it is?
11 Are all the statements in the advertisement positive?
12 Is there plenty of 'you' appeal?
13 Is your copy full of enthusiasm?
14 Have you avoided looking foolish?
15 Have you avoided saying the same thing twice?
16 Have you avoided making it sound like a telegram?
17 Is all the punctuation correct?
18 Have you left out the words 'persons' and 'people'?
19 Are all the accents correct?
20 Have you avoided giving any orders?
21 Have you left out the hotel and catering jargon?
22 Have you been absolutely honest with the clients?
23 Have you read the copy backwards to make sure there aren't any spelling mistakes?
24 Have you used humour where appropriate?
25 Have you used crossheads to break up large lumps of copy?

It is a lot to ask. So let's look more closely at those four rules for good copy we have already identified before we put some flesh on the 25 bones.

Make the copy easy to understand

You need to make the copy absolutely clear and easy to understand.

Simplify the copy

1 Simple language.

It is simple to understand an expression like 'Free drinks before dinner'; it is far more difficult for the reader to understand 'Booked bar'.

2 Simple sentiments.

Say 'to come back again', not 'to return'.

3 Simple words.

Use 'lunch', not 'luncheon, 'help', not 'assist'.

Say 'goes together', rather than 'complements' (which also avoids using 'compliments' rather than 'complements'!), 'very near', not 'adjacent', 'needs', not 'requirements'.

Say 'We're sure you'll agree there's plenty to enjoy', rather than refer to 'an attractive array of offers'.

Don't say 'receive with our compliments'. Say 'get a free ...'

4 Overall simplicity – use 'now', not 'at this point in time'; 'before you leave', rather than 'prior to your departure'.

But there are exceptions:

- Never use the word 'meals'. That diminishes the product.
- On rare occasions, you do need to use the superior word. For example, if you are selling a theme evening for £40, do not describe the decor as the 'props'. Describe the decor as the 'scenery'.

But why doesn't that apply to descriptions of the haute cuisine restaurant? Because £40 a guest for a commercial company party is not a lot of *anybody's* money. The cost of dinner in an haute cuisine restaurant is not expensive for the majority of the guests who use it. The great J.P. Morgan, the American banker, was once asked what it cost to run his yacht. 'If you need to ask,' he replied 'you can't afford it!' Don't be overawed by your own product.

NB: Notice the difference between diminishing the product and lowering the tone.

Keep your sentences short

The first sentence in an advertisement should not exceed 13 words. No sentence in an advertisement should ever exceed 24 words; people just don't understand the message without rereading it.

Always tell them how to buy it

Every advertisement has to tell the public how to buy the product and what it is they are being offered. That means that it has to answer the questions where, when, how much and what the price includes.

Make the copy lively and interesting

Headlines

Headlines should go above illustrations, not below them.

If you are going to offer a benefit in the headline, the body copy has got to support the benefit. For example:

Headline: 'Enjoy the best food in Taunton'
Body copy: '7 times winners of the Somerset Haute Cuisine Competition ...'

Language

Use phrases and words that make the reader take notice of the advert. There are 440,000 words in the English language – four times as many words as in any other language. Use that spread to your advantage.

Use words with meaning – linger, glance, authentic. Consider the phrase 'our resident pianist'. What else could you describe a pianist as? Talented, syncopated, tuneful, dulcet, honey-toned, rhythmic. So widen your vocabulary: not sounds but melodies, chords and harmonies. Not beautiful (music) but mellow, inspiring and haunting.

Don't use the same word twice. This doesn't apply to words like 'and' or 'but'. It means that you don't use a word like 'accommodation' twice. The second time you would use 'bed-rooms'.

Don't use meaningless phrases

For example: 'Air conditioned rooms are available in many of our bedrooms.' How many is many? Which bedrooms? Or 'Valuable assistance is offered in such areas.' What specific assistance?

The décor is described as being of 'strong and elegant character, to take us right into the new millennium'. What does that actually mean ?

Use plenty of enthusiasm

Puddings are served with 'mountains of cream'; tell readers 'you probably love' not 'you obviously like'.

Make sure there is plenty of 'you' appeal

Clients are interested in the benefits of the product to them. They are not interested in us. Therefore, use the words 'you' and 'your' but leave out the words 'I', 'we', 'me', 'my', 'us' and 'our' as much as possible. The former should always exceed the latter by about 4:1.

So you say:

'You'll be delighted to hear', not 'I'm very pleased to announce'.
'You will find enclosed', not 'I am enclosing'.
'Your Head Waiter will be there all evening', not 'Our Head Waiter ...'

This principle applies in other forms as well. For example:

In brochures, say 'you can enjoy' not 'guests can enjoy'.
In Mother's Day advertising, put 'In March it's finally time for your Mum to relax' not 'In March it's finally time for all the Mums to relax'.

Don't be negative if you can be positive

Don't say: 'Rooms cannot be guaranteed before 3pm' but say 'Rooms can be guaranteed after 3pm.'

That's an easy one, but sometimes a negative creeps in by a subtler route. Consider the phrase '... venture down to the nightclub'. The implication is that you're creeping down into the cellar to see what that strange noise was! You need to develop, to its sharpest, your sensitivity to the nuances of words.

Say what the product *does*, not what the product *is*: for example

'Amstrad makes communication much easier.'
'Persil washes whiter.'
'Guinness is good for you.'

Write good English

If you are not very careful, there is a real danger that you can make yourself look foolish. Here are some real examples from past promotional efforts.

- 'We want you to find staying in an [Intergalactic] hotel a pleasure'; followed immediately by 'Major refurbishing has now started at the hotel'.
- '... sparkling brooks and babbling waterfalls' – it should be 'sparkling waterfalls and babbling brooks'.
- '... and never the swain shall meet' – quotations must be correct.
- Words like 'unpreceded' and 'endulge' – which do not exist.
- 'Commemorate Mother's Day' – to do that, Mother would have to be dead!

Understand the meaning of the words you use

For example, you should not say 'the hotel staff are extremely fastidious when looking after guests and their belongings. If that were true, the staff would handle the guests and their belongings with tweezers, wearing masks and protective clothing for fear of infection.

Also, unless you are making a play on words, don't use unusual phrases such as '... for an extended time'. (That one's wrong – it's 'a long time' or 'an extended period'.)

Don't get your singulars and plurals mixed

This can easily happen in a long sentence:

'A full Intergalactic breakfast, with a choice of kippers, cereal, fried eggs and fruit juices cost £7' – it should be 'costs'.

Know your subject

For example, you can't have 'a madras of curry' – Madras is a city in India. I've seen a breakfast menu offering the guests 'tea or coffee, fruit juice, croissant, Danish pastry and condiments'. What would you put the salt and pepper on, I wonder? They meant, of course, 'conserves'.

Avoid tautology

Tautology is saying the same thing twice by using words that mean the same thing or are redundant, for example:

'Serve her meal with our compliments, free of charge'
'... years of age'
'Every evening at 8pm'

Avoid sounding like a telegram

Don't save words in your copy if it means you end up sounding like a telegram. For example, 'Complete attached page', 'Time of year'. It makes the copy sound formal and unfriendly. It implies that you are in a hurry.

Get the punctuation right

If you get the punctuation right, you can't give a bad impression to the client on that score. If you get it wrong, you could easily give the impression that you are sloppy or illiterate; neither quality is likely to inspire client confidence in the rest of the product. A good book by D. Crystal called *Rediscover Grammar* would be useful if you feel you have a problem in this area.

Goodbye 'persons' and 'people'

You aren't a 'worker', you are a member of the 'staff'. At a meeting you are not 'people' you are delegates. When writing copy or letters, don't use the words 'people' or 'persons'. Use 'guests', 'delegates', 'visitors', 'holidaymakers' or 'tourists'; never use 'covers' or 'heads' either.

And write good French!

Either you write dishes in French with the correct accents, or you write them in capital letters which don't require accents. You shouldn't leave the accents out if you don't remember where they go. Look the word up in Sharman and Chadwick's, *The A-Z Gastronomique* (if you can get hold of a copy) or a similar book.

Make it fun

Don't give the clients orders

For example, don't write 'It is essential that ...' or 'Your waiter will inform you of our selection of fish'.

Don't use jargon

Here is just a small selection of jargon phrases that should never be used again:

- full credit facilities
- booking requirements should be made, to the amount of ...
- first consideration
- hospitality and service excellence

- choice of venues
- comprehensive meeting rooms
- restaurant dining
- inclusive of
- perfectly located
- reservations are necessary
- beverages
- standard of service
- 5 star restaurants and bars
- fully equipped
- the choice is yours
- you deserve it
- dance the night away
- and then you retire to your guestroom
- please do not hesitate
- beautifully appointed

What's wrong with jargon and hackneyed phrases such as these?

1 Nobody believes it – 'first consideration'.
2 Nobody understands what it means – 'comprehensive meeting rooms' (what's 'comprehensive'?).
3 Nobody can see any difference between you and your competitors – everybody says they are 'fully equipped', 'beautifully appointed' and 'perfectly located'.

This includes difficult catering jargon as well; for example, words such as melange, carpaccio, balsamic, roesti, Thermidor; or 'Ragout of Fallow Deer'. What's a Ragout? What's a Fallow Deer? (A yellow or brown one is the answer, but does it matter?)

Try bullet points

Compare for impact:
The hotel has a swimming pool, sauna, gym and squash courts

with:

- Swimming Pool
- Gym
- Sauna
- Squash Courts

Some final dos and don'ts

- Always be honest. 'Being honest' with the guests also means putting the best interpretation on the facts, making the hotel case as well as possible. So, if the client has a choice (of night clubs, for example) say so:

  '... in fairness, there are about another dozen competitors as well'

- Don't hype unless you can live up to it. It is no use describing someone as 'an experienced Conference Manager' if the client is eventually going to be dealt with by a young Sales Coordinator. All that will happen is that the Coordinator will fail to live up to the promise and his or her job will be made that much more difficult.

- Don't make threats you wouldn't carry out:

  'If payment is not received within 7 days, this facility will be withdrawn.'

- Don't offer savings if they're so small you're afraid to say what they are.

- Don't go totally OTT:

  'The Intergalactic Luncheon Club has become a legend in its own time.' (Has it?)

  'Rest assured that your well-being is our utmost concern.' (Utmost?)

  'the untamed glamour of the Splendide restaurant'. (Wow!)

- Don't talk about special menus unless they really are special.
- Don't use the word 'just', as in 'the cost is just £5,000'.
- Don't pretend to offer bargains:

  '£100, including complementary car parking'. That's a con.

  '£100 including car parking'. That's a customer benefit.

Starting to write the advertising copy

We have talked about the *elements* of good advertising copy. But what about the whole advertisement, the 'global concept'? There are a number of proven guidelines here as well, which you can follow when settling down to write good advertising copy.

1   Follow the theme:

Headline:	'The Millennium presents you with a great challenge. It's more comfortable to think about it in our bar.'
Follow the theme	'Well, it may take you some time to solve the problems of the world. Time you could devote while snoozing/contemplating in the lovely lobby lounge or eating in the beautiful Garden restaurant. Time spent usefully pondering, while a reliable hotel staff carry out your instructions for the conference or the dinner. The one where the Chairman ratifies your conclusions and warmly congratulates you.'

2   There is a structure to an advertisement. Look at this one for a destination advertisement.

Headline:	'Few of the great natural wonders of the world remain.' Expand by the use of a subhead: 'The Intergalactic offers you two of them – the Great Barrier Reef and the primeval rain forest.' Use *alliteration* (words all starting with the same letter): 'You'll never forget a trip to the Great Barrier Reef; a colossal, colourful collection of fabulous, flecked fish.'

Paint pictures with words: 'Exquisite coral formations, softly shifting sands and the eerie serenity of life under the waves. Equally, the Rain Forest is a marvellously unspoilt vista of spectacular scenery and tropical vegetation.'

Aptness: 'nature at its most natural and wonderful'.

3 Use today's words.

Words with meaning: 'It's a brilliant hotel; fresh and airy, with a terrific pool, an award winning restaurant and friendly staff anxious to offer you a real Australian welcome.'

Use popular phrases: 'The Great Barrier Reef, the Rain Forest and the Intergalactic – They're not making packages like that any more.'

4 Writing advertisements has elements of writing poetry. Consider the effects of metre, as in 'softly, shifting sands' – long–short–long–short–long.

5 There's no law that we have to keep to outdated styles.

Old fashioned: 'Rich oxtail soup flavoured with Tio Pepe sherry.'

Could be: 'There's a delicious Oxtail consommé, if you like a soup with a bite. Laced with Tio Pepe sherry, it's a great heart cockle warmer.'

This is using a phrase that gets them sitting up and has real credibility – not an excellent soup, but a great heart cockle warmer.

6 Lively copy comes from many stratagems. One is to change the spelling of a common word to get in its other meaning.

Cabaret with a comedian – 'the roar ingredients will be on show'

Another is the use of a word with a flavour appropriate to the subject:

'... dive in to the best fish and shrimp'.

Another is to slightly change the spelling of a word in a popular phrase to give a quite different meaning:

'Try a real Winemaker's Dinner – and love to tell the tale.'

Or apply a phrase always associated with one subject to another subject:

Outside catering: 'If you can't come to the Intergalactic, the Intergalactic will come to you.'

Another is called juxtaposition.:

'You don't have to call it a day; stay the night.'

Readers are usually interested in news:

'The new Empire Restaurant opens on July 12th.'

Questions get the readers involved:

'Wouldn't you like to get away from it all?'

7   When you are writing a lot of copy, break it up with crossheads – small headlines. The crosshead tells the reader what is the main customer benefit to be found in the next paragraph.

8   Here's an example of enthusiasm as a selling weapon, combined with a touch of humour.

'For £50 a guest a night, you can try beds so comfortable you could give away your counting sheep to a friend. A standard of luxury so high you might decide that there just might be one place even better than home.'

9   Every piece of promotional material should follow the rules of good advertising. What can you do about the copy you use in the Wine List. Can you do better than 'A necessary accompaniment to any meal'? Both enthusiasm and alliteration are available weapons:

'You can choose from all the great wine growing regions of the world. A big, booming Cabernet Sauvignon from Australia, the tantalizing tastes of the Moselles, the beautiful bouquets of the fine Californian vineyards, the delectable Chateau Yquem 1959.'

You could do better with the public rooms as well:

The lounge: 'A tiny oasis in a hectic world. Hidden away for quiet meetings, much needed drinks or simply a breather.'

And here are some more examples of good copy you could produce for any of the following features or events.

Fast breakfast service in your room:

'Don't go without breakfast.'

Guest Comment Cards

'How would you improve this hotel?
Every hotel should give you exactly what you want.
So was there anything you wanted that you didn't get?
If you'd be kind enough to jot it down on the form, I'll try and see that it's there for you next time, and I'm sorry to have let you down on this occasion.
Thank you for staying with us. Come back soon, and don't forget there's always a warm welcome waiting for you.'

Refurbishment:

> Headline: 'Sorry, but it will look lovely when it's finished.'
>
> 'I'm sorry if you find it awkward, with all the renovations going on around you. The problem with redecorating a hotel is that it can't all be done while the guests are asleep. So please forgive us, but its £50,000 well spent on giving you an even prettier place to stay.
>
> What are you going to get? Well, a very grand entrance for anybody who wants to make a very grand entrance. There's going to be a stunning new lounge where the Empire lounge used to be. The Hawke cafe is being totally revamped and the Reception and Concierge's Desks will be a sea of Carrera marble.
>
> Don't watch this space while it's such a mess, but do come back and see it finished; that will, definitely, be worthwhile.'

Christmas:

> 'Nobody does Christmas better than the Intergalactic. Leave the work to us this year. There are choristers at 11.30 in the morning, singing those well loved melodies just a little more in tune than Uncle Jimmy.
>
> 'Then go and help yourself from a vast buffet, a table crammed with everything you expect and lots of lovely extra dishes to tempt the most jaded palates.
>
> 'For the children, there will be a visit from Santa – with presents for them, of course – and a really funny clown.'

Or:

> 'Once a year it's time to have the very, very best. That means the Empire Restaurant on Christmas Day. Imagine; your favourite drink in the sophisticated Piano Bar any time after 11 o'clock. Then lunch – and what a

lunch – in the stylish elegance of the Empire Restaurant
– voted No. 1 in the Archtamuddy Bugle competition.
'A 5 course menu, with those memorable Scottish specialities, the tastiest Turkey with luscious Macadamia
Nut Stuffing, an enormous Dessert Buffet to choose
from and plenty of Christmas goodies.

'Just in case you don't believe in him, Santa will make
a personal appearance; so will even more authentic
choristers and, of course, there will be a pianist gently
tinkling the ivories throughout.'

In both the pieces of Christmas copy, notice the use of dashes
to accentuate the personal note.

The most powerful words

Some words are more powerful than others. They attract attention more, they are more vivid, more credible, more exciting.
Here are the best words.

Best headline words

Free	Your	Here	How
Now	Bargain	Who	Guaranteed
You	Introducing	Why	New

Most persuasive words

Now	Suddenly	Magic	Sensational
Quick	Offer	Wanted	Hurry
Easy	Remarkable	Free	Announcing
Bargain	Introducing	Compare	Revolutionary
Startling	Challenge	Amazing	Improvement

Best words for introducing news

Modern	Announcing	Novel	Revolutionary
Latest	Introducing	Today	Presenting
Recent	New	Now	Suddenly

Best words for appearance

Classic	Spectacular	Elegant	Captivating
Scenic	Distinctive	Lavish	Fascinating
Exquisite	Attractive	Dramatic	Fashionable
Beautiful	Appealing	Charming	Glamorous
Colourful	Magnificent	Handsome	Flattering

Best words for quality

Good	Unparalleled	Valuable	Unsurpassed
Top	Rugged	Durable	Outstanding
Famous	Greatest	Fine	Personalized
Better	Remarkable	Noted	Imported
Choice	Improved	Superior	Excellent
Special	First-rate	Exclusive	Terrific
Special	Wonderful	Limited	Surpassing
Rare	Outstanding	Unique	Authentic
Genuine	Selected		

Particularly good words for Food and Beverage

Warm	Lovely	Elegant	Comfortable
Cosy	Fine	Home made	Delicious

Not 'rich' or 'heavy'.

Headlines

> If you have a good headline, you have a good ad. Any competent writer can write copy. If you have a poor headline, you are licked before you start. Your copy will not be read. (John Caples, BBDO)

Notice John Caples, a famous advertising agent, didn't say it would make the advertisement weaker or that it would be less effective. He said 'Your copy will not be read.' That's how important the headline is.

Headlines are the parts of an advertisement we remember best; that is why they are the most vital part of an advertisement They should encapsulate the product's main customer benefit. So to write your good headlines you have to decide what is the main customer benefit. Ask yourself 'What does it do?' and 'Who is it for?'

Consider the options for Sunday lunch promotions:

- 'Why bother to cook this Sunday?'
- '27 choices for Sunday lunch – for just £8.50.'
- 'Why haven't your friends told you about Sunday Brunch at L'Escalier?'
- 'If you love luscious desserts, you'll flip over Sunday at L'Escalier.'

Which is the best choice for you? Or there could be a fifth, sixth or seventh choice.

Remember, the name of the product is not a headline. 'Intergalactic Hotels' is not a headline. 'Why not settle for the best?' is.

We know a great deal about how headlines work. Here are some facts:

- Five times more people read headlines than anything else.
- 10 per cent more people read headlines above a picture, rather than below.
- 28 per cent more people remember a headline in quotes (' ') rather than one without quotes.
- A great many very successful headlines used only short, simple words and not more than 10 of them.
- A headline is even stronger if you put a subhead (a smaller headline) underneath it.

Here then are some basic rules about headlines:

1   The structure of the headline should, ideally, include:

- An invitation for the reader.
- The most important product benefit.
- The name of the product.
- An interesting provoking idea.

For example:

> For a great gravy thickener – 'Ah, Bisto!'
> If you want a powerful petrol – 'Esso – Put a tiger in your tank.'

2   The headline should appeal, primarily, to the most important market you are trying to reach. For example, the first advertisement for hearing aids had the headline:

> 'Deaf?'

3   The headline should contain an action verb: '**Head** for the top'; '**Eliminate** your competition'; '**Stop** me and buy one'.

If these rules have been followed, even if the readers stop after the headline, they should know something about the product and its benefit. It's true that a lot of good headlines don't contain all of these points. But if yours doesn't, ask yourself if it would be stronger if it did.

Most good headlines fall into one of the following four types.

1   They present a new benefit. Executive Floors, Award winning Chefs and a New Restaurant are just three examples

2   They promise an existing benefit. *It can't be new every time. It is also powerful to keep offering the same important benefit.*

> 'The Splendide – In the hearts of Blackstead for 100 years.
> Great food when you feel it really counts.'

The third line here would be a subheading.

3   They arouse curiosity or have provocative headlines. For the guests at one hotel in New York, I produced this headline to get more business for their rooftop restaurant.

'If you think the view is sensational, wait till you taste the food.'

4   They address the one main market.

'For everybody who loves great steaks'

Humour

Humorous copy also follows rules.

1   Deflating the pompous:

'Joining the single European currency is a crucial decision. It's more comfortable to think about it snoozing by the pool.'

2   OTT praise:

'The Nobel Prize winners for Pommes Frites.'

3   Mixing metaphors with straight meanings:
'Don't go Dutch. Go Welsh and give your loved one a feast to remember.'

4   Absurdity:

'If you absolutely insist, you can go snake hunting, but we lose more guests that way …'

5   The right word in the wrong context:

An advert in a ballet programme: 'Why not pointe along to the Gallery Brasserie.'

6   Play on words:

A prize of free travel in a food competition: 'First Class Fare.'
Menu items: 'Steak your claim', 'Spice as nice', 'Très Chick'.

Fish: 'Our fish are catching people', 'Don't miss the boat'.
A gourmet attraction: '9 Day Wonder – January 10–18'.

7   Breaking up a common phrase set in concrete:

'Half a bottle of free wine – 'Fancy? It's free!'

8   Parallelism:

'Prepared with cheese and croutons, not to mention élan, chic and savoir faire.'

9   Juxtaposition:

'You don't have to call it a day; stay the night.'

Here's how it can all come together. This might be the copy for an advertisement to sell tickets for a comedian in cabaret in the hotel:

'Tired of the same old Christmas parties?
A funny thing could happen to you on December 15th or 17th.
If you're looking for a Christmas party that's everything but dull, why not come to Charlie Brown in very personal person.
Back by popular demand, Charlie Brown and his acid wit will be in full hilarious flow, Cabaret and the Grand Ballroom before Christmas.
The roar ingredients are on show on December 15th and 17th. So try a little untenderness, anything new and a table for 10.'

This second example shows how the guying of much loved but hackneyed situations can be humorous. This is for a New Year's Eve Party on the theme of 'Midnight in Casablanca'.
'Spend New Year's Eve in Casablanca
Somewhere in this crazy world there must be a great

New Year's Eve Party. Sure, it's at Rick's new place – the Grand Ballroom at the Splendide. Join Humphrey Bogart and Ingrid Bergman and play it again until 2 in the morning.

You must remember this – in a fabulous setting of white tuxedos and the driest of Martinis, you're going to have a wonderful evening.

Who's it for? Here's looking at you, kid.

£50 a guest.'

Typefaces

You have to understand the basic principles of using typefaces. Here are the points you need to remember.

- There are two families of typefaces: Serif and Sans Serif (sans means without). The serifs are the horizontal lines at the bottom of the letters. In small letters, serif typefaces are easier to read.
- Luxury products like Rolls Royce and *The Times* use serif typefaces. So serif = the luxury product is the general principle.
- Typefaces can be printed in UPPER and lower case (capitals and small letters.) In *italics*, **bold**, outline and shadow. Or in a *combination* of them.
- The public won't read the body copy (small letters) in anything smaller than 9 point. (Type is measured in points. This book is in 10 point.
- Some typefaces are recognized by the public as associated with history, FASHION, **Children's parties**, old books and **cowboys**. If you are doing a mediaeval banquet, Mediaeval will look wrong.
- One of the most commonly used typefaces is called Times New Roman. Twenty 9pt Times characters = 2.54 cm (1 inch). Don't forget a blank = 1 character.
- Type is easier to read if there is white space around the text.
- Black type on a white background is easier to read than white letters on a black background: **Typefaces.**

Proof reading

When you see a proof of your advertisement, always read it a second time backwards to pick up any spelling or typesetting mistakes. It is the best way, by far, to spot mistakes. When you read the material forwards, because it makes sense, you miss the errors. Read it backwards, it makes no sense, and the words are seen in terms of their correct spelling.

You will need to mark the mistakes you find or changes you want to make, e.g.:

ꝺ	Take out	,/	Comma	⌐	No paragraph
⋏	Insert at this point	⊙	Colon	...	Stet – let it stay
⊢⊣	Hyphen	;/	Semi colon	⌐⌐	Transpose (swap round)
⌐	Make paragraph	⸱̓	Apostrophe	≡	Capital letters
⊙	Full stop	Ⲩ	Space	≢	Lower case (small letters)

Graphics

Graphics are both typefaces and illustrations; borders, cartoons, etc. Essentially, graphics is everything in the advertisement except the photographs.

Good graphics make all the difference between a good and a poor advertisement in appearance. That's why they are also the job of the professional. There are, however, some useful tips.

1 You need good graphics to have the best chance of attracting the reader's attention.
2 Bright, contrasting and pleasing colours give you more readership potential.
3 The following colour combinations are the most readable (in order):
  – Black on yellow.
  – Green on white.
  – Red on white.
  – Blue on white.
  – White on blue.

– Black on white.
– Yellow on black.
4 The public love cartoons.

Don't forget the possibilities of violators and snipes. These are the technical names for a banner, or slash, or balloon which you may put across part of the ad to say 'Now Open' or 'Special Offer' or 'One Night Only'. They are used to draw attention to a particular point in as forceful a way as possible.

Layouts

The layout is the way the whole advertisement looks. If your layout is acceptable, you have to be able to answer 'yes' to all the following questions:

1   Does the layout communicate the message as simply as possible?

2   Does it have an attention-getting focal point? (Your eye is immediately drawn to the most important part of the message.)

3   Do the picture and the words give the same message?
    For example, you could have a picture of a very complicated dish on a plate; a sea of sauce, beautifully decorated. Geometrically designed pieces of food. Don't then use words to describe it like 'pure and simple'. The picture isn't of pure and simple food. The words and the picture give two different messages; the client will be confused.

4   Does it look like a product your target market will like?

5   Will it be clearly visible to readers when they look at the page?
    Your advertisement should, preferably, dominate the page. That means it will be bigger than the other advertisements. Obviously, you don't have to take the whole page to achieve this.

6   Are you producing just the one ad for all the different media?

It isn't always necessary to produce different sized ads for the different media. They may be slightly different in size but you can enlarge or reduce the size of your ad by up to 10 per cent without spoiling it. If it is surrounded by more white space, it may be even more noticeable. White space separates your ad from the others on the page.

7   Did you make the right decision on colour vs black and white ads?

Research has shown that colour ads result in 50 per cent more enquiries and a 23 per cent higher readership.

8   Have you seen the newspaper advertisement layout on newspaper stock?

Newspapers use poorer quality paper than magazines. Make sure you see the newspaper advertisement on newsprint when you see a proof.

Photographs

You are not supposed to know how to take photographs like a professional photographer. That's a job for an expert and it is perfectly reasonable to hire their services. The photographer, however, is not supposed to know about selling your product. That's your job and, therefore, you have to tell the photographer precisely what effect you want to get from the photographs he or she takes. If you don't do that, the photographer will decide on what shot looks the most attractive to them. But it is you who are the best judge of that.

When, therefore, you decide what the photograph should be, you should be able to answer 'yes' to all the following questions.

1   Is there, within your photograph, a great idea for selling the product?

Your photograph is competing with many others for the attention of the reader. If there is something special about it, you have a better chance that it will catch the reader's attention.

For example, Chewton Glen in the New Forest has a Unique Selling Proposition (USP) that their Leisure Club won the Swimming Pool Association's award as the best in the UK. So the advertisement for their hotel could show the trophy. Nobody else can claim awards to the same extent as Chewton Glen and so these figure strongly in their promotional material.

2   Does your photograph have a story in it?

Every photograph must have a story. The story must illustrate to the client the advantages of using the advertised product.

There are obviously many stories, but when you eliminate those stories that everybody uses – the picture of the Grand Ballroom with all the staff standing straight and smiling, for instance – you have to finish up with a fresh and good one. Here are some examples:

(a)   The conference room

The client holding an important conference is inherently worried that the hotel he or she chooses may make mistakes. They will get the blame but the hotel will really be responsible. Most clients also believe that the cause of a lot of errors is that the hotel doesn't let them do what they want. They are tied down with rules and regulations.

A good conference selling photograph, therefore, shows a conference room in which there are two people; one is obviously a member of the hotel staff because they are in uniform or wear an identifying badge. The other is a client. The one in uniform has a note pad and is seen to be making notes. The other is pointing and appears to be giving instructions. The story in the picture is, therefore, that the client gives the orders in your hotel. That will be a story the client likes.

(b)   The bar

The two main attractions in a bar are:

(i) The chance to avoid loneliness by talking to someone.

The client is reassured that his fears of hotel rules and the possibility of his instructions being ignored, are groundless. The caption reinforces the message (*Source:* Grosvenor House, London)

(ii) The variety of drinks from which you can choose. What we call the gluttony of choice.

A good photograph for a bar will, therefore, get both those elements into the picture. Notice that this means that you will be focusing on a number of people at the bar, rather than showing the size of the bar, or the whole of its decor. That doesn't matter because neither the size nor the decor are likely to be the main customer benefit.

(c)   The food

When you see advertisements, you will notice how often the advertised product is shown with somebody using it; the girl at the wheel of a car or the man drinking the beer, the woman wearing the dress or trying the shampoo, the child eating the sweets or playing with the toys. What is more, the models in the advertisements look like the type of people who will buy the products. You don't get advertisements of little old ladies drinking the beer, women using the power drill, or children using the vacuum cleaner. Another point: the woman using the vacuum cleaner doesn't look like the sort who has a diamond tiara upstairs.

So, when you photograph the food, there have to be:

(i) Guests with the product; the massive buffet without a client in sight is a bad photograph.

(ii) The kind of guests who will be likely to buy the product. A child's birthday party, therefore, would have the child as the centre of attraction, beaming at the cake, and all the close relatives gathered round, obviously equally delighted at the child's pleasure.

3   Does your picture arouse curiosity?

You need an 'angle' for your picture; something which is unusual and attracts the reader's attention. Ice work, sugar work and butter work all do this. Staff in costume do it. An unusual background can do it. Anything odd can do it. People staring out of pictures attracts attention. So do extreme close-ups.

4   Does your photograph show the finished dish, not the ingredients?

Ingredients do not find favour with the customers. They want to see the finished dish or nothing. And remember to take a slice out of a gâteau so that they can see the inside. Of course, you want them to see the attractive lay-out of a dish, but you can show guests with a knife and fork poised over it, or with a small part cut away. The customer benefit is in eating the food, not admiring it.

5   Does your picture show a few individuals and not a crowd?

Crowds don't attract the readers. Nobody can identify with a crowd. You want them to identify with the guest enjoying the meal experience.

6   Is the message easy to understand?

Of course, *you* can understand it. You know exactly what you have in mind. But is it equally obvious to the reader. Try the picture out on your friends – preferably not your colleagues who are also experienced hoteliers and caterers. Only if the general public understand exactly what you are trying to put over, will the picture be a success.

Summary

It is highly unlikely that you have ever worked in an advertising agency. It is also unlikely that advertising and direct mail were taught in depth on a hotel management or tourism curriculum. Nevertheless, these are vital skills for all hospitality management to acquire.

If you are selling to the general public, rather than to group buyers, some form of advertising or direct mail is going to be your best option. On its effectiveness will depend your success.

Case study

This case study illustrates:

- That advertising can work for hotels as much as for any other product.
- That the principles of advertising don't change because it's a hospitality product.
- That the criteria for success can be measured in terms of additional profits.

To find an advertising campaign which has been a resounding financial success in the hospitality industry over many years is not that easy. Measurements of advertising effectiveness are often judged only in terms of the public's additional recognition of the brand. This is known as building the brand but it would be nice to measure massive additional profits as well on occasions.

In Britain there is a national habit of taking short holidays in hotels; 2 night weekends away from home are the most popular. It is a demand estimated to be worth

ADVERTISING

£2 billion to the hotel industry and it has been created by advertising. You can't sell to the general public individually in any other way.

The pioneer campaign was for a product called Stardust Mini Holidays and it lasted for about 20 years. At its peak over 150,000 people bought the package for weekends in London and almost every kind of advertising medium was tried to see which would serve best.

The first piece of promotional material was a poster. It had to make its mark on railway stations where the potential customers were likely to be preoccupied and where competing posters and notices were to be found in profusion. Therefore, the Stardust poster was created in a colour called Dayglo Red. The brief to the agency was to produce a poster that would stop a charging elephant at 200 metres on a dark railway platform on Wigan Station at 11 o'clock on a November evening! Dayglo Red is a very bright red indeed. Eventually, the posters became so recognizable, through long use, that the public could be reminded of the attractions of a weekend in London even if they couldn't read the words across the platforms. The colour provided the message.

One competitor carried out research to find out how their public had heard of their promotion. Thirty-five per cent had first come across it as a poster – and the company in question wasn't using posters! These people were seeing ours! This may seem a disastrous result for Stardust but the aim was to create a national habit; no less. Anything which helped achieve that was alright.

The brochure broke new ground in one particular way. The focus groups who had been asked to comment on brochure proposals said that they didn't know their way around London and needed a map. So the brochure included a map, with pictures of the main attractions. Then the fun element was introduced. The caption for St Paul's Cathedral identified it as 'Recently Wrenovated'! The one for the Albert Hall said 'Named after Mr. Queen

Victoria'. Mild, inoffensive humour to establish that we recognized we were in the fun business too.

Stardust was the first Short Break to go on television. The commercial showed a North Country comedian in Trafalgar Square, exhorting the joys of the capital. It worked very well, but only to widen the market. It was not immediately profitable in its own right. We took the towns in the TV area where it was advertised and saw how much their figures had improved over the previous year. Then we compared that improvement with the rest of the country which hadn't had the TV advertisement. The TV area had done better, producing an additional profit, but the additional profit didn't match the cost of the TV. In future years, if there were no TV, the widening of the market would produce a retroactive profit, but not in the first year.

What worked more immediately was the PR effort in Ulster. Ulster TV being too expensive, we brought four journalists to London for the weekend to sample the package. They wrote favourable articles when they returned home. Belfast, which had been languishing at 85th in the league table of business from cities, suddenly went up to 8th. The only thing that had happened was the PR, so the credit could be given to that.

Stardust outsold its major competitor 5:1. So we tried flooding a single town, Blackpool, with advertising: cinema advertising, local newspaper advertising, bus advertising. The results from Blackpool against the competition went up to 8:1. The difference in profit did pay for the advertising. We could try that again in other towns.

Sometimes the advertising took time to pay off. Most industries expect that advertising will take years to build them a substantial share of the market, but hospitality industries look – often unsuccessfully – for better results than that. So bus panels in a Midlands town produced no results for the season when we ran them. So we stopped – and the following season the results from that town went up substantially. It can take time to convince the public and it is a mistake to give up too early.

The question had to be decided of whether national newspapers, with their higher cost and circulation, were a better advertising investment than buying the smaller but cheaper circulation of the local press. We always found that the local press was the better bet. The reason was that we always linked the local advertising with the best local travel agent and the local public had more confidence in them than in an amorphous national body.

The result of advertising inviting the readers to cut out coupons and send for brochures was more difficult to assess. From one major magazine series we had 24,000 coupons returned and had one member of staff who only spent their time dealing with them. All the application forms in the brochures had been coded in order to know who had booked as a result of getting the brochure. The answer was a miserable 720 – 3 per cent. But what if they had been convinced by the brochure but booked their weekend on another application form? That was almost impossible to prove. So we didn't do it again. There was a strictly enforced rule that if you couldn't prove whether it worked, there was no point in doing it again. Failure wasn't the problem; ignorance of the results was.

When the hotel company was broken up, there was no longer a product to be sold and Stardust disappeared. During its lifetime, though, it helped the industry to prove that hospitality advertising is just as effective as it is for any manufacturing company.

10 In-house promotion

Chapter 9 discussed the rules of advertising. Now we have to apply those rules to the promotional material and marketing plans we use in-house. The most important area is normally restaurant promotion, so let's look at that first.

Restaurant promotion

If you are running a good restaurant, you deserve to have the public flock to your door and queue round the block. Often they don't because it's an unfair world. So, if quality is not enough, you need to add a soupçon of restaurant promotion to get the results you want. Let's have a look at the full checklist.

Ambiance

1   Is there a plan for what music tapes to use at specific times of the day?

It is easy to ignore this point; it may seem too trivial for words. But if you want your restaurant to attract business people, words are the problem – specifically, hearing them. The process of going deaf – which happens to a greater or lesser extent as you grow older – is usually not that you have problems hearing people whisper to you. The two of you in an otherwise empty room, should have little trouble in communicating at a low decibel level. The problem comes when you try to distinguish the voice you want to hear from a hubbub of voices all around you. If the music tape has a singer, that creates precisely that problem. Background music gives the ear less trouble, but a competing voice makes life very difficult. So make sure you don't use music with vocals. And give thought to the kind of music which is appropriate for different times of the day. The Massed Bands of the Brigade of Guards is hard to take at breakfast!

If all this seems obvious, why doesn't it happen? Well often, in a hotel at least, the responsibility for what music is played is given to Reception staff, who have their own pop favourites. Managers only usually give instructions on the music for specific periods, like Christmas. Even then, if you have guests staying for a few days over Christmas, remember there is a definite limit to the number of times you can enjoy 'Jingle Bells'! Vary the music.

2   How are guests welcomed at the door?

First impressions do count. They set the tone for the whole eating out experience. It is traditional to use a phrase like 'Have you made a reservation?' This implies, however, that, if you haven't, you may not get a table. It creates uncertainly in the guest, which isn't a pleasant experience. It also suggests that the guest may have done something wrong in not booking. The guest may then be embarrassed in front of colleagues or clients.

The right approach – because you have to check if there is a reservation – is to smile and say something like 'Hello. How nice to see you. Did you happen to make a reservation?' Suggesting that it is possible the guest did, but not that important.

If you don't get off on the right foot, the client is far more likely to find cause for complaint, just in order to get their own back for the initial unpleasant experience. While not all clients are that sensitive, you can't afford to make mistakes with those who are.

The menu

3   Is the menu attractive to look at?

A menu is a sales document. It is designed to encourage

people to buy the food. So why hasn't it got any attractive photographs? It's a truism that a good photograph is worth 1,000 words. The answer is that when the 'modern' menu was first devised – over 100 years ago – the technology for producing colour photography didn't exist. So colour photography could not be used then, and most restaurants still are not doing so today. It used to be argued that it was a question of cost, but the prices for printing in colour have come down over the years and most operations could afford photographs now.

So, if you specialize in particular dishes and want to sell more of them, put photographs of those dishes into the menu. Some would argue that your menu would then resemble that of a Burger Bar. This doesn't follow at all. Just because a small car manufacturer advertises their products with photographs, that doesn't stop Rolls-Royce doing the same. You distinguish your product by the quality of the graphics, by the colours and the typefaces you use. The lower the market you are aiming for, the more you should use primary colours; red, blue, yellow, green. The use of pastel shades appeals more to the higher socioeconomic groups.

To put photographs into your menu would set you apart from almost all your competitors. Can they all be wrong? Well, if they are not, *every other industry must be*. Furthermore, in the Far East, where they are not terribly concerned about the printing technology of Victorian England, they use photographs for international, luxury hospitality products.

It is usually the case that, if you are prepared to tear up the traditional rule book, you have a much better chance of producing good promotional material. Almost all the typical restaurant promotional material is very old fashioned.

4   Is the menu accurately spelt?

You are trying to make the menu reflect the high quality of the food you are offering and it doesn't reflect well on the food if the wording is misspelt. It doesn't enhance your image if the French accents are missing or incorrect. I recall one luxury hotel in Edinburgh which had a wine list with 13 château bottled wines on it. The word château was spelt with an umlaut every time. Nobody seemed to know that château isn't a German word.

IN-HOUSE PROMOTION

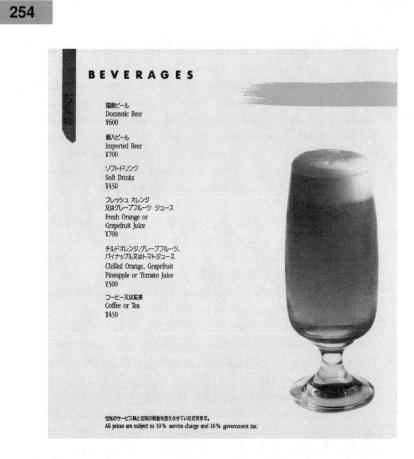

In Asia top quality restaurants use menus with tremendous photography. A picture is worth a thousand words (*Source:* Tokyo Bay Hilton)

5   Are there some items of food in which the restaurant specializes?

Over the years, eating out in restaurants generally has increased out of all knowledge. But eating out in hotels, as a percentage of the eating out market, has declined year on year. From the mid-1980s to the mid-1990s, eating out in Britain went up 75 per cent. Eating out in hotels went down 15 per cent (Health Education Authority figures). So, if you are a hotelier, what are you doing wrong?

The most common cause of failure is that the public don't know why they should come. You might ask your partner

NOODLES IN SOUP

トンクーサイシンメン
椎茸と青菜入りそば
"Ton-ku Saishin Men"
Noodles with Shiitake Mushrooms
¥1,100

ショウズータンメン
炙焼肉辛子入りそば
"Sho-Zu Tan Men"
Noodles with Spiced Minced Meat
¥900

エビワンタン
海老入りワンタンのスープ
"Ebi Wan Tan"
Shrimp Won Ton in Soup
¥1,100

タカナそば
豚肉細切りとタカナ入りそば
"Takana Soba"
Noodles with Shredded Pork
and Mustard Greens
¥900

whether they fancy pizza, a curry, a steak or a Chinese. You don't ask them if they fancy a restaurant with 'a wide range of national and international dishes'. You need to specialize in something and it doesn't matter too much what it is; the best steaks, the finest fish, puddings-to-die-for. When you have a speciality, you have something on which to hang your advertising.

Now you can work on those catchy headlines; free lunch for the under-5s becomes 'The Heir is Free.' If you specialize in a single fish, it could be 'Come on in, just for the halibut.' Or with the pasta menu, 'All the Italian you need to know.' Those 4 seconds you have to grab attention can now be used to good effect.

6 Are you describing the dishes on the menu with enthusiasm?

IN-HOUSE PROMOTION

FRIED NOODLES

炒めたヤキソバ
"Kata Yakisoba"
Deep-fried Noodles
¥1,100

五目ヤキソバ
"Gomoku Yakisoba"
Fried Noodles with
Assorted Toppings
¥1,100

イーヤンツァオメン
二種類の炒め焼そば
"E Yan Tao Men"
Two kinds of Fried Noodles
¥1,300

牛肉ヤキソバ
牛肉細切り入り焼そば
"Gyuniku Yakisoba"
Fried Noodles with Shredded Beef
¥1,200

バンバンジー冷麺
特製ごまソース冷麺
"Ban Ban Jie Ryan Men"
Noodles with Special Cold
Chicken Sesame Sauce
¥1,300

COLD NOODLES

五目ひやし
"Gomoku Hiyashi"
Noodles with Assorted Toppings
¥1,200

ジャージャー麺
豚肉挽肉と甜麺醤のキューブ添え
"Jya Jya Men"
Noodles with Minced Meat
and Sweet Bean Paste
¥1,100

ラクサペナン
海鮮入りとろみマレーシア風カレーそば
"Laksa Penang"
Malaysian Noodles
with Seafood in Curry Soup
¥1,300

五目そば
"Gomoku Soba"
Noodles with Chop Suey
¥1,100

ポーツァイ チャーシュータンメン
ホウレン草とチャーシュー入りそば
"Po-Tsai Char Siu Tan Men"
Noodles with Spinach and Roast Pork
¥1,100

ネギそば
細切りチャーシューと香ネギ入りそば
"Negi Soba"
Noodles with Roast Pork and Leek
¥900

パーコーメン
揚げロース入りそば
"Pai-Koh Men"
Noodles with Pork Cutlet
¥1,200

牛肉そば
牛肉細切りとシメジ入りそば
"Gyuniku Soba"
Noodles with Shredded Beef
and Shimeji Mushrooms
¥1,100

パイユーチータンメン
蒸鶏入りそば
"Pai-Yu-Chi Tian Men"
Noodles with Steamed Chicken
¥1,200

ジャンツァイアーターンメン
鴨の燻製入りそば
"Jian-Tsai-A Tan Men"
Noodles with Smoked Duck
¥1,200

The dishes on the menu are normally explained: why should a client know the garnish for Filet de Sole Emmanuel X, or what Oreilles à la Rouennaise are? But then you find that 'Filet de sole Veronique', for example, is typically described as 'Filets of sole with a white wine sauce and green grapes.' That is no way to sell your best dishes. That's the recipe, not selling copy. Where is the enthusiasm? If you are not enthusiastic about the dishes, why should the customers want to try them? That sole could be 'Fresh filets of delicious sole, with an excellent white wine sauce and succulent green grapes.' You may not like that kind of approach, but the public does. And if you are worried about running out of adjectives, there are a very large number in Roget's Thesaurus.

The wine list

7   Are your descriptions of your wines likely to increase sales?

There is a genuine problem with trying to sell wine – it is a very difficult product to describe. Most of the descriptions in common use are meaningless. Phrases like 'a supple texture', 'full bodied', 'robust and complex', 'a big wine' are being used to describe a liquid. A gymnast may be supple, a mathematical equation complex and Lennox Lewis big, but what do these adjectives mean to the general public when it comes to wine?

It doesn't help to concentrate on the grape varieties either. How many can distinguish between the grenache, chardonnay and cabernet sauvignon varieties? Could your staff cope immediately if the guest said 'I'm particularly fond of the grenache grape? Which wines would you recommend?'

Few know that you can't even rely on the Cru classifications because they came into being in 1855 and the vines – and, therefore, the wine – were substantially altered in quality by the phylloxera epidemic which attacked them some years later.

The description of each wine needs to be aimed at a particular market. Take a sparkling white Bordeaux. Not everybody's taste by any means. Who is most likely to drink it and why? It seems that young women like it. If they are not particularly knowledgeable about wine, they are impressed by the fact that it sounds French and, therefore, safe. Also, it adds to the fun of the meal and is like one of their favourite drinks, Coca-Cola, because it has bubbles. The copy then writes itself – 'French, fun and fizzy'. Those are the three main customer benefits.

It is perfectly feasible to describe wines like that. 'A good quaffing wine' for the club member; 'Better drink this one sitting down' for those who always get someone else to drive home; 'Winner of the Montelimar Prix d'Or' for those who want the quality of the wine endorsed by someone other than you.

8   What are the staff told to say to introduce the subject of wine to the guests?

There is the common practice of handing out wine lists after asking the question 'Would you like wine this evening?' That, you will now recognize, is the principle of maximum choice; 'yes' you win and 'no' you lose. The correct question – if question there must be – is 'Would you like red or white wine this evening?' That's the principle of minimum choice and you win whatever the positive answer.

9   How do the guests get hold of a wine list?

So let's start again. The objective is to sell wine and, to do that, the client has to look at a wine list. A separate wine list is desirable to give the subject added importance. Sticking the wines at the end of the menu makes ordering wine very much an afterthought and the profit on a bottle of wine can be a substantial percentage of the total profit you get.

Now put the wine list on the table. Until the clients pick it up, they are thinking of whether to have wine, beer or bottled water. You want to move them to which wine? Why should they pick it up? Almost every wine list has a plain cover with a somewhat less than brilliantly imaginative headline: the headline is 'Wine List'. The cover has all the romance, excitement and appeal of a stock list for nuts and bolts.

So what's the alternative? A powerful headline or some cartoons associated with wine drinking. People love to look at cartoons.

10   What's the best way of selling wine?

Give the clients time to mull over their choice. Don't rush them. If you are offering vintage wines, tell them what scores

Wine lists are normally dull pieces of promotional literature. Here's a cover which helped to increase wine consumption by 15 per cent (*Source:* Diageo)

they achieved out of 7. But never list a wine as something like Nuits-St-Georges 1994/1995, because 1994 was 4 and 1995 was 6 and to charge the same for both vintages either shows you don't know one from another, or that you are charging the price for 1995 but are only going to deliver 1994. Some may think 'ah, but how many people are going to know that?' But not you; because that isn't ethical.

11   Are there wines for specific tourist markets?

American, Australian, Italian, Spanish, French, German, South African, Austrian, Portuguese, New Zealand. People know their own products better than the ones that come from abroad. Americans will drink Gallo wines, but may be less enamoured with Pomerol, if they haven't come across it before.

It is also worthwhile considering having the wine list printed in the language of the tourist. It may be difficult for the Japanese to choose between your Chablis and your Sancerre. To have to make up their minds, with the descriptions in a foreign language, is often asking too much.

Individual guests

12   Have you considered a singles table for individual guests? That is how we got *table d'hôte* – the host's table. The Victorians recognized that individual guests in a hotel could be lonely and the manager invited them to join him for a drink and dinner, so that the guest had congenial company. The restricted menu became necessary because everybody came in to dinner together.

You would need a host from the hotel in the evenings and a free drink or two in a private room, to be really successful.

Cigars

13   Do you have a humidor and a decent selection of cigars, in good condition and not over-priced?

You may not allow smoking in the restaurant, but 25 per cent of the population in the UK smoke. If the guest is offered the contents of the humidor, at least see that they are in fine condition. If you want to offer the best value for money, you will offer cigars from the Dominican Republic or Spanish Honduras. They score very well in international competition and are less expensive than those from many other sources.

Promotions

14   Do you have plans for special occasions?

Not just Christmas, New Year's Eve, Burns Night, Mother's Day, Father's Day and Easter Sunday, but Sunday brunch, Billy Bunter pudding menus for Monday night, etc. etc. A restaurant, open 7 days a week, wants to fill up on 14 meal occasions. Hotel restaurants fill at breakfast because there are guests in the bedrooms, so we'll leave breakfast aside. There are 7 lunch occasions and 7 dinner. You normally will attract different markets at different times. You need to devise what attractions you can offer and then back them up with special occasion attractions during the year.

For example, you may want to attract business people from Monday to Friday for lunch, families for Sunday Lunch and hold Dinner Dances on Saturday evening. That leaves you with Sunday evening, Saturday lunch and the other evenings. You may decide that Monday night you will offer Senior Citizens a reduction, Tuesday night is all the pasta the guests can eat, Wednesday night is Pudding Night – very popular, puddings – etc.

Then you need to identify your customer benefits. Take business entertaining. The prospective client is likely to want peace and quiet, unobtrusive service, the opportunity to offer their guest the food and drink the guest particularly favours, no music and a fuss made of the guest. The price is less important because successfully entertaining the guest is of far greater value.

15 Is there a dining club?

People like belonging to clubs and you want your guests to feel they belong in your restaurant. So create a club and offer them benefits from being a member of it: wine tastings, gourmet dinners and for club members; perhaps, the first drink free, occasional parties on very quiet nights during the year and the opportunity to buy wines at inexpensive prices at Christmas. I have known Michelin 3 Star restaurants do this.

16 Does Reception try to sell restaurant reservations when the guests register at your hotel?

It is an appalling criticism of hotel restaurants how many guests brave the driving rain, the sleet and snow, the breathalyzer, breakdown vans, parking problems, overcoats, taxis and cloakroom attendants – anything to get out of having to use the hotel restaurant. Well, the quality of the food you offer may be the reason, but that's nothing this book can help with. What you can do is take advantage of the problems the alternative to eating in the hotel brings. Your best headline for the restaurant is 'Why bother to eat out tonight?' And get the reception staff

IN-HOUSE PROMOTION

who check the guest in to try to get a booking for the evening.

You could also try offering an *à la carte* menu. Now this does not mean a wide range of attractive dishes. It means offering the client anything they want to eat if they order it a while in advance. Alright, they can't have jugged hare or baked octopus, but within reason. Why should guests go out if they can have their favourite dishes where they are.

17 Is there a free drink promotion when guests eat in the restaurant, offered to them when they register? You will need a suitable card for this: 'We'd like you to celebrate staying at the hotel by accepting a free drink of anything you like when you sit down to dinner.'

18 Have you considered offering a set menu at a reduced price for guests who sit down to eat at 6.30 or 7 o'clock?

The older generation are quite happy to eat early. Families with young children don't want them to go to bed too late.

19 Have you considered producing a General Manager's dinner dance by writing with details to a mailing list?

This can work very well if you know your local market. Write to them and announce that you and your partner are going to have a party and, if they'd like to join you, the tickets will cost this and the menu will be that, and the entertainment will be the other. As you're going to be there yourself, it is guaranteed to be a good evening.

20 Have you considered Speakers' Dinners, sponsored by the local paper, on Sunday nights?

These can work well if you have a ballroom. You need to attract different markets on the different occasions. Perhaps a local paediatrician talking about the health problems of children, or a pensions consultant on how to deal with dropping annuity rates. A famous hockey international would attract the local hockey players and a well known fisherman the lovers of the piscatorial chase.

21 Have you thought of a 'Cook with the Chef' promotion?

The local paper may well sponsor that as well. The better

your chef, the more likely people are to want to learn from him or her.

22   What about inviting local boutiques to have their mannequins showing new collections to restaurant guests on advertised occasions?

-You will need a mailing list of women who would be interested in this. The local boutiques should know their own customers. It could be a regular feature for Friday lunch.

23   Have you thought of creating a POETS Club for Friday? Push Off Early – Tomorrow's Saturday: it's a Friday afternoon drinking club.

24   Is there a link with the local theatre or cinema for pre- and post-theatre suppers? 'A meal 'n' a movie' is a successful promotion in many parts of America. There's a lot of pre- and post-theatre dining.

25   What about dishes named after your local celebrities?

The dishes would be chosen by the people concerned. It brought the leaders of fashionable society to the Savoy Hotel in Victorian times – consider Poire Belle Hélène, named after the Duchess of Aosta and Peach Melba, the way Nellie Melba, the opera singer, liked her peaches done – and it has been successfully done elsewhere.

Advertising

26   Do you have an advertising campaign in the local paper advertising the restaurant?

Remember that this campaign needs to concentrate on something that makes your restaurant special. You know from the chapter on the Marketing Plan how to assess the value of the campaign. What you still need to identify is what works best to improve your profits; which day is it best to advertise on and what is the optimum amount of space you should buy? Should you be on the Restaurant page, the Women's page or the City page?

You will be inundated with all kinds of offers to advertise.

You can't choose them all, so how do you decide? As a generalization, the drip-drip approach is most likely to succeed in the long run. Keep doing the same thing week after week and wear the market down. Like direct mail, there is a cumulative effect.

27   What should the advertisement look like?

It is quite common for a chain operation, in particular, to set down rules for the appearance of advertisements produced locally by the branches. To use such-and-such a typeface, such-and-such a layout. That's fine if the product you are selling fits the typeface. If it doesn't, you diminish the effect considerably.

Consider the difference between FASHION Show and **Fashion** Show. Which says models and catwalks to you? Or what about 𝔐𝔢𝔡𝔦𝔞𝔢𝔳𝔞𝔩 𝔉𝔢𝔞𝔰𝔱 and Mediaeval Feast? It is just ink on paper but the shape of the letters makes a substantial difference to the image.

Remember the type must not be smaller than 9pt and you need to provide all the information the reader will need to decide whether to buy the product.

28   Are you advertising the awards won by members of the staff?

Which restaurant is most likely to be able to cook well? One where you are told the chef has won an award in open competition – and the award is specified – or one where the offering is described as 'superb cuisine'?

29   Can you display pictures of famous local and national personalities using the restaurant, in the restaurant area?

30   Is there a proper poster advertising the restaurant both outside and within the building?

What should an attractive display contain? Not just a menu on an easel too near the ground, or in a box behind reflective glass and backlit, so that it dazzles the reader. At the right height, behind non-reflective glass – if you have to use glass at all – preferably with spotlighting from the front, with a powerful headline and with some popular specialities.

In hotels these menus are usually to be found outside the

restaurant entrance and in boxes in lifts. Unless guests walk past the restaurant door, they don't see it.

When guests are in the lift, they gaze at the panel showing the numbers of the floors, in order not to miss the doors opening. So, again, they are not going to study your menu at that point.

The places to put menus to achieve their maximum effect are where clients have to stand still for some reason and have time on their hands. When waiting for a lift is ideal. Or when waiting to register. When waiting to buy tickets in a theatre or in a queue for admission to a stately home. These are times when something to occupy you when you are waiting is always attractive.

31   Is there a headline which encapsulates the main attraction of the restaurant? 'The Empire Restaurant' is not a headline.

32   Do you have a mailing list of business people to advertise business entertaining?

A complete list of Directors, addresses and phone numbers is available in your locality's section of the Kompass Register, Windsor Court, East Grinstead House, East Grinstead, Sussex (tel.: 01342 326 972).

33   Do you have a mailing list for social eating-out? Are you collecting names and addresses from as many local guests as possible?

Tent cards

34   Are you using tent cards to improve turnover?

Tent cards are used for what is known as impulse purchasing. You had no intention of buying the product, but you saw it advertised and bought it on impulse – it's why they stack sweets by check-out counters in supermarkets. So you can use tent cards to sell your products in the same way. Take a product like a liqueur coffee. Berni Inns was a chain of pub restaurants that served over 20 million covers, 30 years ago. Twenty-five per cent – 5 million – of their customers had a liqueur coffee. They sold them by putting a tent card on the table, advertising them.

IN-HOUSE PROMOTION

Now, if you follow suit, remember not to put the tent card on the table at the beginning of the meal. When people sit down in a restaurant, they are thinking about soup or hors d'oeuvres, not liqueur coffees. As the staff remove the entrée plates, they should crumb the table down and put the tent card onto it. That will maximize sales.

Dessert menus are akin to tent cards and you can use the cards in lounges to sell afternoon tea, or a drink after dinner, or to suggest the clients make their next booking before they leave.

A tent card should not take up too much room on the table but it can be as high as you like. It needs a powerful headline like anything else; one for liqueur coffees is 'The end of a perfect day!' That gives you the two meanings of either it has been a very nice day, or a liqueur coffee would compensate for a dreadful day.

That was 34 things for you to think about, and when you have all those under your belt, you have a good chance of improving your restaurant turnover. It is, of course, a sizable task, but few restaurants fill up quickly enough for the owners. Effective marketing speeds up the process very satisfactorily.

Guest Directories

You find these in hotel bedrooms, and they can usually be much improved. What do you want to achieve by providing a Guest Directory?

1   You want the guests to use it. The headline is usually 'Guest Directory'. That, as you now know, is what it is, not what it does. So it breaks that important rule of advertising.
How much better is:

'Got a problem about anything in the hotel? Here's the answer.'

2   You want to take this additional opportunity to set the tone of the hotel. Are you friendly, formal, laid-back, fun, per-

sonal, dictatorial or what? It is your decision, but you can't tell everybody to smile and be friendly to the clients and then put into the Guest Directory something like 'Personal cheques cannot be accepted by the management unless accompanied by a valid Banker's Card.' Or 'The company takes no responsibility for guests' valuables unless deposited in the hotel safe.' The result is to totally confuse the customer. Just what sort of place are you running?

So the wording of the guest directory should reflect your stance. If you want to be warm and friendly, then the same points can be covered by 'We are very happy to take personal cheques if you have a Banker's Card' and 'We can take full responsibility for anything valuable you would like to leave in the hotel safe.' You could add 'Unfortunately, insurance companies won't cover us if anything happens to them anywhere else.'

See what a difference it makes.

3 You want to offer the clients the best service you can. Who is going to offer that service? Your staff. Well, you will always find the telephone extensions you need in a Guest Directory but seldom are there any names of people who can be contacted personally. Guests don't like impersonal service, any more than you do. So provide the names of the people they should ask for.

Does that mean that every time a member of staff leaves, you have to reprint the Guest Directory? No. Just put in a fictitious name. 'If you would like an extra blanket, just ring Sally Smith in the Housekeeper's office on extension 74.' Someone rings Housekeeping and asks for Sally Smith and whoever answers the phone knows it's a guest request. 'Sally is out at the moment but let me help?' is the answer. Untrue, but harmless.

4 You want the guests to understand how to use the facilities of the hotel. Well, can they by reading the Guest Directory? Certainly not if they are foreign tourists and can speak just about enough English to ask the way to the nearest castle. It would be perfectly possible to have an abbreviated version of the Guest Directory in different languages and to hand out the appropriate document at Reception when you collect the pass-

IN-HOUSE PROMOTION

port details. What could be more thoughtful – and which type of document would be more likely to get the client to buy more of your products.

Even to those for whom English is their first language the wording of many Guest Directories is convoluted and difficult to understand. A good way of testing whether the information is simple to follow is to get a 14-year-old to read the document. Then you ask questions like 'How would you phone Australia?' If, having read the appropriate section, they can say something like 'Dial 8 for an outside line, 6 for an international line, 0061 for Australia and then the city code, followed by the number', you will know the information can be understood by your guests. If the 14-year-old hasn't a clue, simplify the wording.

It helps to put in an Index too.

Bedroom advertising

There are many hotel products you may want to try to promote. These may include the hotel's restaurant and bar, the mini-bar in the room, room service, in-house films, return visits, Special Events, extending stays, Beauty Treatments in the Leisure Club, Tennis, Golf and, potentially, a lot more.

So, apart from the Guest Directory, how good is the promotional material? For the use of the mini-bar there is usually a form the guests are asked to complete when they take goods from it. They are invited to become stock control clerks. There is no suggestion that they will enjoy the goods inside the mini-bar, nor that it can satisfy any of their wants; just a form.

You can do better than that. You need a tent card on the mini-bar which attracts their attention and sells the products. The best headline is 'Hungry? Thirsty?' Those are the two customer benefits on offer. The guests can satisfy both hunger and thirst if they use the mini-bar.

A lot of the other products are only listed in the Guest Directory. If the guest doesn't open up the Directory – and they usually only do so if they have a problem – your sales arguments are not going to be heard through that route. You will need to have some form of advertising in the room. One of the best is a plastic carousel with four panels, enabling you to advertise four products. You put the flyers behind the frame cover and then you can replace them with new ones as time goes by.

Make the flyers in the panels bright enough to attract attention. As they are for immediate consumption, using the fashionable colours of today is appropriate.

Remember again that point about headlines. 'Tea and Coffee Making Facilities' is what it is. 'Settle back with a free hot tea or coffee in the privacy of your own bedroom' is what it does. What about a headline for the top of the carousel? 'Goodies' would probably attract attention. After all, that's what you're offering them.

If you want your guests to extend their stay, you need a suitable letter for everybody who is due to leave on the morning of the quiet night. The letter would explain that you are able to offer a reduced price, and this letter would be put onto the bed so that it was seen as soon as the guest walked in.

Posters

One of the most important and effective ways of advertising in-house is by the display of attractive posters (we have already touched on this in discussing restaurant promotion). Like everything else in advertising, there are strict rules you need to follow to make your posters as effective as possible.

1   The first job of a poster is to be seen. That doesn't just mean it has to be attractive. It can be as attractive as you like, but if you put it in some dark corner of a little used lounge, it is a waste of your money. If I say it has to be a visual scandal, it gives you some impression of the impact it needs to make instantly.

2   Remember the poster has to be a reason for stopping what the guest is doing, distracting them from what they are thinking, and getting them to concentrate on the message in the poster instead.

3   The poster represents your organization.

(So do signs for that matter. And a sign, written by hand, which announces 'Out of Order' reduces you to the level of a second class boarding house. So, incidentally, does the word 'Gents' on the door of a male cloakroom. Use 'Gentlemen'.)

A bad poster is worse than no poster at all. Make sure the poster uses up-market graphics, typefaces and colours.

4   The headline is vital in the process of stopping people in their tracks. Suppose your tariff doesn't include a full breakfast. So you want the guests to buy full breakfast, rather than continental. The right headline is: 'Gracious living starts with an English breakfast.' That's the main customer benefit – gracious living, rather than swallowing coffee and a croissant as you dash to work.

5   Posters are read from top to bottom. So put the important information at the top.

6   If you can, have a model in the picture using whatever product you are selling. Someone having a facial in your Health Club, for example. Don't make the model too glamorous. The public have to identify with the model and see themselves enjoying the same experience.

7   The pictures and the words must send the same message. There is no use in having the models dressed informally if the wording then announces that 'Guests may take advantage of the facilities if their requirements are communicated to the appropriate department.'

8   A large picture is better than several small ones. But if you are using a large picture of a model, the head shouldn't be larger than a normal head. Large heads are not liked by the public.

9   The poster headline should be at eye level; about 1.7 metres (5 ft 8 in) off the ground.

10   Most posters are to be found in boxes and back lit, which means that light is shining out and can dazzle the reader, who

then doesn't look at it as long as if the light was behind them. It may cost more to spotlight the poster, but you don't find anything back lit in an art gallery.

11 You need to distinguish between two kinds of poster. First, the one you can read at length because you've got nothing much better to do; second, the one you pass as you are walking along.

When you are waiting for the hotel lift, you have one eye on the sign that tells you that the lift is coming, or on the light that comes up when it has arrived. If there is a poster in front of you and the lift is 10 floors away and stopped, what better way to pass the time than to read the poster. Not behind you or on a side wall, but in front of you.

If you are on the move, you have only time for a fleeting glance. The task of the poster is then to give you the customer benefit you need in no more than seven words. Look at the headline for the breakfast poster again – 'Gracious living starts with an English breakfast': seven words.

12 Locate every poster where it is most likely to get attention. That does not mean on side walls. Think about yourself walking down a corridor: it is perfectly true that you could turn your head to look at a poster, but you are usually preoccupied with locating whichever room you want and avoiding any obstructions or people walking towards you. So mostly, you gaze straight ahead.

Now if the corridor ends with a blank wall and on that wall there is an attractive poster, then you begin to wonder what the poster is about. When you reach the end of the corridor, you are likely to give it a second glance.

So, there's a dozen golden rules for posters and you need to apply them all to give yourself the best chance.

Brochures

As you now realize, when you look at a typical brochure, the rules of advertising are being broken again. Do they have headlines, 'you' appeal, captions, wit, fashionable colours, colloquial language and crossheads? No, normally they are missing out on a variety of those key points. The same goes for Conference and Banqueting Packs. Consider what Professor Makens of Cornell University in the USA wrote on this subject after interviewing a considerable number of conference buyers.

> Each prospect or client represents a unique buyer with customized needs. Unfortunately, these needs are seldom heard by the sales representative. Instead of listening for clues that describe specialized needs, the sales representative finds it easier to send out a standard packet and hope that the client will pick out something useful. Meetings planners and conference organizers often complain that it is virtually impossible to differentiate among a stack of hotel 'fulfilment kits'.

In my experience that applies every bit as much in Britain. If your brochures met the standards set by the advertising industry, you would shine out like a lighthouse to distressed mariners. You need a combination of properly designed promotional material and a good sales letter.

Always remember that the public break no laws by not reading your promotional material. You need to jolly them along. If that happens when they least expect it, so much the better. Take something as dull and uninteresting as the matrix you find in all banqueting brochures of the rooms available, together with their sizes and capacities. Almost always the heading is 'Dimensions and Capacities'. An alternative is 'Before you decide on the menu, here are some numbers to crunch'. It is the sheer unexpectedness of the wit which stands you in such good stead. They read on to see if there is anything else amusing coming up.

Obviously, most hospitality products need promotional material, but it can never be designed specifically for an individual customer. So the covering letter becomes more important than the promotional material; not vice versa.

Summary

To produce good promotional material you must be prepared to believe that the basic industry designs can be improved; that the style of many menus, wine lists, etc. are inappropriate for today's market because they omit many of the best parts of advertising material.

Promotional material is designed to sell products and not to just give information about them. To do that you have to get the potential clients to look at them. No matter how good the promotional material, it must be carefully placed where it will attract the most attention.

Remember also that your promotional material will be most effective if it always follows the rules of advertising. Do not spend time reinventing the wheel.

With restaurant promotion, you are normally appealing to the general public rather than the group buyer. Promotional material, therefore, becomes even more important, as that is the best way of reaching the market. So use as many methods of persuading them to buy as you possibly can.

Case study

This case study illustrates:

- How the principles of advertising can be applied to a hospitality product like anything else.
- How to adjust a typical piece of hotel literature to proper advertising standards.

One of the greatest banqueting hotels in Europe is the Grosvenor House in London. Its largest ballroom can seat 1,500 guests and it has a wide range of excellent small suites as well. In creating a new Banqueting Brochure for the hotel in the late 1990s, the problem that had to be overcome was the one identified by Professor Makens at Cornell University: that the average client couldn't tell one hotel from another, because all the brochures looked alike and sounded alike.

When you look at your Banqueting Brochure, you probably do have the same kind of facilities as everybody else. The name of the game is to make them look and sound different and better. So at Grosvenor House we set out to do just that.

The first necessity with any piece of promotional material is to get the client to read it. So the brochure needs to have strong headlines on each page. You also have to remember that a great deal of banqueting is held strictly for enjoyment – weddings and Christmas parties, annual dinners and reunions. If the wording in the brochure is more appropriate for a funeral, it doesn't measure up to the client's mood.

So in the Grosvenor House brochure there was a modicum of humour. Typical headlines in the new brochure read 'Why Grosvenor House?' (explaining the customer benefits) but there was also one which announced 'You've got to start meeting like this' (giving details about the conference rooms). 'Let's talk about value for money' (saying why it was good value), but also 'It's probably better to start your diet the day after' (talking about the food), and 'The story of the rest' (talking about the bedroom accommodation).

When people read newspapers, they read the headlines, look at the pictures and read the captions under the pictures. Those are the three most popular elements of the paper. More people read captions than body copy. So the Grosvenor House had captions as well, such as 'Add a touch of business theatre' underneath a picture of a beautiful piece of ice work. Or 'Whatever the product, reveal it in style' under a picture of the launch of a new car. There was a particularly clever one for a picture of a wine steward by a wine rack: 'We started planning your enjoyment years before you fixed the date.' The caption points up the merits of laying down a cellar and of knowing the finer points of wine. But it does so light-heartedly, not formally with information about types of grapes and technical information about the 'acid base'.

Every brochure says how good the product is. The Grosvenor House brochure didn't rely solely on its ability to flatter itself. There was a page devoted to the comments of clients; Typical was one from Deloitte & Touche, a major consulting group. It read '... best one yet! Everything went even better than planned'. How much more powerful is that than your own hype? Additional credibility also comes from mocking the stylized language used in the industry. On bedrooms, the copy read 'Once upon a time there was a dank, subterranean dungeon which was not described in the castle brochure as a "superbly appointed bedroom", but that's about the only one on record.' Notice that if you said that to someone, you wouldn't have to change a word: it's exactly as people speak.

The photographs were right as well. You put yourself in the place of the organizers and ask yourself what you would want in their position. You would want somewhere quiet to work out any problems. Grosvenor House has a quiet lounge. So the picture of the client sees a man in a comfortable armchair, his face cupped in his chin, with a background of rich book cases. The caption reads 'Appreciated for its peace and comfort.' The picture of a beautiful boardroom has a caption 'If you're planning a seriously important meeting' using a modern phrase, rather than 'superb' this and 'magnificent nineteenth-century' that.

The wording can be colloquial too, because we use colloquialisms when we talk. 'This is the spot to ... go through your own presentation for the umpteenth time.'

The saying goes in selling, 'the more facts you tell, the more you sell'. Talking of leisure facilities, most brochures refer to something like 'superb state-of-the-art facilities'. The Grosvenor House talks about '6 reflex modular exercise machines, 2 Concept and 2 rowing machines, 4 Cybex and 2 Life Cycle exercise bikes and 4 Power Sport treadmills'. I haven't the faintest idea what any of them do, but they are state-of-the-art and the guests who are enthusiastic about exercise, will.

The Grosvenor House brochure is definitely different. It keeps to the rules of the advertising industry.

So why are so many brochures indistinguishable from each other? You have a choice of indolence, a lack of experience, playing safe, worrying about what the bosses will say and being old fashioned. All one can really say is that, if the average hotel brochure is structured correctly, then the advertising industry's efforts for other kinds of organization are all wrong.

11 Public relations

In hospitality marketing, public relations is normally one of two things: press relations or guest relations. Both are very important to you, and your costs – in terms of money – are not great. It does take time and you need to master the principles, but the results of good publicity can be spectacular. If the Savoy in London is one of the most famous hotels in the world, it is substantially because of excellent public relations, carried out over very many years. They have the best hotel archive in the world, packed with the evidence of the free publicity they have received.

Public relations has a major advantage over advertising; the public believes what it reads in the editorial of papers, far more than what it sees advertised. Advertise you give exceptional service by highly qualified staff and the public will discount your claims by a large percentage. Let a newspaper journalist say the service was good and everybody believes that it was; you're seen as biased and they're not.

Of course, public relations can be a two-edged sword. You can get damaging PR as well as favourable. Stopping or ameliorating potentially bad PR is part of your task.

For example, a bomb-making terrorist was inefficient and the device went off causing a substantial fire in a hotel at 10 o'clock at night. You can imagine the potential headlines – 'Hotel guests flee massive explosion'. The problem then is that, unless the public read the stories carefully, they may think it was your fault. How do you turn it round? Find a positive story, even in such difficult circumstances. In this case, after I told the press what had happened they published '500 hotel guests evacuated in 5 minutes' – proof that the fire drills worked excellently in an emergency.

Or take the dreaded possibility that a guest contracts salmonella after a meal with you and this is proved in court. The headline 'Diner hospitalized after eating out' could do you immense damage. What's the alternative? 'We very much regret this isolated incident. It's the first time it's happened in the 15 years the restaurant has been open. During that time we have served well over a quarter of a million meals, without any problems.'

The secret to creating good publicity out of bad, is to decide well in advance what you are going to do and say if there is an emergency. Don't try to make it up on the spot. Learn your lines before the problem ever crops up. I agree you may never need the solutions you come up with, but you can't afford to take the risk. Then, if the worst comes to the worst, you know how to react. Above all, make sure that nobody else speaks to the press in an emergency except the executive qualified to do so.

Press relations

Press releases

All the media are ambivalent about press releases. On the one hand they resent giving free publicity to commercial organizations. On the other, they have to be realistic; as businesses, they need to keep the wage bill down and press releases are a very cheap way to fill editorial space.

So how do you produce a good press release? It provides the answers to the questions, who, what, why, when, where and how much? Let's look at a simple example:

Who?	The Redminster Civic Museum
What?	will be holding an exhibition of Roman treasures
Why?	to help local school children studying early British history.

When?	The exhibition will run from October 17th to December 12th
Where?	in the Chester Hall.
How much?	Tickets will cost 75p.

Now that's simple enough, but of course, the media get a large number of press releases all the time. You will have to do better than that if you want more than a small notice on the 'What's on' page. So now you have to consider what more you can do to get more space.

Well, in this instance, you could send a picture of one or more of the Roman treasures. If they print that, you would be far more strongly featured. The treasure could be held by a typical school child. And how about getting the Professor at the local University to endorse the attraction of the exhibition? You have to work out how to make a bland announcement into a news story. The paper can do that for themselves, but a little help is no bad thing.

Every sort of gimmick has been used to sharpen up press releases. Christmas programmes have been sent out with everything from Christmas cake to crackers. They have been delivered by balloon, abseiled off high buildings and sent by carrier pigeon. You won't be going that far, but you can still be imaginative. You have to make it more noticeable than those of your competitors.

For restaurants, the local restaurant critics are of prime importance. They have to produce a column every week, so they need plenty of interesting subjects to write about. Again, you need to work out the angle; the story that will make it a good column. Has your chef won an award, are you having an Albanian Gourmet Week, is there a wine tasting of the new Bulgarian vintages? It may take you a long time to get the critic to visit you, but keep at it. Persistence pays off.

You can send two kinds of press releases. You can send a brief one, which just gives the bones of the story. Or you can send a long one, which saves the paper from doing any more work than printing it verbatim. In your short one, avoid the error of making value judgements. Don't say 'a wonderful tasting champagne'. It is for the journalist to decide whether it is wonderful or not. But you can say – if it is true – '70,000 bottles of this champagne were sold in the UK last year'. Facts you can provide; opinion you can't. There is no harm in sending both kinds of press release together if you feel so inclined.

There are other pointers to remember with press releases.

1 Those 4 seconds you had to get the attention of the readers with your direct mail has gone all the way up to 5 seconds when it comes to press releases! You need a strong headline just as much for the latter as the former. It has to include the key point of the story and, hopefully, some clever wording to make it even more arresting.
2 Keep the sentences short. That's the way most news stories are written and you are saving the journalist the time it takes to cut up long ones.
3 Don't be vague. Don't say 'yesterday' or 'tomorrow'. Give the dates. Provide the facts.
4 Don't put more than three paragraphs on the first page.
5 It is always good to have a quote from the person who is in charge at your end: 'Chef Auguste Morel said ...'; 'General Manager, Howard Plant, commented ...'
6 At the bottom, put in a contact name, so that you can be contacted to provide more information.
7 If you don't want the story to be published before a key date, just put 'embargoed until (date)' at the end.
8 When you type the press release, always do it with double or 1.5 spacing, so that it is easy for the journalist to alter or amend the copy.
9 Put 'Ends' at the end, and the date on which you sent the release.

It looks far more professional if the press release is sent to the media on paper headed 'News Release' or 'Press Information'. With the radio, it's called a Radio Cue Sheet. If you want it on TV, you need the story summarized in one or two paragraphs – so that the news reader can just read it out as it is. Also, with TV, highlight the visual attraction of the story. The name of the game is to persuade the News Editor to read your release; that, with a spot of polishing, a few words added and subtracted, it can be used, thus saving newsroom staff time and trouble.

But life isn't always that easy. You need to follow up that your release has been studied at all. And be sure to label any photographs you send, so that if they are mislaid, they can be attached to your release when they surface again. Keep at the media, offering more information if they want it. If it doesn't work, ask them what would interest them.

If you want to send your material to a number of media organizations, you could consider paying companies like Two Ten Communications or PIMS to send it 'down the line'. At a cost of around £100 they will send the material to several hundred media for you. You can also use them to produce a Radio Lynx day for you. For £300 to £1,000 they will arrange a live link-up with up to a dozen radio stations in your area to promote your story.

Building relations with the media

You should build up a picture of the media people you deal with and the way their company works. You need to keep detailed records of their deadlines, but also their personal characteristics. With magazines, you need to know when they decide on their features. The Features List is normally produced at the beginning of each year and plots the future issues. Try to fit in with them: if the feature is on Mexican cooking, try to provide a Mexican recipe associated with your own restaurant.

If you keep a list of the deadlines and the copy dates, it helps you not to bother them just when these are approaching and they need some peace. Remember, some parts of a publication are immediate; the news pages, for example, but some can be planned and even printed days in advance; the magazine pages, for instance. You need to plan well ahead. A magazine may decide on a feature several months in advance and you need to know about it from the start, if it fits in with your product. Beaujolais Nouveau may only arrive in November, but the story about it may well be planned in July.

Try to establish relations with media people, so that if there is a quiet period for them, they might ring you to see if you have an interesting story.

Always talk to the press, whatever the circumstances. If you don't, they'll do the story with whatever accuracy they can manage and it probably won't be as favourable to you. They may even ask your competition to comment on the story and that could do you even more damage. Your competitor might comment 'That would never happen in a well run organization'!

Image

You can get into the media in all sorts of ways. One restaurant did so by producing a number of April Fool menu items, like Soup in the Basket and Brussels Sprout Trifle. That did no harm. One town got enormous publicity for a story that it was the most boring place in the world to spend a weekend. That wasn't so good. You have to be careful: it is not true that all publicity is good publicity.

One of the main objectives is to achieve the reputation of being the centre of the local social scene. You can go a long way towards that by such efforts as:

● Allowing important local associations to meet free on quiet days in your conference rooms. Consider the low prices given to Rotary Clubs.
● If you have a quiet night in your ballroom, give it to a local charity to raise funds. You could just charge them cost for the food and drink.
● Give hospitality at Christmas to the deprived, the disabled and the elderly.
● Bring in sixth formers from the local schools to see your work at first hand. Give them the opportunity to consider your part of the industry as a future career. Arrange for photographs of the group with you for the local paper.
● See if you can get a live broadcast from your hotel or restaurant.

Recipe columns

A substantial part of the costs of any of the media is the staff. If you can do the work of the staff efficiently for nothing, the publisher, editor or whoever is happy. The weekly recipe column comes under that heading. Offer to provide it. If your offer is accepted, you have a medium which is, effectively, saying that yours must be a good product otherwise it wouldn't be allowed to be a part of their excellent publication

Visiting journalists

Tourism organizations are equally keen on good publicity. They get approached by a lot of journalists for cooperation when the journalists visit their region. If you can house or entertain the journalists, you have a better chance of being mentioned in the forthcoming story. Tourism organizations are always glad of the help of the local industry.

Media photography

A first consideration is whether the publication wants black and white or colour. Normally send photographs 25.5 cm × 20.5 cm (10 in × 8 in), with a gloss finish. Colour is best done from transparencies and these cost around £30 each. Hopefully, the publication will be satisfied with a colour photo.

Use a professional photographer unless you are good at it. The local press photographer is a good idea.

Take plenty of photographs to make sure you have got some good ones. Paste on the back of the pictures what the subject is. Name the people in the photograph and give the publication you are sending it to a contact name and phone number.

What makes a good photograph for the media?

- People doing something – not a group just smiling at the camera.
- Action across the whole picture – if the action is centred in the middle, the photo will be cropped (the sides cut off) to eliminate the dull bits. Put your product's name in the middle of the picture – if the picture is cropped, your name will still be there.

PUBLIC RELATIONS

- Make sure your people are wearing distinctive badges – these will come out clearly.
- Use models the readers will identify with – for example, if the photograph is for a publication in Japan, use Japanese models.

Press launches

1 Send out the invitations a couple of months in advance if you can. Journalists are busy people.
2 Try to make the subject of the launch unusual, interesting, intriguing and to the point. They have to read the invitation for you to succeed. Follow-up afterwards to make sure they did read it.
3 Keep the presentation short. The audience just want the message and the hand-outs. They will ask questions if they want to, and then do the rest.
4 If you want to get into the national press Picture Desk diary, you will probably need to send out a photo-call notice 2 weeks in advance, i.e. tell the national press when the photo opportunity will be taking place.
5 Make up a comprehensive press pack and send it also to people who can't or don't come.

Guest relations

There is a lot you can do.

History board

If the competition are more modern, make a virtue of your age. Put up a history board, emphasizing how experienced you are and how long you have been serving the community.

Management photographs

Customers like dealing with people rather than organizations. Put up photographs of your key staff, so that the customers can recognize who they are talking to. Everybody behaves that little bit better as well, if they are not anonymous.

However, such things as Staff Member of the Month displays are meaningless to the customers and have no role to play. The guests didn't choose the staff member, so your opinion carries no weight with them. Such displays are better found in the staff area.

Internal publicity

1   Have you tried displaying special menus, photographs of VIPs who have used you in the past, a notice board of recent events, creative banqueting ideas and awards the staff have received. It all reinforces your message of being that little bit better than the competition.

The good effect of these displays can be spoiled, however, if the displays themselves are cheap and nasty. The sort of person who can help you here is a window dresser for a good local shop. They are experts on display.

2   Keep a press cuttings book which you can display for guests.

3   If you host an important conference and the company will be distributing its own press material, including photographs of speakers at the podium, make sure the podium has your operation's name clearly on the front.

4   Equally, if an organization has not thought of the possible photography publicity angles, you can bring them to its attention. The media would probably not be overwhelmed to receive a photograph of yet another new product, but if what they were seeing was made of ice cream and 2 feet tall, it could be a different matter.

Newsletter

A newsletter circulated to customers is a relatively inexpensive way of promoting the hotel's image, keeping in touch with the clientèle and selling all kinds of products. A good example of

Cook with the Chef to repeat sell-out success

Ken Ham pictured with Pierre and Martin

THE CHANCE to cook with Pierre Chevillard last December was a sell-out within 48 hours of it being announced. Well, how often do you get the chance to improve your cooking under the paternal eye of a Michelin starred expert. You now have another chance on Monday, May 15th. The price is £235 if you're by yourself and £310 if two of you are going to come. That includes the classwork, a wonderful 3 course lunch with wine, a night staying in the hotel, English breakfast and VAT. Pierre wants you to get personal help, so numbers will be kept to 10; hurry, hurry, hurry.

Book a chair for The Chair

GRAND NATIONAL Day is Saturday, April 8th.

It is only right and proper that the world should know how you always manage to pick the winner of the Grand National. This advice should not be restricted to the immediate family. You should bring the pin with you to the hotel's Grand National Day Lunch and watch the world's greatest steeplechase on the big screen. You can then look forward to walking up and collecting your prize. Prizes, but no betting, so deliver your coup de grâce to your bookies before you come. Pierre actually uses quinces for his coup de grace, you might try it some time.

£50 includes the reception, a thundering 3 course lunch, wines, coffee and VAT.

Great dresses I have known

IF YOU have ever wondered how they get the clothes right in TV costume dramas, put Wednesday, May 17th in your diary. Joy Meier, who has been involved in costume design on TV for 25 years, will be letting you into the secrets. A lot of the clothes go on to be popular collector's items and Joy has a fund of stories of the peccadilloes of the rich and famous. Fashion design has always been a fascinating topic and it's always a good day when you can listen to an expert. The cost will be £40 for the reception, one of Pierre's fine lunches, as well as wine, coffee and VAT.

Summer Lunch on Sunday, August 6th

I KNOW it's freezing cold and winter, but one day it will be August – freezing cold August. No I jest. August 6th, 2 days after the Queen Mothers 100th Birthday, we're going to have the sort of party she would enjoy. All blazers and boaters and a Dixieland Jazz band to chase the clouds away. Great summer food, Pommery's Summertime Champagne and all's well with the world. £55 for all the above including wines and VAT.

Chewton Glen washes whiter

WELL, it makes a change from Persil and it's all because, at vast expense, we've built a new laundry over the kitchen. If you've ever blanched at the thought of the size of the Monday morning wash. How would you deal with 60,000 pillowcases, 30,000 sheets, 200,000 towels and 40,000 bathrobes a year? No, emigration is not an option. Just get yourself a washing machine the size of an average elephant and ironing equipment of such complexity that you need an Electrical Engineering degree to operate it. Worry not; your linen will, in future, be even more perfect.

Only 29,999 to go

A good newsletter has to look and read like a newspaper (*Source:* Chewton Glen)

how a newsletter can be used is provided by the acclaimed Chewton Glen hotel, which is the subject of the case study at the end of this chapter.

In the limelight

Which executive is going to represent your organization as its spokesperson? Is he charismatic? Does she have a pleasant personality? Are they terrified of being in the public eye? Who is going to write their speeches? Do they know how to make a speech?

The executive chosen has a tremendously important job. If you make a mistake in the privacy of your own organization, few people may know. Make it on a platform, before a major audience, and the business can be ruined. Remember Mr Ratner at the Institute of Directors conference, talking about his jewellery.

So, whoever is going to undertake the task, should be prepared to go back to school and learn the subject thoroughly. There are experts who can help. You can get courses on how to appear on TV, there are professional speechwriters, there are stage management companies, there are books.

Specialist *public relations consultancies* exist of course, and are normally effective; but they are expensive – maybe £1,000 a day in London. They need very detailed briefing because your industry is not, necessarily, something they know much about.

Speeches

If you have to make one, do:

1 Type it out in a size you can easily read.
2 Make sure that you have a high enough lectern.
3 Use a tie microphone if you can, so that you don't have to bother about the amplification.
4 Underline the words of the speech you want to emphasize.
5 Put a vertical line after words where you want to take a breath or a pause. So:
   'Old King *Cole*/ was a <u>merry</u> old soul/ and a <u>merry</u> old
      soul, was he.'
6 Try to vary the speed and the tone of your voice. A dull drone doesn't help keep the audience's attention.
7 The bigger the audience, the bigger the gestures have to be, if you want to get over the message.

Summary

Public relations is a powerful weapon and probably one of the least expensive. It does demand, however, that you carry it out professionally, because the work will be scrutinized by professional media executives and not just by the general public.

Case study

This case study illustrates:

- How a small, individual hotel can achieve a great deal of press coverage.
- The right way to go about producing a newsletter.
- The importance of awards.

According to *Gourmet Magazine* in the United States, Chewton Glen in the New Forest in England is the best country house hotel in the world. Michael Winner, a particularly vitriolic press critic of everything second rate in hotels, judges it his favourite hotel outside London. Michelin has given the restaurant a star and the motoring organizations their highest accolades. So it is a seriously good operation. This is the result of 30 years' hard work by its founder, Martin Skan, whose ambition was always to create a great hotel and did so.

Chewton Glen only has 60 bedrooms and it is situated a long way away from the major population centres in Britain. It never advertises but Martin Skan spends a lot of time and effort on public relations. Having a fine product is only half the battle; the other half is to get people to buy it. It is particularly hard if you are a small company up against the major chain operators.

One of the principal ways in which Chewton Glen keeps in touch with its clientèle is by producing a newsletter. You will have seen an illustration of part of it in the chapter. Any hospitality organization could produce something similar – indeed, a large number of them do. It is not particularly expensive and it is a good medium for selling all kinds of products. Many of Chewton Glen's special offers are taken up in large quantity as soon as the newsletter is sent out.

The name of the game, however, is to make the newsletter an effective promotional effort. You will notice from the illustration that the Chewton Glen newsletter looks like a page of a newspaper. What is more, the use of serif typefaces makes it look like an upmarket paper. Sans serif typefaces are more commonly used by tabloids.

A newspaper wants its readers to be interested in the stories it publishes. So it uses striking headlines to obtain their attention. They are informative, often witty and they bring out the main customer benefit. Of course, you have to give the readers credit for understanding the references: 'The Chair' is a famous fence on the Grand National Steeplechase course; 'Chewton Glen washes whiter' is a throwback to one of the most famous advertising slogans ever, 'Persil washes whiter'.

The way you read a newspaper is by first reading the headlines, then looking at the pictures, then reading the captions under the pictures. So most of the Chewton Glen newsletter pictures have captions.

The writing is light-hearted, because a hotel is in the fun business. The journalism needs to reflect this image. Notice, I say 'journalism'. A newsletter is another form of newspaper, so the rules of journalism have to apply. This, first of all, involves the graphics and the layout. If your newsletter doesn't look like a newspaper, it loses a lot of its impact. The stories are important too and if the writing isn't as good as a journalist produces, then the reader loses interest and the newsletter goes into the wastepaper basket.

Journalists write to a set of rules. The best summary of these is in a book produced by The Economist magazine, called *The Economist Style Guide*. You can buy it in a book shop.

The writing involves facts; it doesn't go in much for bland phrases and generalizations. Remember that saying, 'The more facts you tell, the more you sell.' It also keeps the reader involved by making humorous remarks. Readers who are amused go on reading in the hope that there will be other jokes coming up.

Public relations also involves the media writing favourably about your product. Martin Skan concentrates on the most influential media. He has secured articles on the hotel in popular travel magazines all over the world. It is a long process because everybody wants the magazines to write up their products. Martin is prepared to work on a magazine for several years before he finally achieves his objective; which can be six or eight pages in the magazine devoted exclusively to his hotel. He will invite the journalists to stay at the hotel and be particularly careful to ensure that they really enjoy themselves. After all, they have to compare their reception at Chewton Glen with all the other products they sample. He will contact them again and again.

Public relations also involves the hotel in attracting the local market. If you have a particularly fine hotel with a famous restaurant, it is possible that the local citizenry get intimidated by the perceived superiority of the product. You have to make it appear local and human to them, even if you are competing on an international scale. So Pierre Chevillard, the great chef at the hotel, also writes a recipe column in the local newspaper. He writes about the simple dishes that the public would like to cook better.

If you want to create a good image locally, you also have to support the local community. The hotel is often chosen as the venue for charity fund raising. The hotel's normal profits are cheerfully sacrificed to good causes. Indeed, not just local charities. Every year, a group of children from Chernobyl in Russia visit the district and are entertained to lunch at the hotel. It is a happy memory they will be able to contrast with the difficulties they normally have to encounter.

The hotel sets out quite deliberately to win awards. It is difficult to convince potential customers that you have a fine leisure club if you simply say in your brochure that you have something like 'superb leisure facilities'. If you can say that you won the National Award for the Best Leisure Club in the UK, this is far more convincing.

It also uses endorsements from its clientèle in its promotional material. If a captain of industry writes that the conference went well, a reproduction of his words of praise says far more about the property than all the hype the hotel writes for itself. Chewton Glen adopts a modest tone in describing its facilities. It relies on the words of other, unbiased, critics to speak for it.

You may well not have as good an operation as Chewton Glen. That doesn't prevent you from adopting much the same approach to improve your own image. And the best thing about good public relations is that it seldom costs a fraction of the money that would have to be spent on advertising to get the same results.

12 Special Events and Short Break Holidays

Special Events

Special Events are the business we invent. They have a very long history in the hospitality industry. The Monte Carlo Rally was invented to provide business for Monte Carlo in the winter. The Cresta Run brought people to St Moritz in the winter too. Both were nineteenth-century marketing. Similarly, with the Cannes Film Festival, the Hong Kong Rugby Sevens and skiing in the Canadian Rockies. As the builder of the Banff Springs hotel in Canada said at the beginning of the last century 'If we can't bring the scenery to the tourists, we'd better bring the tourists to the scenery.'

All hotels and restaurants might benefit from Special Events. Their importance can best be seen when you contemplate a low point in your business cycle. Not only have you not got enough business, but your competitors are not doing so well either. You can't take enough business from them to fill your gaps and so you are left to rely on that most exciting of possibilities – inventing new business for yourself.

Special Events fall into two main categories:

- Business based on events created by others; going to concerts at the Royal Festival Hall and staying overnight; groups coming for sports events, exhibitions and fairs.

- Creating the events yourself and then selling them to people interested in the subjects; an antiques weekend, a bird watching weekend, a bridge tournament, a wine tasting, cook with the chef or creating conferences at colleges during vacations.

What makes a successful Special Event?

There are six elements you need, ideally, for a successful Special Event:

1 An expert.
2 A way of publicizing it.
3 A sponsor.
4 A programme.
5 A piece of promotional material.
6 Enough time to get it off the ground; a year is the optimum.

There are occasions when you might get away without one or other of the elements. If you are selling people on going to the opera, you may not need an expert. If a newspaper or magazine can be persuaded to do a Special Event as a reader trip, you may not need a piece of promotional material; the editorial in the media may be enough. Almost always, however, you need all six.

Why do you need an expert? Because the market is usually the fanatic; the real enthusiast. It is the real enthusiast who is prepared to go the long distance and spend the money to follow his or her favoured pursuit. If you are creating a bridge tournament, do you offer Swiss Pairs or Teams of Four? What would an attractive fly fishing programme include? How would you set up a crossword championship? How much beer should you have available for a darts tournament? Nobody can know it all. Retain an expert who does know.

Why do you need a way of publicizing it? Because you have to tell the serious enthusiast that the event exists. If good media are not available to enable you to reach them, you are unlikely to be successful.

Why do you need a sponsor? Because you will have

expenses and it is better to have them covered by somebody else. If you are doing a teach-in for university students, a bank may sponsor it because they want the students to have their accounts with the bank. An antiques auction house may sponsor an antiques weekend. You will already have heard of companies offering corporate hospitality, bringing favoured guests to sporting events.

Why do you need a programme? To attract the enthusiasts.

Why do you need a piece of promotional material? To explain what's on offer.

Why do you need enough time? Because there is usually a lot to do and you don't want to fail, or make the wrong decision because you ran out of time. If you get it right the first time, it will build. If you don't, you probably won't get a second chance; you can recover from failure, but it is easier to build on success.

Do all Special Events work?

No, they don't. But if you are going to lose a fortune in a low season period, the worst that can happen if you try a Special Event is that you lose a fortune plus the cost of the Special Event. You are going to lose a fortune anyway – and for the next umpteen years too. Short Break holidays in Britain are now said to be worth £2 billion a year to the British hospitality industry. They were started back in the 1960s on exactly this premise.

What sort of Special Events could help your hotel?

Well, in Hampshire, you could run Classic Car events, using the fantastic collection of Classic Cars in Lord Montagu's Motor Museum in Beaulieu. Near Glasgow there are rhododendrons flowering in January in the Younger Botanic Gardens. If you are running a hotel overseas, the underground caves in Puerto Rico would attract any number of potholers and the orchids in Borneo are fantastic.

The key to deciding which special event to try is knowing how many people are seriously interested in the subject. If you want 200 participants, you need a market of 10,000. If a specialist magazine has an audited circulation of 10,000, that should be sufficient (quilt making, for example). A generalist magazine should have a circulation of about 50,000 (gardening, for example).

Which kind of Special Event should you try first?

Start with one that takes advantage of an existing event in your location. When you are comfortable with the promotion of that, try inventing one for yourself. Don't wait for the results of an existing event before starting to plan one of your own; the empty seats, tables and rooms need filling as soon as possible.

What if you don't sell enough tickets?

If the only way you can run a Special Event linked to an attraction of some sort is to buy tickets for the show in advance, how do you justify the investment if you don't sell the tickets?

The point to recognize is that this revenue should be considered like a win on the Lottery. It is not part of your normal income. The business you do day after day is designed to pay for your fixed overheads – rent, staff, heating, etc. To those fixed costs have to be added the marginal costs of having the guest with you – the food they eat, the additional laundry, etc. You don't expect the revenue to pay the same proportion of the fixed costs as usual. If you don't do the event for those quiet periods, you won't have any revenue for those empty beds or empty seats. The revenue you will now get makes you a profit. That profit makes a contribution to fixed costs, but not as great a contribution as you expect from normal business. So, you may indeed need to buy the tickets for the event you are running; sporting Special Events are a typical example.

So let's say that you want to buy 100 tickets at £10 each – an investment of £1,000. Add to that an investment of £200 for direct mail – you send out a letter and need to pay for the paper, envelopes and postage. Total: £1,200. Let's say that each package costs the guest £100, including the ticket, and of that £100, you make a profit of £40 after covering your marginal costs.

You are aiming to sell 100 tickets. If you sell 30 of them you will recover the whole £1,200 investment, i.e. you make £40 out of the 30 guests = £1,200. So your break-even point is 30% of the potential sales. That doesn't seem too hard a target.

Don't forget that we are assuming that you lose all the cost of the other 70 tickets. That you don't sell them back to the venue or to any of your staff or guests. But you may well recover at least a proportion of your outlay. If you've chosen a popular event, the possible risk of a loss should be very small.

How do you go about setting up a Special Event?

1   Decide which one you want to try. As I say, it would probably be best to begin with an existing event in the town; one where there is a potential to fill the hotel, but where there isn't anything like it happening at the moment.

2   Identify your expert. Have him or her to lunch with a view to tapping their brain and with the suggestion that, if you can come to an agreement, they might like to be paid for their advice.

3   When you lunch the expert, find out:
    (a) Where is the market is to be found in bulk?
    (b) What media do they read specifically about their hobby?
    (c) What kind of programme would be of interest to them besides attending the event? With a sports event, for example, they might be attracted if they could meet the players. If they are visiting an exhibition, perhaps they would like a speech on the subject from an expert on the night before their visit.
    (d) Who might be a suitable sponsor. If it was a darts tournament, then somebody who makes darts. If it was something to do with a seniors market, then perhaps a cruise company who want their holiday budgets.
    (e) What would the right sort of cost be?

4   If you are happy with what the expert tells you, agree their fee, subject to the Special Event going ahead. Agree a final decision in a couple of weeks.

SPECIAL EVENTS AND SHORT BREAK HOLIDAYS

HOSPITALITY SALES AND PROMOTION

5   Work out a possible Profit and Loss account. How much would you be spending and how much profit could come from filling the programme?

Try to work on spending, as a budget, about 10 per cent of the potential profit. Then your break-even point isn't too high. Talk to your financial experts and get the marginal costs of one client staying – laundry, cleaning the rooms, etc. Then when you produce your P&L account, nobody can argue with the figures.

6   You could offer the programme to the suggested media as a Reader Trip. If you can't get agreement with the market leader, try the others. If you are doing an orchid event, a newsletter for a National Orchid Society is likely to be more productive than a magazine called *Gardeners' Universe*.

7   Try to get a sponsor now that you have the expert and the publicity medium.

8   When you have the expert, the publicity medium and the programme, decide your timetable. Remember, a sponsor is very welcome but not essential. Try to give yourself ample time to get the programme off the ground. If the publicity medium comes out monthly, it may set up the pages 3 months in advance. Then you will need to provide the programme 4 months in advance and the issue you are interested in will be 3 months before the event. You could repeat the publicity at 2 months and 1 month if you don't sell out at 3 months. But the 3 months before issue is vital. Don't start 2 months out; it is likely to be too late.

9   You will probably need a piece of promotional material as well, unless the medium chosen is publicizing all the details. The essential thing in such a piece is that the programme is *attractive*. All-singing, all-dancing promotional material tends to put off the enthusiasts, who are interested in their hobby, not in the hype.

10   Make sure that whoever is going to deal with enquiries for bookings knows all about the event and that there is somebody

with this knowledge available whenever the enquiry comes in. People could be ringing on Sunday and you may only have that one chance to get them to book.

11   It is perfectly reasonable for people to pay for these packages in advance. Not vital, but reasonable.

12   Always ensure that there is a hotel representative available throughout an event, if it is held in the hotel. The expert will run it, but you need to have someone on hand in case something goes wrong. Produce a Guidelines document for the hotel in advance, so everybody knows exactly what is supposed to happen.

There are different categories of Special Events; these are sports, hobbies, education and business. If you are trying to get by without paying an expert, then you need answers to the following questions.

How do you find the enthusiasts?

There may well be Yearbooks or Membership Lists produced by the relevant organizations. For example, the Royal Horticultural Society produces *The Gardener's Yearbook*. In it you can find everything from the Daffodil Society to the Association of Botanic Gardens. There are nearly a dozen different rhododendron societies in the UK.

What are the different customer benefits?

With hobbies and sports the answer to this is simple; the enthusiast wants to learn more about their subject. There is also another major advantage, though; enthusiasts often find great difficulty in arousing interest for their favourite subject among their family and friends. The opportunity of spending time with people who are similarly inclined, is very attractive.

When you come to an event with an educational purpose, there have to be advantages to the prospective attendee, to the individual paying the bill (who can be a relative) and to the person who is going to disseminate the information.

For the pupil or student, this is a chance to learn more about the subject from experts. It is also an opportunity to spend time in a different town in a nice hotel. If the parent is paying, then it is an opportunity to give their child a better chance of getting good marks in the subject discussed. For the teacher there is the opportunity of picking up hints from experts and also, when the child or student gets good marks, the credit will normally go to the teacher; everybody will have forgotten the benefit of the special event.

Business is different again. One of the largest Special Events ever was a 3 day teach-in for the owners of hairdressing salons. The attraction was Vidal Sassoon, a great hairdresser. Two thousand hair salon owners came to London from all over the world. They came because the cost of the teach-in was far less than the additional profits they could legitimately hope to make from the experience of listening to Mr. Sassoon. The promotions were carried out all over the world by British Airways who wanted to sell airline tickets in January – there's the sponsor. The programme was devised by Mr. Sassoon – there's the expert. The media were the hairdressing magazines.

Are there smaller events you could try?

Of course, there are events on a smaller scale than this for you to try. Trivial Pursuit evenings in pubs are a kind of Special Event. You could invite the local boutique to stage a fashion show in your restaurant one lunch time when new fashions have just become available. The restaurant doesn't have to be restricted to the boutique's customers. It would be an attraction to women who had never been near the shop.

Wedding Fairs are Special Events. Here you get representatives of the various services that are needed for a wedding to come together for an exhibition in the hotel on a Sunday. The brides-to-be can make many of their arrangements in one place: car hire, wedding cake, toastmaster, printing, morning dress hire etc. You get more potential wedding customers and the cost of promotion can be defrayed by all the other, non-competitive, organizations who are also taking part.

There are fairly small Special Events taking place in hotels all the time: these are the annual functions of sports clubs, school reunions, etc. There are things you can do for them which would increase your profits. The more people who buy tickets, the more money you make. Do you help them sell tickets? Do you help them with attractive posters for the pavilion, or with their direct mail or their local advertising? Why should an Old Boy's Association committee know the first thing about advertising or direct mail? Yet, on their success in attracting guests, depends your profit. So help them.

The correct sales approach when creating a Special Event

As always, your main concern is to identify what benefits there are for the customer. In terms of Special Events, you have an easy task. The guests are going to have a good time, or be better equipped to achieve their financial or educational aims. You have a genuine quality product to sell, but the people to whom you are selling are often very nervous of commercial organizations of any kind. The mere idea that they are going to be sold anything puts their hackles up. You do not approach a Head Teacher or a Gardening Society Chairman like a New York Travel Agent.

So what's going to reassure the client? Primarily, the fact that you have done similar things before. Not because this illustrates your expertise but because the enthusiast is not being asked to do something new. Most enthusiasts are concerned that a new idea is going to take too much of their time, involve them in costs the club or society can't afford, expose them to criticism if it doesn't work and hurt their reputation if their members don't support the idea.

Notice that the problem is seldom cost; the money that people spend on hobbies and sports cannot be justified, as you may justify buying a new carpet. They pay hundreds of pounds for pieces of nylon thread, wood and metal, called a fishing rod. Many of them are worried at the prospect of getting involved with the world of commerce; most of the people you deal with in Special Events lead sheltered lives.

It, therefore, becomes extremely important that they learn quickly that you are entirely trustworthy, that your word is your bond and that you have nothing up your sleeve except a wish to fill hotels. You must reassure the organizers that they run no risk if they agree to do a Special Event with you.

Now, obviously, this does not apply to business Special Events. It doesn't apply to newspaper editors. The benefit to the newspaper is to offer reader a better service than they will get from a competitor publication. When I was first setting up the National Crossword Competition, I visited *The Times* and asked them to sponsor it. They asked me why they should. I told them that, if they didn't, I would go to the *Daily Telegraph*. They then understood why they were sponsoring it; as far as crosswords are concerned, *The Times* and the *Daily Telegraph* have been in deadly competition for readers for years.

Another important element in the sales approach is to take the subject of the hobby or sport very seriously indeed. The idea that people may be absolutely engrossed in the nocturnal habits of the badger may seem to you ludicrous. That isn't the point. If badger lovers want to spend time in your hotel – or pub, or conference room, or ballroom – because of their interest in this branch of the Mustelidae family, thank your lucky stars. There is nowt so queer as folk, but Special Events enthusiasts are an ideal class of guests, so long as they are left alone to get on with what they enjoy.

What about prices?

It is because you cannot justify the money you spend on your hobby in rational terms, that price is not a major factor in the success of Special Events. The quality of the event is. The way pop fans want to see The Spice Girls is mirrored by the way in which quilt makers want to see their heroines. The bigger the attraction, the more you can charge for it – like any other kind of entertainment

Short Break Holidays

With Short Break Holidays such a well-established feature nowadays, you may wonder if it is still possible to set up your own Short Breaks programme? The answer is that it would be, but we need to start at the beginning.

What does a Short Break programme include?

1   The constituent parts of a Short Break Holiday are simply a hotel to stay at, with a full breakfast; people like a proper breakfast. Essentially, it's B&B.

2   Don't try to add anything else to the package. It just reduces your potential market. If the potential guests have to pay for a package that includes a sightseeing tour, they won't come if they don't like sightseeing.

3   Don't include dinner. They may want to eat dinner out of the hotel. We don't make enough profit out of dinner to increase the selling price of the package. The cheaper the total price, the more customers you will attract. This policy would run counter to perceived industry wisdom, but the argument hasn't been refuted.

4   You should offer a number of optional extras which can be bought at the same time as the basic package. Besides dinner and sightseeing, it could include forms of transport and theatre tickets, for example.

5   Since the guests have to reach you, there is a cost for transport. The smaller the price for transport, the cheaper the total price of the package. And the larger the share of the price the hotel gets. So your best market isn't too far away.

Where will the customers come from?

6   The distance people are prepared to travel before refusing to go home again without sleeping overnight is different in different countries. In the UK it is about 100–150 miles. This doesn't mean that nobody will travel further, or stay after a shorter journey; it just indicates where your major market is likely to be.

7   Their income has to be sufficient to be able to afford your

package. When you have decided the cost, you can estimate who can afford the price.

How are you going to sell the package?

8 For this you need friends. A friend in this context is somebody who wants to make more profit and can do so by working with you. That means railway companies and bus companies to carry the visitors. It means travel agents to book the clients and take their commission from so doing. The smaller the travel agent, the more they need the commission from you providing the additional business. Now it can include the Internet as well – specialist companies, like lastminute.com.

The smaller agents also should know their district better. They know how to approach the people who might like to buy the package. Momma & Poppa agents are likely to be good friends when it comes to Short Break Holidays. So, you are looking for Momma & Poppa agents in towns with plenty of your kind of customer, at the right distance to travel and stay overnight. This doesn't mean that you won't try to deal with major travel agent companies. You can build a network of people selling for you much quicker if you do. But they will probably be much tougher to work with, their branches have big demands for other products and you are simply less attractive to them than you are to the smaller company.

9 If you want to get the smaller agents to sell the package for you, you could invite them to come to the hotel for a weekend conference which would include that subject. To attract them, make it a two night stay but the conference is for one morning only. For the other session you need to offer them a major topic they are far more interested in than Short Break Holidays. One that has proved very popular in the past is avoiding paying tax! You just produce a tax expert to talk to them.

10 You are a natural partner for a transportation company – an airline, railway operator, etc. You are the other part of the equation; you can provide marketing resources to add to their own. Often, you may have worked with the transportation company before.

If you can reach agreement with the railway company, and have the packages sold at the stations, just like railway tickets, that would be very good.

11 You need a brochure. A few tips about a Short Break Holiday brochure:

- Do remember you are selling a fun weekend. No formal hotel jargon please.
- Get yourself a good strapline. Not 'Intergalactic Short Break Weekends' but 'You deserve an Intergalactic Short Break Weekend'.
- Keep it simple. A good way is to divide the copy into question and answer segments – 'What is included?', 'Can I go by train?', 'What is the price for children?'
- People read captions to photographs more than they read the body copy. Put in good, descriptive captions.

12 You need good advertising. Most of the Short Break market travels as couples. They can best be approached by advertising.

13 Examples of good advertising media are:

- Posters to be put up at railways stations, in travel agent windows and bus terminals. Hopefully, the space will be provided free by your transportation partner.
- Local newspaper advertising.
- Displays within the hotel. Not just a brochure in a rack, but a display.
- TV travel programmes.
- Local radio, linked to a local travel agent, to buy the product.
- Leaflet drops in your kind of area.

As the market grows and you get more customers, you can consider things like television advertising, but not at the outset. It is usually too expensive.

At the outset, you probably won't know what will work. There are a lot of potential media and you may have no previous experience of their potential. So try each in one town only, to see which works and which doesn't. Monitor the demand from that town as the applications come into the hotel.

Why do people want to come on a Short Break Holiday?

14   When you realize that for the price of a Short Break Holiday you could have a week's holiday in Spain, it seems odd that people should decide to spend that amount of money on two days in a city in their own country. Why do they do so?

Because Mum wants a break from routine. She's sick and tired of working, 7 days a week and wants a weekend away. Or because a young couple can get away for a romantic weekend, but not for a week. Or because there is something they want to see in your city over the weekend and you are providing them with the best way of doing it. The overworked mother does seem to be the main market.

What's the right price?

15   What is the right price for two nights, breakfast and taxes? The ideal price for maximum demand is about half the weekly salary of junior management or senior blue collar staff. You would have to go higher if you run a luxury product.

What's the right policy for children?

16   It is usual to make no charge for children sharing their parents' room. If they are under 16 they can have their own room at 50 per cent, according to availability, of course.

Setting up Special Events can be scary. You can be fearful of the results of failure. Always keep in mind, though, that unless a Special Event works, you are probably subject to poor trading for the period of the year you have selected until the crack of doom. You are going to lose money every year. With Special Events you may lose less or, if it is successful, make a profit instead.

HOSPITALITY SALES AND PROMOTION

Of course, they don't all work. Trying to run ski tuition in Warrington didn't work. Bird Watching on the Yorkshire Moors in January did though. A Welsh Castle Special Event didn't work, but looking for UFOs on Welsh hilltops did. As I say, there's nowt so queer as folk.

Summary

Special Events may seem an extreme way of solving revenue problems. When you get down to the really difficult periods, however, they are one of the best solutions. They take up as much of your time as you want to spare, because you are inventing them at your own speed; or you know a long time in advance that the events are going to take place.

Another major advantage is that it is normally possible for you to set the price without a lot of competitors cutting rates. That isn't true of the type of Special Event that has become very popular – bridge tournaments, for example. It would still be true of shell collectors or Byron societies.

You have to balance the likelihood of success when you are tapping into a very large market – bridge players – and when you are going for an equally enthusiastic but smaller market – toy soldier collectors. No matter how obscure the subject, there will probably be a large group of enthusiasts wanting to gather and talk about it.

Case study

This case study illustrates:

● The way to set up a Special Event for a small company.
● The need to adjust the product for different cultural markets.
● The way to create partnerships.

Short Break Holidays are a national habit in Britain. The

value to the hotel industry is estimated at over £2 billion a year. Short Breaks have been consistently and effectively promoted in the UK for 40 years now and the question arises of whether they could be equally popular elsewhere and whether a small hotel company could get a package off the ground.

Some years ago I was responsible for three hotels in Amsterdam with a total of about 400 bedrooms. The hotels did well in the summer but suffered over weekends in the winter. So we decided to launch a Short Break Holiday programme to solve the problem.

You might imagine that there was little demand for a weekend in a hotel in Holland. After all, it is easy enough to get home in most parts of the country. The distance from Rotterdam to Amsterdam is only around 50 miles. The point is, however, that in a small country, 30 miles is considered a long way. In Britain the most popular distance to travel and definitely stay is more like 150 miles. In America it is much longer and any number of Americans will travel 60 miles for a picnic. So you have to take national assessments of what is a long distance into account.

The other reason for supporting a Short Break package is that a lot of people don't want to go home anyway. Rather than do the housework, cooking and chores, they would move in with the people next door!

So we felt that the package had possibilities. The next problem was how to tell the Dutch that it existed? If you have to choose between men and women, all the research shows that more women push for Short Break holidays than men. It is still the case that more of them need the break. So we decided to negotiate with one of the best women's magazines.

Why should the magazine – it was called *Libelle* – want to run a Reader Trip that would fill my hotels? Remember, you always have to work out what's in it for your partner. The obvious answer here is to make the magazine more popular: if you read *Libelle* you get all kinds of offers. *Libelle* wanted to prove that if you read other magazines, you got fewer or less attractive offers. Short Break holidays are popular with the public.

The magazine could see that they would improve their standing *vis-à-vis* their competitors. So that was the key consideration. The next thing was to reassure them that they would not have a heavy additional administrative burden if they worked with us. Hotels should look for free publicity from the media, but they are far less likely to receive it if the media have to do a lot of extra work. So we reassured *Libelle* that all the correspondence would come to us, they would not have to ticket anybody, we would deal with the queries and complaints, they would not have to pay for the cost of printing or postage, etc. What they would get was commission on the bookings; another important customer benefit.

Of course, few of these costs actually come up unless you are doing business. The magazine publicity produces the demand initially and then it is simply the administrative cost of dealing with the results.

You can increase the interest in a promotion like this with good public relations. You offer one or two prizes in a competition and the people who take part learn about the product. You can increase your database because those who take part are probably potential Short Break Holiday customers and, in submitting their entries, they give you their names and addresses. You can do human interest stories for the magazine, following a typical family during the course of their weekend.

Naturally, all the publicity for the promotion was in Dutch. That was a considerable advantage because a lot of organizations overestimate the public's ability to speak other people's languages. Talking to the Dutch Friends of British Tourism, they complained that too much material was in English. They said that the Dutch could deal with simple daily events in English but if there was anything

SPECIAL EVENTS AND SHORT BREAK HOLIDAYS

complicated to grasp, they prefer to have the information in their own language.

Then, of course, you need to define 'language'. All languages change over time. If you are translating material from one language to another, you must take into account the modern idioms. If you use translators who have been away from their own country for some years, it is easy to get out of touch. You find them either using traditional verbiage – 'excellent facilities' and 'superb cuisine' – or phrases like 'jolly good'. Remembering that you only have to make one mistake to turn off a lot of customers, you need someone who is *au fait* with the current usage and vocabulary.

Sometimes you can link the promotion with Special Events taking place in the city. One November weekend when the hotels in Amsterdam were very quiet, I was delighted to find we were full. I asked how we had managed that and was told that there was a big concert at the Concertgebouw and we had bought enough tickets to fill the hotels. The opportunity of coming to see the concert and staying had proved very attractive.

Once you have the basic package, you can adjust it to take all sorts of events into account. It tends to grow of its own volition as well; people who would have gone to a city for an event and made their own individual arrangements, buy the package instead. With the backing of the partner's name, it is also possible to get other organizations to listen to you who may not have done so otherwise.

The hotels did extremely well out of the *Libelle* programme but, of course, the competition could easily have done the same thing with other magazines or in other ways. There was a meeting of the Amsterdam hoteliers one evening and our Managing Director was quizzed about the *Libelle* initiative. He could have had a fine time winning the admiration of his colleagues for the cleverness of the promotion, but he told me the message he gave them was somewhat different. He told them: 'You know what the British are like. They think that just because things work in Britain, they'll work in Holland. They won't listen to reason and they just chuck money away and then ask us to reach unreasonable profit targets. It hasn't worked and it's just been a waste of money!'

Bibliography

Bennie, Michael, *How to do your own advertising*, Northcote House, 1990.

Berman, Shelley, *A hotel is a place ...* Price, Stern, Sloan (USA), 1972.

Bird, Drayton, *Commonsense direct mail*, The Printed Shop, 1982.

Bird, Drayton, *How to write sales letters that sell*, Kogan Page, 1994.

Black, Sam, *Practical public relations*, Pitman, 1962.

Bowden, Gregory Houston, *British gastronomy*, Chatto & Windus, 1975.

Buttle, Francis, *Hotel and food service marketing*, Cassell, 1986.

Carnegie, Dale, *How to win friends and influence people*, The World's Work, 1995.

Cone, Fairfax M., *With all its faults*, Little, Brown (USA), 1969.

Crystal, David, *Rediscover grammar*, Longman, 1996.

Dewitt Coffman, C., *Hospitality for sale*, American Hotel & Motel Association (USA), 1980.

The Economist style guide, Profile Books, 2000.

Fairlie, Robert, *Direct mail*, Kogan Page, 1979.

Feltenstein, Tom, *Foodservice marketing for the 90s*, Wiley (USA) 1992.

Fewell, Arnold and Wills, Neville, *Marketing*, Butterworth-Heinemann, 1992.

Freud, Sigmund, *Two short accounts of psychoanalysis*, Penguin, 1957.

Greene, Melvyn, *Marketing hotels into the 90s*, Heinemann, 1982.

Holloway, Christopher and Robinson, Christopher, *Marketing for tourism*, Longman, 1995.

Ismael, Ahmed, *Catering sales and convention services*, Dalmar, 1999.

James, Walter, *A word book on wine*, Phoenix House, 1959.

Kotler, Philip, Bowen, John and Makens, James C., *Marketing for hospitality and tourism*, Prentice Hall, 1999.

Lewis, Robert and Chambers, Richard, *Marketing leadership in hospitality*, Van Nostrand Reinhold (USA), 1989.

McCormack, Mark H., *McCormack on negotiating*, Arrow, 1995.

Middleton, Victor, *Marketing in travel and tourism*, Butterworth-Heinemann, 1998.

Ogilvie, David, *Ogilvie on advertising*, Crown (USA), 1983.

Pease, Alan, *Body Language*, Camel (Australia), 1981.

Reddin, J., *Managerial effectiveness*, McGraw-Hill (USA), 1970.

Roberts, John, *Marketing for the hospitality industry*, Hodder & Stoughton, 1993.

Roman, Kenneth and Maas, Jane, *The new how to advertise*, Kogan Page, 1992.

Ruder, *Getting the sales from sales training*, Sales Executives Publications, 1958.

Seaton, A.V. and Bennett, M.M., *Marketing tourism products*, Thomson, 1996.

Sharman, Fay and Chadwick, Brian, *The A-Z Gastronomique*, Papermac, 1989.

Strunk, William and White, E.B., *The elements of style*, Macmillan, 1979.

Sumner, J.R., *Improve your marketing techniques*, Northwood, 1982.

Taylor, Derek, *Hotel and catering sales promotion*, Iliffe, 1964.

Taylor, Derek, *How to sell banquets*, Northwood, 1979.

Taylor, Derek and Thomason, Richard, *Profitable hotel reception*, Pergamon, 1982.

Taylor, Derek, *Sales management for hotels*, Van Nostrand Reinhold (USA), 1987.

Taylor, Derek, *Hotel and catering sales – a complete guide*, Heinemann, 1988.

Taylor, Derek and Taylor, Hugh, *Hotel and restaurant advertising*, Dewberry Boyes, 1997.

Vorderman, Carol, *Guide to the Internet*, Prentice Hall, 1998.

Index